观海文丛——华东师范大学外语学院学者文库

语言研究掇拾

——语言学与外语教学研究文集

张吉生　主编

南开大学出版社

天　津

图书在版编目(CIP)数据

语言研究掇拾：语言学与外语教学研究文集 / 张吉
生主编. —天津：南开大学出版社，2021.11
（观海文丛. 华东师范大学外语学院学者文库）
ISBN 978-7-310-06163-1

Ⅰ. ①语… Ⅱ. ①张… Ⅲ. ①语言学－文集②外语教
学－教学研究－文集 Ⅳ. ①H0－53②H09－53

中国版本图书馆 CIP 数据核字(2021)第 227790 号

语言研究掇拾：语言学与外语教学研究文集
YUYAN YANJIU DUOSHI
——YUYANXUE YU WAIYU JIAOXUE YANJIU WENJI

南开大学出版社出版发行
出版人：陈　敬

地址：天津市南开区卫津路 94 号　　邮政编码：300071
营销部电话：(022)23508339　营销部传真：(022)23508542
https://nkup.nankai.edu.cn

天津午阳印刷股份有限公司印刷　全国各地新华书店经销
2021 年 11 月第 1 版　　2021 年 11 月第 1 次印刷
230×155 毫米　16 开本　17.25 印张　2 插页　245 千字
定价：88.00 元

如遇图书印装质量问题，请与本社营销部联系调换，电话：(022)23508339

前　言

　　华东师范大学外语学院在语言学与外语教学研究领域成绩斐然，本研究文集仅收集了近几年的代表作 13 篇，包括发表在 *Language Testing*、*Language Sciences* 等国际著名学术期刊和《中国语文》《外语教学与研究》等国内顶级语言类学术期刊上的一部分文章。所选文章研究范围涉及功能语言学、认知语言学、音系学、语用学、语言测试、语料库语言学、二语习得、教师教育、基础教育、外语课堂教学等领域，作者均为华东师范大学外语学院不同语种的系部，包括英语系、日语系、法语系、大学英语教学部的老师们。他们中有的在理论语言学领域有很深的造诣，理论前沿、视野开阔，学术成果具高屋建瓴之势，是国内相关领域著名学者；有的在外语基础教育、教师教育及课标研究方面经验丰富，重大问题有独到见解，是国内相关领域著名专家；有的是教学经验十分丰富的教师，他们长期在外语教学领域辛勤耕耘，他们既有系统的外语教学理论知识，又有实际课堂教学的经历和经验，他们始终能很好地把科研融入于课堂教学之中；有的是归国不久的洋博士，他们满腹新学又满腔热血，他们立志科研报国，怀有教育强国之理想，是外语学院的中坚力量。

　　华东师范大学外语学院有很大一批优秀教师从事语言学与外语教学研究，他们的学术成果累累，该文集由于篇幅有限无法全部刊出。文集的出版只是代表性地展示一下该外语学院在语言学与外语教学领域近年来的研究成果，在"十四五"规划的实施中，华东师范大学外语学院在语言学与外语教学研究领域将有更多更新的成果问世出版，值得期待。

编　者

2021 年 8 月 6 日于上海

目　录

分位数回归原理析解

陈芳　Micheline Chalhoub-Deville[1]

摘　要：教育领域常用的回归模型是基于最小平方的线性回归（LMR）。但这种回归分析有一些重要的假设前提，比如正态分布和方差齐性等，而且 LMR 适用的是就平均而言的变量间的关系。但实际上一方面数据不一定支持这些假设，另一方面如果不同变量之间的关系因其在整体分布中的不同位置而各自不同，LMR 和它基于平均的分析就不能提供准确的结论。分位数回归就是适宜于这类分析的一种比较新近的统计模型。虽然相关的想法早已有之，但一直到近代计算机的普及和运算的发展才使得它的广泛运用成为可能。分位数回归在生物、地理、医药、经济学等领域已经比较普及。美国的"不让一个孩子掉队"法律也推动了分位数回归在教育评估中的应用。比如被认定为教育绩效权威证据来源的学生成长百分位模型（SGP）就是利用了分位数回归的优势来分层预测学生的进步。分位数回归对于研究基础不同的语言习得者的能力发展，设计更合理的教育测试，探索语言能力与学科能力之间的变动关系等等都有重要的价值。为了推动分位数回归在这些领域的运用，本文用简洁的语言介绍了它的历史、原理和相关软件。本文用一个真实的数据演示了分位数回归下的数据分析步骤、图表呈现和数据解读等等，并将其与 LMR 对比，希望能借助读者熟悉的 LMR 模型来帮助理解和使用这个新的统计工具。

关键词：分位数回归；关系；数学和阅读能力

---

① The University of North Carolina at Greensboro.

Introduction

Traditionally, when the research interest is to examine the relationship between and among variables or when one wants to estimate how independent variables influence changes in a dependent variable, least-squares mean regression (LMR) is the standard tool. However, it is sometimes difficult in the social sciences to meet two of the required regression assumptions, i.e., normality and homoscedasticity (where the standard deviations of the error terms are assumed to be constant, or expressed differently, residuals are considered to be approximately equal for all predicted dependent variable scores). QR relaxes the need for these assumptions (Hao and Naiman, 2007). Also, regular regression focuses on the mean. However, with changes in higher order moments such as skewness or kurtosis of the distribution, the median is likely to be a more appropriate measure of central tendency than the mean (Edgeworth, 1888; Fox, 1997; Hao & Naiman, 2007; Koenker, 2005). In reality, it is also commonly observed that the relationship between variables can change at different points in the distribution. In that case, a single, average pattern cannot adequately represent a complex relationship that shifts rather than stays constant along the distribution.

So, if assumptions of normality and homoscedasticity are violated or previous research suggests the need to explore the relationship of variables across the distribution, quantile regression (QR) is a better alternative. This article aims to introduce this powerful statistical tool to the language testing community. It is hoped that this introduction will encourage researchers to examine the usefulness of this tool to further their explorations and to expand the knowledge base in the field.

To demonstrate the application of QR, the present paper employs data from the National Center for Education Statistics, specifically The Early

Childhood Longitudinal Study Kindergarten Class (ECLS-K) Program (http://nces.ed.gov/ecls/). The data set used is the released full sample data posted on the website http://nces.ed.gov/ecls/kinderdatainformation.asp. The variables of interest in this paper include gender and reading, serving as independent variables, and math as the dependent variable. The present application comes from a larger study in progress, in which several independent variables are investigated. Given the illustrative purpose of this paper, however, we limited the number of variables in the model to better explicate the principles of the methodology.

Historical Overview of Quantile Regression Research

Linear programming and technology advances have made efficient computation a manageable task and facilitated the use of QR with large scale applications. QR has become a common statistical tool in many fields such as medicine (Abreyeya, 2001; Austin et al., 2005; Cole, 1988), biology (Wei, et al., 2006), environmental studies (Pandey & Nguyen, 1999), survival analysis (Koenker and Geling, 2001; Yang, 1999), finance (Chevapatrakul et al., 2009), and economics (Koenker and Bilias, 2001). It is regarded as "the standard tool in wage and income studies in labor economics" (Yu et al., 2003, p.339) because of the less stringent assumptions and the advantages mentioned above.

The use of QR in the educational field is relatively new. Most of the earliest QR investigations focused on equality issues and appeared in journals of education economics (Haile & Nguyen, 2008; Levin, 2001; Prieto-Rodriguez, Barros, & Vieira, 2008; Wößmann, 2005). For example, Haile and Nguyen (2008) studied the achievement gap among different ethnic groups and the impact of gender. Results from traditional LMR analyses were consistent with established findings that Asian students scored on average better than White students in mathematics, regardless of gender. The QR results, however, offer a more nuanced depiction of this relationship. The QR analyses revealed that out of the five quantiles investigated (0.1, 0.25, 0.5, 0.75, 0.9), a significant score difference was found between Asian and White males only at the 0.1 quantile. On the other hand, Asian female students outperformed their White counterparts at four quantile levels, 0.25, 0.5, 0.75 and 0.9.

In recent years, Damian Betebenner and colleagues (Betebenner, 2009; Linn, Baker, & Betebenner, 2002) have used QR to formulate an innovative growth model of student achievement, called Student Growth Percentiles (SGP), which has been enthusiastically embraced for accountability purposes in the U.S. In 2005, former U.S. Secretary of Education, Margaret Spellings (Spellings, 2005), endorsed the Growth Model Pilot Program as an alternative for states to comply with NCLB achievement mandates. [For a detailed discussion of NCLB, see the special issue of *Language Testing* (Deville & Chalhoub-Deville, 2011).] Basically, and as opposed to simply reporting the percentage of proficient students every year, SGPs have been adopted by many states because, with the help of QR, it allows the documentation and investigation of the relative amount of growth all students make across the distribution.

As mentioned, QR has proven to be a useful tool in numerous studies in diverse disciplines. Despite interest among language testers in empirical research to document growth and performance, the use of QR in the field has been absent. The present article seeks to introduce the QR methodology to help spark interest among language researchers to explore its potential to answer germane research questions such as how variables relate to one another at differentiated levels of language proficiency.

Technical Overview of Quantile Regression and Software

Quantile is an equivalent term to percentile, where the median is the 50th quantile. Similarly, 25th and 75th quantiles correspond to the first and third quartiles. QR modeling is a term for a series of QR alternatives. Roger Koenker (2005), the author of the first book devoted to QR, traced the procedure back to the mid 1700s by a Jesuit priest, Boscovich. This means that QR actually predates the introduction of least squares regression. In that first attempt to "ever *do* regression" (Koenker, 2005, p.2), Boscovich estimated the slope coefficient through a process, which Laplace (1818) later noted as the "method of situation" because the model was an interesting mixture. While the slope was estimated based on the median, the intercept was still estimated as a mean. In 1888, Edgeworth improved Boscovich's and Laplace's ideas by proposing a process to minimize the sum of absolute residuals in both intercept and slope parameters. Thus, QR formally started.

Quantiles are order-statistics and more resistant to outliers. If errors follow a normal distribution, results of LMR and the QR at the median coincide. If errors are not normally distributed or homoscedasticity does not hold, QR provides a more efficient and accurate estimate of parameters. Additionally, QR can better handle the unequal variation observed with one or more independent variables at various points of a dependent variable. For example, Koenker and Hallock (2001) studied the determinants of infant birth weight. The use of LMR helped show that baby boys weighed in excess of 100 grams more than girls on average. Although this direction of disparity in birth weight was consistent across the weight distribution, QR analyses revealed that the magnitude of the disparity was less at the 5th quantile (with 45 grams' difference) than at the 95th quantile (135 grams' difference). In short, in comparison to LMR, QR can uncover differences in the nature of a relationship at different points in the distribution.

In a publication by one of the authors, (reference deleted here to preserve anonymity for review purposes) shows that the relationship between reading proficiency and math achievement is not constant, but varies depending on students' math ability. The conventional approach to explore the differential relationship between reading and math is to divide the population into subgroups based on students' math scores and conduct a series of classical regressions. Heckman (1979) argues strongly that such an approach could create biased parameter estimates. Figure 1 provides a visual presentation of the issue.

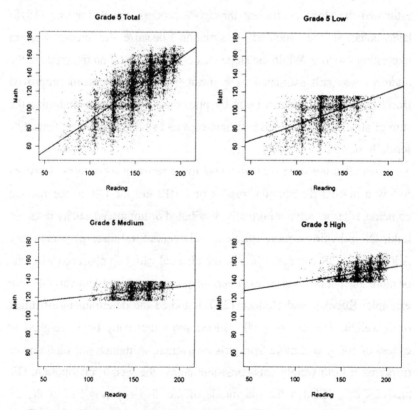

Figure 1   Total mean regression versus subgroup mean regression plots

Figure 1 includes four LMR regression plots, including the total group and three subgroups, which document the relationship between reading and math for a sample of grade 5 students in U.S. schools. The LMR total data plot shows a stronger relationship between the reading and math scores. The relationship looks different, however, when the students are divided into three math ability groups with equal numbers. Compared to the overall regression line based on the complete data, the flatter regression lines in the subgroup analyses indicate a weaker relationship between reading and math scores. Such results suggest that the truncated LMR fails to discover the strong relationship between reading and math scores at different ability levels. QR is a more appropriate analytic tool to study a changing relationship, such as the one observed in the present example. (The alert reader will discern that the graphical results are expected based on the restricted range in the three subgroups. The point, however, is that QR can model the relationship among the variables more efficiently—namely with one analysis—and can ascertain where within the distribution the relationship of the variables differs.)

Several software packages are available to perform QR analyses. These include commercial programs such as SAS and Stata. Free programs are also available, e.g., the Quantreg package in R (cran.r-project.org/ package= quantreg) and Blossom (http://www.fort.usgs.gov/products/software/ blossom/). R has the most complete and easy-to-carry-out functions. Quantile process plots can be obtained with all these programs. The ggplot2 package in R (cran.r-project.org/package=ggplot2) is especially useful for tailored plots. Appendix A provides R or Stata code to run the analyses reported on in the present paper. Code for the Figure 3 example is too long to be included but is available upon request. In summary, "With today's fast computers and wide availability of statistical software packages…, fitting a quantile regression model to data has become easy. However, we have so far had no introduction … to the method to explain what quantile-regression is all about" (Liao, 2007, p. vii). This quote represents quite adequately the state of affairs with regard to QR, especially in fields such as language testing. The present paper seeks to remedy this situation.

The Basics of the Quantile Regression Methodology and an Application

Data and data layout

Before we delve into the specifics of the methodology, a brief description of the data used to explicate the methodology is provided. The present QR illustration employs the grade 5 ECLS-K data, which is a partial set of the Kindergarten-Eighth Grade Full Sample Public-Use Data File especially prepared for longitudinal studies. More information about this dataset can be located in the Combined User's Manual for the ECLS-K Eighth-Grade and K-8 Full Sample Data Files and the Electronic Codebooks (Tourangeau, et al., 2009) and the ECLS-K Psychometric Report for the Eighth Grade (NCES 2009-002) (Najarian, Pollack, & Sorongon, 2009). The ECLS-K was developed under the sponsorship of the U.S. Department of Education, Institute of Education Sciences and National Center for Education Statistics. The selected data set includes 11,265 cases students in grade five.

For the purposes of the present paper, grade 5 reading and math scores based on assessment instruments designed especially for the ECLS-K program are used. Scores are derived using the three-parameter IRT model and are vertically scaled from kindergarten to the 8th grade. The score range for reading is 64-203 and for math is 51- 171. The reliability of the Grade 5 reading and math scores are .93 and .95, respectively. In terms of the gender variable, the data are coded 0 for males and 1 for females.

The data for LMR as well as for QR are organized in a similar fashion for analyses to be carried out. It is the computation algorithm, not the data setup, that makes the difference in the types of analyses conducted. Figure 2 provides a snapshot for the data layout used in the current paper. Finally, to help the reader better anchor the QR concepts introduced, LMR modeling is presented first and a comparison is made between the two statistical tools.

ID	READING	MATH	GENDER
0023015C	168.14	154.7	0
0023016C	163.78	144.01	1
0023017C	181.47	156.64	1
0023018C	189.18	157.15	0
0023019C	170.03	147.18	1
0023020C	148.57	127.11	0
0023021C	151.83	131.96	1
0023022C	123.31	138.57	1
0023023C	166.14	119.04	1
0023024C	87.67	55.42	1
0023025C	92.64	112.55	0

Figure 2   A snapshot of data layout for QR regression

Finally, and with regard to the quantiles chosen in the present application, seven quantile points are selected. These quantiles, commonly seen in the QR literature, (Buchinsky, 1994; Koenker and Hallock, 2001; Wößmann, 2005; Haile and Nguyen, 2008; Konstantopoulos, 2009), include .05, .10, .25, .50, .75, .90 and .95.

Equations

Using one independent variable, as an example, a simple LMR model can be written as

$$y_i = \beta_0 + \beta_1 x_i + \varepsilon_i \tag{1}[1]$$

---

[1] The methodology sections benefit from and correspond to the structure found in Hao and Naiman (2007).

β_1 is the slope, i.e., steepness of the regression line, which represents the strength of the relationship between variables x and y and β_0 is its intercept on the y axis. For the ECLS-K example, the formula is written as

$$MATH_i = \beta_0 + \beta_1 READING_i + \varepsilon_i \tag{2}$$

Conceptually, we wish to investigate the relationship between reading proficiency and math test scores. The data are used to find a single regression line that minimizes the error term (thus also the least squared function). Algebraically, the goal is to find the point where the first derivative of the mean squared deviation is zero with respect to the mean. Graphically, the resulting regression line minimizes the sum of squared vertical distances of all response observations. The best fitting line is the one that passes through the expected means of the response distributions conditioned at every value of the independent variable.

In comparison, a QR model can be written as

$$y_i = \beta_0^{(p)} + \beta_1^{(p)} x_i + \varepsilon_i^{(p)} \tag{3}$$

Or using the ECLS-K example,

$$MATH_i = \beta_0^{(p)} + \beta_1^{(p)} READING_i + \varepsilon_i^{(p)} \tag{4}$$

The only notational difference between Equation 1 and 3 is the extra superscript 'p', which specifies the pth QR model. [1] Usually a predetermined set of QR models are compared to detect the different effect of the independent variable on the dependent variable at various quantiles of the response distribution. It is important to note that all the data points are used for every QR modeling[2]. Taking the ECLS-K as an example, where the reading score is the independent variable and math the dependent variable, the best fitting line for $p=.5$ passes the conditional 50th percentile (the median) of the math score distribution. In other words, half of the math

---

[1] Koenker and other authors use the letter τ rather than p. For ease of communication, p is used here to reference a given percentile value.

[2] It is a misconception that only a subset of the observations is used for every quantile regression. It is standard procedure to use all observations in a given data set to locate a quantile given that it is the the pth value in the ordered observations. Also, the quantile regression analysis is a minimization of the weighted sum of absolute residuals for all the observations.

scores lie above the median regression line and half below the line. For the regression line at p=.75, 75% of the cases are below the best fitting line and 25% are above. Similar interpretations apply to other QR *p*s.

Figure 3 shows the plots of the LMR as well as seven QR lines for the ECLS-K example. The seven QR lines correspond to, from the bottom up, the regression modeling with conditional math percentiles at. 05,. 10,. 25,.50,. 75,. 90 and .95. The LMR line (the dotted line) is very close to the median QR line (the solid line in the middle). However, the other 6 QR lines (solid gray) all have different intercepts and slope coefficients. The slopes indicate that there is a differential relationship between reading and math scores at different part of the distribution. For instance, the relationship is stronger for students with low math scores (see the bottom line) than for those with high math scores (see the top line). Additionally, unlike the subgroup LMR models in Figure 1 and regardless of math score levels, there is a strong relationship between reading and math scores. This is indicated by the relatively steep slopes for all the regression lines.

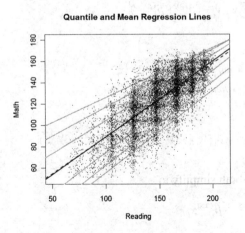

Figure 3   Quantile and Least Square Mean Regression Lines

Parameter Estimation

In LMR modeling, estimates of the intercept and slope coefficients of the best-fitting line are the ones that minimize the sum of squared errors and is written as

$$\sum_i^n \varepsilon_i^2 = \sum_i^n (y_i - (\beta_0 + \beta_1 x_i))^2$$

(5)

The estimates can be shown to be $\hat{\beta}_0 = \bar{y} - \hat{\beta}_1 \bar{x}$ and $\hat{\beta}_1 = \dfrac{\sum_i^n (x_i - \bar{x})(y_i - \bar{y})}{\sum_i^n (x_i - \bar{x})^2}$. When the assumptions of linearity, constant variance, and independence of x values are met, ordinary least square estimation provides the best, unbiased estimators of the population parameters.

In QR modeling, estimates of the intercept and slope coefficients that correspond to the best-fitting line are the ones that minimize the *weighted* sum of *absolute* errors

$$\sum_i^n w_p |\varepsilon_i| = \sum_i^n w_p |y_i - (\beta_0^{(p)} + \beta_1^{(p)} x_i)|$$

(6)①

Where

$$w_p = \begin{cases} p & when \quad y_i \geq (\beta_0^{(p)} + \beta_1^{(p)} x_i) \\ 1-p & when \quad y_i < (\beta_0^{(p)} + \beta_1^{(p)} x_i) \end{cases}$$

Or

$$p \sum_{y_i \geq p} |y_i - (\beta_0^{(p)} + \beta_1^{(p)} x_i)| + (1-p) \sum_{y_i < p} |y_i - (\beta_0^{(p)} + \beta_1^{(p)} x_i)|$$

(7)

When $p=.5$, both simplify to

$$\sum_i^n |y_i - (\beta_0^{(0.5)} + \beta_1^{(0.5)} x_i)|$$

.

---

① Koenker's notation for this concept is $\sum_{i=1}^n \rho_r(y_i - \xi)$. The notation used in this paper is more consistent with notations commonly seen in equations for least squares regressions in the social science literature.

The solution that minimizes the weighted sum of absolute distance is when $\hat{y}_i = \beta_0^{(p)} + \beta_1^{(p)} x_i$ equals the pth percentile. For more detailed information on QR parameter estimation, see Koenker (2005) and Hao and Naiman (2007).

Several algorithms are available to estimate the QR parameters, e.g., simplex (Koenker & d'Orey, 1987), interior point (Portnoy & Koenker, 1997), and the smoothing method (Chen, 2007). The default algorithm in both the Quantreg package in R and SAS is simplex. However, this method is computationally demanding and thus not recommended for large sample sizes. For sample sizes larger than 5000 observations and 50 variables, interior point is considered more efficient (SAS, 2008, p. 5400).

The estimates for the QR coefficients using the interior point algorithm are summarized in Table 1. The slope for the reading score in LMR is .69, which is only an average slope. QR, on the other hand, provides the slopes of the reading score for different math ability students. These vary from .77 (at the .05 quantile) to .47 (at the .95 quantile). The value is larger at lower quantiles than at higher quantiles. This means the relationship between reading and math is stronger for low math scoring students and weaker for high math scoring students. In comparison, LMR seems to underestimate the relationship for low math ability students but overestimate it for high math ability students. The Table also includes standard errors and significance levels. These are explained in the following section.

Table 1   Slope Coefficients

	LMR	Results at Different Quantiles						
	Results	.05	.10	.25	.50	.75	.90	.95
Intercept	20.44	-21.47	-15.88	-1.93	18.38	42.80	63.19	79.29
Slope	.69	.77	.78	.77	.71	.62	.54	.47
SE	(.01)	(.01)	(.01)	(.01)	(.01)	(.01)	(.01)	(.01)
p	.00	.00	.00	.00	.00	.00	.00	.00

Standard Errors and Confidence Intervals

Once the coefficients are estimated, standard errors are calculated to help test the statistical significance of the strength of the relationship, i.e., the slope coefficient estimate $\hat{\beta}_1^p$. The null hypothesis specifies that the slope coefficient is equal to 0, which means there is no linear relationship between the independent and dependent variables. In this section, the discussion focuses on the standard errors and the confidence interval estimation. The section that follows presents this information in a graphical form. Subsequent sections address hypothesis testing and goodness-of-fit.

In LMR, the standard error for the coefficient β_1 is calculated by assuming a normal distribution of the error term. That is, the ε_i in equation 1 is regarded as independently and identically distributed across all covariate values with a mean of 0 and a constant variance of σ_ε^2 (In fact, the subscript "i" can be dropped.). The σ_ε^2 is not known but the variance of the residuals, s_ε^2, provides an unbiased estimator of σ_ε^2 (Fox, 1997).

$$s_\varepsilon^2 = \frac{\sum \varepsilon_i^2}{n-2} = \frac{\sum [y_i - (\beta_0 + \beta_1 x_i)]^2}{n-2} \tag{8}$$

The sampling variance of β_1 can then be estimated as

$$V\hat{a}r_{\beta_1} = \frac{s_\varepsilon^2}{\sum (x_i - \bar{x})^2} \tag{9}$$

and the estimated standard error of the slope coefficient is just the square root of the sampling variance.

$$SE_{\hat{\beta}_1} = \frac{s_\varepsilon}{\sqrt{\sum (x_i - \bar{x})^2}} \tag{10}$$

$(\hat{\beta}_1 - \beta_1^{null})/SE_{\hat{\beta}_1}$ is assumed to follow a Student's t distribution with n-2 degrees of freedom and thus the $100(1-\alpha)\%$ confidence interval for β_1 is given by $\hat{\beta}_1 \pm t_{\alpha/2} SE_{\hat{\beta}_1}$. The confidence interval helps assess the precision of the estimated $\hat{\beta}_1$, i.e., the extent to which our estimated slope coefficient represents the population value.

As reported in Table 1, the LMR slope $\hat{\beta}_1$ is .69 and the standard error is .01. For the 95% confidence interval, $t_{.05/2}$ is almost the same as $z_{.05/2}$ which is 1.96. Thus, the final 95% confidence interval falls between .69-1.96×.01 and .69+1.96×.01, which correspond to .67 and .71. This narrow band of confidence interval can be clearly seen in Figure 4 by the solid horizontal line and the dotted lines closely above and below it. This is also consistent with the significant p values (p=.00) in Table 1 which implies high precision of estimation.

One reason for using QR modeling over LMR is that the conditional response distribution is skewed rather than normal. In such cases, the traditional approach for calculating the standard error is not appropriate for QR modeling. Instead, it is recommended to use bootstrap methodology (Efron, 1979), such as the xy-pair technique, which does not require a specific distributional form[①]. The observed data set is regarded as the population and the algorithm bootstraps pairs of observations (e.g. a reading score with a corresponding math score) from the data repeatedly and generates multiple samples. Every sample gives a parameter estimate, which yields a distribution of the $\hat{\beta}_1 s$. The standard deviation of these $\hat{\beta}_1 s$ is taken as the standard error of the parameter β_1. As the number of bootstrapped samples increases, the sampling distribution of the $\hat{\beta}_1 s$ is approaching normal distribution[②], and the confidence interval follows the form of $\hat{\beta}_1 \pm z_{\alpha/2} SE_{\hat{\beta}_1}$ (Koenker & Bassett, 1982).

---

① Other techniques are available such as the Parzen, Wei, and Ying's (1994) version of the xy-pair bootstrap and the Markov chain marginal bootstrap by He and Hu (2002) and by Kocherginsky, He, and Mu (2005). Non-bootstrap methods have also been developed. For more details about these methods, the reader is referred to Koenker (2005).

② The normal distribution here refers to the distribution of the $\hat{\beta}_1 s$ from all the bootstrapped samples. This is related to the features of sampling distribution, which as the central limit theorem describes, will lead to a normal distribution of the $\hat{\beta}_1 s$ if we repeat the sampling procedure enough times. This is different from the mean regression normality assumption of where the error terms are required to be normally distributed.

Another approach to determining the confidence interval that does not require that estimates be normally distributed and capitalizes on the set of bootstrap samples obtained entails taking the empirical values from the distribution of the estimated $\hat{\beta}_i s$ and locating the corresponding empirical percentiles. For example, the 95% confidence interval of the parameter β_1 starts from the 2.5th percentile of all the $\hat{\beta}_i s$ from the empirical samples and ends at the 97.5th percentile of the estimated $\hat{\beta}_i s$ from these samples.

The standard errors of estimation for the ECLS-K example are provided in Table 1 in parentheses. These estimates are produced, by default, in Stata by randomly sampling the data (Stata Base Reference Manual, 2009, p. 1457). As the table shows, all the standard error values are .01, which indicates that when these confidence bands are plotted, they will be very close to their regression lines. This is clearly the case, as depicted in Figure 4, which is discussed in the next section.

Graphs

For LMR and QR, when there is only one independent variable, as shown in equation 4, the regression lines can be plotted out directly. The difference is that in LMR, there is only one regression line representing the mean pattern of relationship between the dependent and independent variables while in QR, there are usually many quantile regression lines corresponding to the relationship at several quantiles of interest (see Figure 3).

For quantile models that involve at least two independent variables or covariates, a unique form of graph called *quantile process plot,* is used to present the complex set of regression lines that depict the changes in the slope coefficients at each quantile. This *quantile process plot* can show more clearly how the coefficients differ across quantiles. Both the *quantreg* package in R and SAS can produce process plots.Figure 4 is an example of a *quantile process* plot based on the QR model defined by equation 11. This model includes an additional variable, Gender, as a covariate.

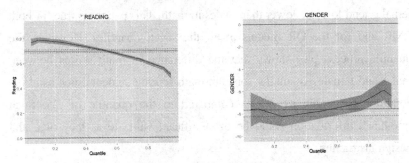

Figure 4　Quantile Process Plots

$$MATH_i = \beta_0^{(p)} + \beta_1^{(p)}READING_i + \beta_2^{(p)}GENDER_i + \varepsilon_i^{(p)} \qquad (11)$$

In Figure 4, the x-axis includes the seven quantiles from .05 to .95 and the y-axis presents the corresponding slope coefficients from these QRs. The black solid line with gray areas represents the quantile regression slope estimates at each quantile and the confidence interval for the estimates respectively. The horizontal solid red line with dotted lines above and below represents the mean LSR regression estimates and confidence band. The horizontal line at zero is the reference line for hypothesis testing against a slope value of 0.

Figure 4 shows that the reading slopes are all positive (all the values are above the 0 reference line). The slope coefficients for reading decrease from .77 to .50 as students' conditional math ability moves up in quantile values. The narrow confidence band (gray area), similar to the standard errors addressed above, indicates that the estimations are quite precise. The plot also shows little overlap with the LMR confidence band (area between the two dotted horizontal lines), which illustrates how LMR and QR differ in modeling the relationship between math and reading. In comparison to

QR, the LMR model underestimates the relationship for low math-scoring students and overestimates that relationship for high-math-scoring students.

The slope coefficients for the Gender variable are all negative. Since males are coded as 0 and females as 1, the negative slope coefficient means females tend to score lower than males in math. This pattern is true for both LMR and for the QR models at all the seven quantiles. However, the quantile process plot shows that the difference in math scores between males and females is smaller for high math-scoring students such as at the conditional quantile of .90 as compared to the quantile of .25. Such fine-tuned information could be of significant value to as they plan and design instruction.

Comparing the plots for the two variables, it is evident that the confidence band for the Gender slope coefficients, i.e., the width of the gray area reveals less precision of estimation compared to the estimation of the reading effects. The Gender coefficients are still statistically significant since the confidence band does not cross the 0 reference line (hypothesis of the slope coefficient being 0). Finally, the interaction effect between Reading and Gender is not modeled here, but it can be explored and graphed.

Hypothesis Testing

With LMR, hypothesis testing for the significance of a single independent variable draws on the central limit theorem and follows regular regression procedures. The t-statistic is calculated as follows

$$t = \frac{\hat{\beta}_1 - \beta_1^{null}}{SE_{\hat{\beta}_1}} = \frac{\hat{\beta}_1 - 0}{SE_{\hat{\beta}_1}} = \frac{\hat{\beta}_1}{SE_{\hat{\beta}_1}}$$

(12)

and the result is compared against the critical t with $n\text{-}2$ degrees of freedom under the null distribution. The hypothesis testing for a single independent variable in QR follows the same pattern with the only difference that $SE_{\hat{\beta}_1}$ is estimated based on bootstrapped samples as described in a former section.

So using the model in equation 4 again, the results of the hypothesis of $\beta_1^{null} = 0$ is summarized in Table 1. All the Reading slopes are statistically significant at the level of p=.00 be it LMR or QR.

However, in QR, because several quantiles are modeled, additional hypotheses are of interest, such as the equivalence of the various slope coefficients across quanitles. In QR, the xy-pair bootstrapping method described previously is used to produce a covariance matrix of the cross-quantile estimates, which can then be employed to perform this hypothesis testing, known as the test of equivalence.

For a given variable, the covariance matrix allows the examination of whether any difference between the slope coefficients of any pair of quantiles is statistically different. For example, we can investigate whether there is a statistical difference in how reading performance predicts math scores when, the students are at the 75th versus the 90th percentile of the math score distribution. The Wald statistic, equation 13, is used for the test of equivalence.

$$\text{Wald statistic} = \frac{(\hat{\beta}_1^{(p)} - \hat{\beta}_1^{(q)})^2}{\hat{\sigma}_{\hat{\beta}_1^{(p)} - \hat{\beta}_1^{(q)}}^2} \tag{13}$$

In this equation, $\hat{\beta}_1^{(p)}$ is the parameter estimate from the pth QR model and $\hat{\beta}_1^{(q)}$ is the parameter estimate from the qth quantile regression model, i.e., any given pair of quantiles. The denominator is the variance of the difference between the two coefficients for the pth and qth quantile regressions. Obviously, the Wald statistics can be extended to a joint test of equality of slopes at the same time. In that test, the null hypothesis becomes $H_0 : \beta_1^{.05} = \beta_1^{.10} \cdots = \beta_1^{.90} = \beta_1^{.95}$ which is an omnibus test.

In a regression model with one independent variable, the Wald statistic follows a χ^2 distribution with one degree of freedom. In a model with p

independent variables, the Wald statistic follows a χ^2 distribution with p degrees of freedom (Koenker & Machado, 1999). Thus the Wald statistic can be readily extended for more complicated models for the test of equivalence of coefficients between quantiles. The Wald test is readily available in computer programs such as Stata and the Quantreg package in R (Koenker, 2009). Stata uses the *sqreg* command and Quantreg uses the command *anova.rq* to test the equivalence of coefficients between quantiles.

Table 2   Test of Equivalence

Varible		Overall Equivalence	Pair-wise Quantile Comparison					
		ANOVA	.05=.10	.10=.25	.25=.50	.50=.75	.75=.90	.90=.95
READING	F	86.86	1.75	4.14	82.67	187.63	78.40	33.22
	p	.000	.186	.042	.000	.000	.000	.000
	sig.	***	NS	NS	***	***	***	***

*** indicates significance level at or below .01. NS means not statistically significant.

Using the ECLS-K data, Stata produces the results based on the model in equation 4 in Table 2 on the equivalence of coefficients. The overall statistics is the omnibus test, which shows that there is statistically significant difference between some or all of the slope coefficients. More interestingly, pair-wise Wald tests reveal that the reading slope is statistically different between quantile .25 and .50 (w=82.67, p=.000). This means the relationship between reading and math scores is different between students whose conditional math ability is at the 25th percentile versus those at the 50th percentile. Further, there is a significant difference between all upper pairs. This differential relationship between math and reading at different points of the math score distribution is typically not detected in analyses that target the mean of the distribution. In conclusion,

QR is a more appropriate methodology when differential rather than an average relationship is thought to exist between and among variables.

QR Goodness-of-fit Index

For LMR, R^2 is the usual measure of goodness-of-fit. It is defined as:

$$R^2 = \frac{SSR}{SST} = \frac{\sum_i (\hat{y}_i - \bar{y})^2}{\sum_i (y_i - \bar{y})^2} = 1 - \frac{\sum_i (y_i - \hat{y}_i)^2}{\sum_i (y_i - \bar{y})^2} = 1 - \frac{SSE}{SST} \tag{12}$$

R^2 is the ratio of the sum of squares due to regression (SSR) and the sum of squares of the total model (SST). As is commonly known, R^2 represents the proportion of variance in the response variable being explained by the independent variables in the regression model. Inversely, R^2 can be seen as the proportion of error variance (SSE/SST) subtracted from 1 (this notion comes into play in the following paragraph). R^2 ranges between 0 and 1. Higher values indicate a stronger relationship.

In QR, a similar index is suggested by Koenker and Machado (1999), which is the likelihood ratio of the sum of weighted absolute distances for the full pth QR model $V^1(p)$ and the sum of the weighted absolute distances for a model with only the intercept $V^0(p)$. Stata labels this ratio *pseudo-* R^2 to distinguish it from the LMR R^2. The default Stata output includes R^2 and *pseudo-* R^2. The equation for *pseudo-* R^2 is[1]

$$Pseudo-R^2 = 1 - \frac{V^1(p)}{V^0(p)} = 1 - \frac{p \sum_{y_i \geq \hat{y}_i} \left| y_i - (\beta_0^p + \beta_1^p) \right| + (1-p) \sum_{y_i < \hat{y}_i} \left| y_i - (\beta_0^p + \beta_1^p) \right|}{p \sum_{y_i \geq \hat{Q}^{(p)}} \left| y_i - \beta_0^p \right| + (1-p) \sum_{y_i < \hat{Q}^{(p)}} \left| y_i - \beta_0^p \right|} \tag{13}$$

For the model $V^0(p)$, the intercept is the sample pth quantile $\hat{Q}^{(p)}$ of the dependent variable. In the ECLS-K example here, the intercept for the pth quantile regression is the reading score at the pth percentile. Both

---

[1] In Hao and Naiman (2007), this is denoted as R(p).

$V^0(p)$ and $V^1(p)$ are nonnegative since they are the sum of absolute values. $V^1(p)$ is always equal to or smaller than $V^0(p)$ since a covariate is supposed to explain some variance of the dependent variable. Similar to the R^2, the *pseudo- R^2* range is 0-1, with a larger value indicating better model fit.

The goodness-of-fit results of the ECLS-K data for the two models defined by equation 4 and 11are summarized in Table 3. The results show that based on both the LMR results (R^2) and QR results (*pseudo- R^2* at each quantile), the gender variable does not contribute to the explanation of the total variance in the data once reading is controlled for. With respect to R^2, reading helps to explain 54% of the variance in math scores and gender only explains an additional 2% (the difference between.56 and.54 in column 1) of the total variance.

The results show that the R^2 is always higher than *psuedo-R^2*'s. Such a pattern is typically observed in quantile regression studies (see Drescher and Goddard, 2011). These values are interpreted as measures of the relative effectiveness/goodness of the model in fitting the data for the pth quantile.

Table 3 R^2 and *Pseudo- R^2*

	LMR R^2	QR Pseudo- R^2 at each p						
		.05	.10	.25	.50	.75	.90	.95
		$MATH_i = \beta_0^{(p)} + \beta_1^{(p)} READING_i + \varepsilon_i^{(p)}$						
Model 1	.54	.34	.36	.36	.33	.29	.24	.20
		$MATH_i = \beta_0^{(p)} + \beta_1^{(p)} READING_i + \beta_2^{(p)} GENDER_i + \varepsilon_i^{(p)}$						
Model 2	.56	.36	.37	.38	.35	.31	.26	.22

Summary and Final Remarks

It is often the case in language testing that statistical distributions do not have a uniform variation. For example, in the English language learner

(ELL) literature [see the special issue of *Language Testing* (Deville & Chalhoub-Deville, 2011)], it has been argued that ELLs across grades as well as within a grade are likely to vary in their performance on achievement test. Such variation is prompted by their differing background variables (e.g., first language literacy, second language literacy, educational attainment in English, among others). The application example used in the present paper is part of a larger research piece that investigates how ELLs and non-ELLs with varying reading abilities perform on math tests.

In a traditional LMR, a single, mean-based slope is estimated to describe the relationship between a dependent, response variable and an independent, predictor variable(s). With this approach to modeling, the statistics are restricted in terms of their portrayal of a relationship since the focus is on the mean of the conditional distribution. In such analyses, we cannot address whether the variables show significantly different patterns of association at points other than at the mean.

The traditional LMR analysis at the conditional mean is expanded with QR to provide a richer picture of relationships. QR, a statistical technique that capitalizes on familiar LMR concepts, is considered a methodological improvement because it can depict a more detailed picture of the relationship between variables by estimating multiple slopes along the entire response distribution. So QR is a useful statistical tool especially in applications where averages are not of or the only interest.

In recent years, researchers have been paying more attention to the development and the utilization of QR. The methodology is more powerful than traditional LMR. The field of language testing needs to consider how QR can best be utilized to help advance our research and to enrich our understanding of phenomena of interest. The purpose of this article is to introduce the QR methodology and to show researchers in the field how it can be utilized when multiple quantiles in a conditional distribution of the response variable are of interest. The paper summarizes how to compute QR estimates and related statistics through a modification of the LMR parameters. We would like to end the article by mentioning a couple of issues to pay attention to when using QR. For example, it is worth stating that given the multiple viewpoints of a relationship QR affords, interpretation can be somewhat challenging. As to be expected, the more complicated the model, i.e., with more independent variables or for QR, with more regression analyses done at the same time, the more information that can be gleaned but the more difficult to summarize.

This paper introduces only the parametric linear models, but as with LMR, non-parametric and non-linear QR models are also workable. While this information is beyond the focus of the current paper, those interested in learning about the development and applications of these models are referred to Koenker (2005).

References

Abreveya, J. 2001. The effects of demographics and maternal behavior on the distribution of birth outcomes. *Empirical Economics*, *26*, pp. 247-257.

AERA, APA, NCME. 1999. *Standards for educational and psychological testing*. Washington, DC: AERA.

Austin, P., Tu, J., Daly, P., & Alter, D. 2005. The use of quantile regression in health care research: A case study examining gender differences in the timeliness of thrombolytic therapy. *Statistics in Medicine, 24,* pp. 791-816.

Ballou, D., Sanders, W., & Wright, P. 2004. Controlling for student background in value-added assessment for teachers. *Journal of Educational and Behavioral Statistics, 29* (1), pp. 37–65.

Betebenner, D. 2009. Norm- and criterion-referenced student growth.

Educational Measurement: Issues and practice, 28(4), pp. 42-51.

Buchinsky, M. 1994. Changes in the U.S. wage structure 1963-1987: Application of quantile regression. *Econometrica, 62*(2), pp. 405-458.

Cade, B. S., & Noon, B. R. 2003. A gentle introduction to quantile regression for ecologists. *Frontiers in Ecology and the Environment, 1*(8), pp. 412-420.

Chen, C. 2007. A finite smoothing algorithm for quantile regression. *Journal of Computational and Graphical Statistics, 16,* pp. 136-164.

Chen, F. 2010. *Differential language impact on math achievement.* Unpublished dissertation. University of North Carolina at Greensboro.

Chevapatrakul, T., Kim, T., & Mizen, P. 2009. The Taylor Principle and monetary policy approaching a zero bound on nominal rates: Quantile regression results for the United States and Japan. *Journal of Money, Credit and Banking, 41*(8), pp. 1705-1723.

Cole, T.J. 1988. Fitting smoothed centile curves to reference data (with discussion). *Journal of the Royal Statistical Society, Series A (Statistics in Society), 151*(3), pp. 385-418.

Deville, C. & Chalhoub-Deville. 2011. Special Issue: Standards-based assessment in the United States. *Language Testing, 28*(3), pp. 307-321.

Drescher, L.S. and Goddard, E. W. 2011. Heterogeneous Demand For Food Diversity: A Quantile Regression Analysis. Research in Agricultural and Applied Economics—AgEcon Search, http://purl.umn.edu/114484. http://ageconsearch.umn.edu/bitstream/114484/2/Drescher_Goddard_GEWI SOLA.pdf

Edgeworth, F. 1888. On a new method of reducing observations relating to several quantities. *Philosophical Magazine, 25,* pp. 184-191.

Efron, B. 1979. Bootstrap methods: Another look at the jackknife. *Annals of Statistics, 7,* pp. 1-26.

Fox, J. 1997. *Applied regression analysis, linear models, and related methods.* Thousand Oaks: Sage Publications.

Good, P.I., & Hardin, J.W. 2006. *Common errors in statistics (and how to avoid them)*, 2nd Ed. Hoboken, New Jersey: John Wiley & Sons.

Haile, G.A., & Nguyen, A.N. 2008. Determinants of academic attainment in the United States: A quantile regression analysis of test scores. *Educational Economics, 16* (1), pp. 29-57.

Hao, L., & Naiman, D.Q. 2007. *Quantile regression*. Thousand Oaks, CA: SAGE publications.

He, X., & Hu, F. 2002. Markov chain marginal bootstrap. *Journal of the American Statistical Association, 97*, pp. 783–795.

Heckman, J. J. 1979. Sample selection bias as a specification error. *Econometrica, 47*(1), pp. 153-161.

Khmaladez, E.V. 1981. Martingale approach in the theory of goodness-of-fit tests. *Theory of Probability and its Applications, 26*, 240-257.

Kocherginsky, M., He, X., & Mu, Y. 2005. Practical confidence intervals for regression quantiles. *Journal of Computational and Graphical Statistics, 14*, pp. 41-55.

Koenker, R. 2005. Quantile regression, Econometric Society Monographs (48). *Econometric Society,* Cambridge University Press.

Koenker, R. 2009. Quantreg: Quantile regression. R package version 4.27. Retrieved on May 5th, 2010 from http://CRAN. R-project.org/package =quantreg.

Koenker, R. & Bassett, G. 1982. Robust tests for heteroscedasticity based on regression quantiles. *Econometrica*, 50(1), pp. 43-61.

Koenker, R. & Bilias, Y. 2001. Quantile regression for duration data: A reappraisal of the Pennsylvania Reemployment Bonus Experiments. *Empirical Economics, 26*, pp. 199-220.

Koenker, R., & d'Orey, V. 1994. Remark AS R92: A remark on algorithm AS 229: Computing dual regression quantiles and regression rank scores. *Applied Statistics, 43*, pp. 410-414.

Koenker R. & Machado J.A.F. 1999. Goodness of fit and related inference processes for quantile regression. *Journal of the American Statistical Association, 94*(448), pp. 1296-1310.

Koenker, R., & Geling, R. 2001. Reappraising medfly longevity: A quantile regression survival analysis. *Journal of American Statistical Association, 96*, pp. 458-468.

Koenker, R., & Hallock, K.F. 2001. Quantile regression. *The Journal of Economic Perspectives, 15*(4), pp. 143-156.

Koenker, R., & Xiao, Z. 2002. Inference on the quantile regression process. *Econometrica, 81*, pp. 1583–1612.

Konstantopoulos, S. 2009. The mean is not enough: Using quantile regerssion to examine trends in Asian-White differences across the entire achievement distribution. *Teachers College Record*, 111(5), pp. 1274-1295.

Laplace，P. S. de 1818. Deuxième Supplément a la Thèorie Analytique des Probabilitiés. Paris: Courcier. Reprinted (1847) in Oeuvres de Laplace 7, pp. 569-623. Paris: Imprimerie Royale; (1886) in Oeuvres Complètes de Laplace 7, Paris: Gauthier-Villars, pp. 531-80.

Levin, J. 2001. For whom the reductions count: A quantile regression analysis of class size and peer effects on scholastic achievement. *Empirical Economics, 26*, pp. 221-246.

Linn, R. L., Baker, E. L., & Betebenner, D. W. 2002. Accountability systems: Implications of requirements of the No Child Left Behind Act of 2001. Educational Researcher, 31 (6), 3-16. No Child Left Behind Act of 2001, Public Law No. 107-110, 115 Stat. 1425.

Najarian, M., Pollack, J. M., & Sorongon, A.G. 2009. *Early childhood longitudinal study, kindergarten class of 1998-99 (ECLS-K), psychometric report for the eighth grade (NCES 2009-002).* National Center for Education Statistics, Institute of Education Sciences, U.S. Department of Education. Washington, DC.

Pandey, G. R., & Nguyen, V.T. 1999. A comparative study of regression based methods in regional flood frequency analysis. *Journal of*

Hydrology, 225, pp. 92-101.

Parzen, M. I., Wei, L.J. & Ying, Z. 1994. A resampling method based on pivotal estimating functions. *Biometrika, 81*, pp. 341–350.

Portnoy, S., & Koenker, R. 1997. The Gaussian hare and the Laplacian tortoise: Computation of squared-error vs. absolute-error estimators. *Statistical Science, 12*, pp. 279-300.

Prieto-Rodriguez, J., Barros, C. P., & Vieira, J. A. 2008. What a quantile approach can tell us about returns to education in Europe. *Education Economics, 16*(4), pp. 391-410.

Raudenbush, S. W. 2004. What are value-added models estimating and what does this imply for statistical practice? *Journal of Educational and Behavioral Statistics*, 29 (1), pp. 121-129.

SAS Institute Inc. 2008. *SAS/STAT® 9.2 User's Guide.* Cary, NC: SAS Institute Inc.

Spellings, M. 2005, Nov. Secretary Spellings announces growth model pilot [Press Release]. U.S. Department of Education. (http://www.ed.gov/news/pressreleases/2005/11/1182005.html)

StataCorp. 2009. *Stata: Release 11.* Statistical Software. College Station, TX: StataCorp LP.

StataCorp. 2009. *Base Reference Manual.* Statistical Software. College Station, TX: StataCorp LP.

Tourangeau, K., Nord, C., Lê, T., Sorongon, A. G., & Najarian, M. 2009. *Early childhood longitudinal study, kindergarten class of 1998–99 (ECLS-K), combined user's manual for the ECLS-K eighth-grade and K–8 full sample data files and electronic codebooks* (NCES 2009–004). National Center for Education Statistics, Institute of Education Sciences, U.S. Department of Education. Washington, DC.

Wei, Y., Pere, A., Koenker, R., & He, X. 2006. Quantile regression methods for reference growth charts. *Statistics in Medicine, 25*, pp. 1369-1382.

Wößmann, L. 2005. The effect heterogeneity of central examinations: Evidence from TIMSS, TIMSS-Repeat and PISA. *Education Economics, 13*(2), pp. 143-169.

Yang, S. 1999. Censored median regression using weighted empirical survival and hazard functions. *Journal of American Statistical Association,, 94*, pp. 137-145.

Yu, K., Lu, Z., & Stander, J. 2003. Quantile regression: Applications and current research areas. *Journal of the Royal Statistical Society, Series D (The Statistician)*, 52(3), pp. 331-350.

Appendix A: Codes for most of the analyses for the examples

Code using R program:

 # Code to generate the LSR line for the total group in Figure 1 #

```
G5<-read.csv("G5all.csv")
attach(G5)
G5Slm<-lm(MATH~READING,data=G5)
plot(READING,MATH,cex=0.25,type="n",xlab="Reading",ylab="Ma
th",main="Grade 5 Total",xlim=c(50,210),ylim=c(50,180))
points(READING,MATH,cex=0.25,col="blue")
abline(lm(MATH~READING),lwd=2,col="blue")
```
 # Code for the LSR line for Grade 5 Low math ability #
```
G5low<-read.csv("G5low.csv")
attach(G5low)
G5Slmlow<-lm(MATH~READING,data=G5low)
plot(READING,MATH,cex=0.25,type="n",xlab="Reading",ylab="Ma
th",main="Grade 5 Low",xlim=c(50,210),ylim=c(50,180))
```

```
points(READING,MATH,cex=0.25,col="blue")
abline(lm(MATH~READING),lwd=2,col="blue")
```

 # Code for the LSR line for Grade 5 Medium math ability #

```
G5medium<-read.csv("G5medium.csv")
attach(G5medium)
G5Slmmedium<-lm(MATH~READING,data=G5medium)
plot(READING,MATH,cex=0.25,type="n",xlab="Reading",ylab="Ma
th",main="Grade 5 Medium",xlim=c(50,210),ylim=c(50,180))
points(READING,MATH,cex=0.25,col="blue")
abline(lm(MATH~READING),lwd=2,col="blue")
```

 # Code for the LSR line for Grade 5 High math ability #

```
G5high<-read.csv("G5high.csv")
attach(G5high)
G5Slmhigh<-lm(MATH~READING,data=G5high)
plot(READING,MATH,cex=0.25,type="n",xlab="Reading",ylab="Ma
th",main="Grade 5 High",xlim=c(50,210),ylim=c(50,180))
points(READING,MATH,cex=0.25,col="blue")
abline(lm(MATH~READING),lwd=2,col="blue")
```

#Code to generate Figure 3 #

```
plot(READING,MATH,cex=0.25,type="n",xlab="Reading",ylab="Ma
th",main="Quantile and Mean Regression Lines", xlim=c(50,210),
ylim=c(50,180))
points(READING,MATH,cex=0.25,col="blue")
abline(rq(MATH~READING,tau=0.5),lwd=2,col="blue")
abline(lm(MATH~READING),lty=2,lwd=2,col="red")
taus<-c(0.05,0.1,0.25,0.75,0.9,0.95)
for (i in 1:length(taus)){abline(rq(MATH~READING,tau=taus[i]),
lwd=2, col="gray")}
```

 # Code to generate Figure 4#

```
G5Flm<-lm(MATH~READING+GENDER,data=G5)
```

G5Full<-summary(rq(MATH~READING+GENDER,tau = 1:19/20, data=G5, method="fn"),se="boot",R=500,bsmethod="xy")

"method='fn'" stands for the Frisch-Newton interior point estimation, "se='boot'" means the SE is estimated using the bootstrapping method, "R=500" means 500 samples are generated, "bsmethod='xy'" means the specific bootstrapping method used here is xy-pair.

plot(G5Full)

abline(lm(MATH~READING+GENDER),lty=2,col="red")

savePlot("G5Full",type="jpeg")

Code in Stata:

 # Code to run the model with one covariate and produce statistics inTable 1 #

insheet using " G5all.csv";

set seed 12345;

regress math reading;

sqreg math reading, q(.05 .10 .25 .5 .75 .90 .95) reps(500);

 # Code to run the model with two covariates and produce statistics inTable 2 #

set seed 12345;

regress math reading gender;

sqreg math reading gender, q(.05 .10 .25 .5 .75 .90 .95) reps(500);

test [q5]reading=[q10]reading;

test [q10]reading=[q25]reading,accum;

test [q25]reading=[q50]reading,accum;

test [q50]reading=[q75]reading,accum;

test [q75]reading=[q90]reading,accum;

test [q90]reading=[q95]reading,accum;

test [q5]reading=[q10]reading;

test [q10]reading=[q25]reading;

```
test [q25]reading=[q50]reading;
test [q50]reading=[q75]reading;
test [q75]reading=[q90]reading;
test [q90]reading=[q95]reading;
log close;
clear;
```

Principles of Quantile Regression

and an Application

Abstract: Newer statistical procedures are typically introduced to help address the limitations of those already in practice or to deal with emerging research needs. Quantile regression (QR) is introduced in this paper as a relatively new methodology, intended to overcome some of the limitations of least-square mean regression (LMR). QR is more appropriate when assumptions of normality and homoscedasticity are violated. Also QR has been recommended as a good alternative when the research literature suggests that explorations of the relationship between variables need to move from a focus on average performance, i.e., the central tendency, to exploring various locations along the entire distribution. Whereas QR has long been used in other fields, only recently has it gained popularity in educational statistics. For example, in the ongoing push for accountability and the need to document student improvement, the calculation of Student Growth Percentiles (SGP) utilizes QR to document the amount of growth a student has made.

Despite its proven advantages and its utility, QR has not been utilized in areas such as language testing research. This paper seeks to introduce the field to basic QR concepts, procedures, and interpretations. Researchers familiar with LMR will find the comparisons made between the two methodologies helpful to anchor the new information. Finally, an application with real data is employed to demonstrate the various analyses (the code is also appended) and to explicate the interpretations of results.

Keywords: quantile regression; relationships; reading and math

此文发表于 *Language Testing* 2013 年第 1 期

文化指示方式的解释

——以当代美国英语话语为例

何刚

摘　要：指示方式是在观察和分析话语指示现象后提出来的一个语用学概念。作为一个话语现象，表达指示的单位在语义上存在某种不确定性，影响话语整体的理解。因此，消解这种不确定性，就是要把话语和它所在的语境关联起来。指示语和语境的联系是我们分析文化语境指示、指示语以及指示方式的理据。文化语境有别于直接语境和社会语境，其大部分信息都处于隐含的状态。相应地，文化语境的指示方式、话语单位、超话语单位（如会话）要比一般的明确指示和指向更加复杂和隐蔽，有时只能推导出来。文化指示是文化得以向话语渗透，实现其现实人际社交价值、社会价值、自身重构、复兴的主要途径和方式。

关键词：语境；指示方式；文化的情境介入；当代美国英语

指示现象（deictic phenomenon）主要是一种话语现象，与话语中某个成分的意义或解释有关。它一方面反映出语言对更大系统的索引，另一方面则是把话语所依赖的语境激活。作为语言表达式，指示语构成话语单位，是话语信息的重要组成部分；作为语境连接，它所激活的相关信息构成对话语及行为用意的强有力支撑。比如："××先生，可以**请教**您一个问题吗？"在中国文化中，"请教"激活的是一种文化关系，即带有对被问者（有知识、有德行、受尊敬者）的尊敬。如果是平辈之间，起码也表示谦恭，而谦恭是中华文化主张的美德之一。可见，此话语中的动词具有很强的文化语境指示功能，因为它激活的是人们就特定事件展开的文化联想。本文所要探讨的就是语言形式对文化语境进行编码、激活并与之关联的方式问题。文章从美国话语的鲜活实例入手，探讨美国英语在具体情境中如何指示主流美国文化，并由此释放话语的文化能量。本研究基于笔者对语境的三分（即刻情境、社会语境和文化语境）模型，探讨说话者如何通过话语的指向、激活、暗示等方式实现语言和文化语境的关联。

1. 指示及指示方式

指示语（deixis）是语言学尤其是语用学重点关心的问题之一。根据莱文森（Levinson）的观点，指示语涉及"语言将话语或言语事件的语境特征编码或语法化的方式"，因此也涉及"话语解释如何依赖语境分析"的方式问题。随后，莱文森和其他语言学者，如菲尔墨（Fillmore）、安德森（Anderson）及基南（Keenan）、希德内尔（Sidnell）、奥尔（Auer）也分别指出，语句（话语）的某些语言成分的解释必须参照所在话语发生的语境。从上述观点可以看出，对指示语的理解涉及话语构成成分的语义或语用信息的不确定或待确定状态，而消除这样的状态必须通过语境关联。因此，指示方式是存在于话语之中或话语背后的、用于确定相关形式的语义或语用价值信息的关联方式、方法和手段的总和。

指示方式凝聚着语言和语境的力量。从语言角度讲，它可能涉及不同层次的语言单位（词、短语、构式、甚至整个语句或会话），表明语境是何以得到指示、标识、辨别、激活与利用的；从语境角度而言，通过话语表面成分（单一、联合、混合等），可以揭示有哪些语境结构、成分和特征（集）得到了提及、暗示、指示、激活与利用，因此，也就会产生不同类别的指示场。指示场（deictic field）是一个概括话语激活的语境成分或特征集的关联域，比具体特征要高一层次，是相关语境特征话语体现的总和。比如，指示者（中心）、指示对象、听话者、旁观者、时间、空间、指示方向、运动轨迹、方式、目的地等。请看下面的例子：

（1）a. *We* are *strong women*.（说话者，自信）/ *Why should I* **deny** it？（说话者，无畏）

b. Lillian, you're a nurse. / *Why should you need* to *become* what you already *are*？（没必要改变自己，动词 become 指示变化过程）

c. *That* girl is not like the rest of *us*.（心理间距，异样）

d. *She* lives in Berkeley, and *this* is a book. she is writing about my life.（对象，彼此关系）

e. *Back* to business.（注意回转）

f. So what were *they* building in *Moscow*？（对象，过去，空间处所）

g. *I'll* take *you* to visit *Stalin*./ *You* come *alone*.（指示中心，听话者，目标，听话者，来的方式）

上面例子中 "I/we/my/you/your/she/they" 都属于 "人称指示语"，但从自我出发，体现出不同的距离感，听说者 "you" 距离较近，谈及对象 "they/she" 距离最远。同样，指示代词 that/this 也体现出与说话者的距离远近；Back to/come/take 都表示动作/移动的方向性：靠近或远离指示中心（说话者）。而且，that 多少有点排他性[那个女孩和咱们（包容）其余的人就是不一样]。Were/used to/did 等表示过去动作和状态，其实也是对以前发生的事件的指示。如：I used to be the chair.（现在不是了）/She *did* borrow my dictionary.（她确实借过我的辞典，我没骗你）。作为话语中特定指示语所激活的语境信息特征集，指示场的每一特征都是通过相关的聚合系统选择出来的。这些聚合系统可以类聚各自相关指示信息及成对的特征，构成不同的指示子场（sub-fields）：

人称场：我/我们/咱们/咱/你们/你/小子/他/她/他们/它们/家伙/哥们/兄弟/姐妹

时间场：现在/过去/曾经/以往/遥远/将来（now/then/long time ago/just now/from ...on）

空间场：这里/那里；国外/国内；楼上/楼下；窗外/窗前；房前/屋后；前门/后门/正门/边门；屋里/屋外；厅堂/厨房；后台/前台；左右；咫尺/天边（here/there; upstairs/downstairs; inside/outside; away/close）

动向场：来/去；往返；拿走；回来；过来；上来；下去；滚；取回；离别；回归/团聚（come/go; return/take/fetch/come back/come over/get out/leave）

社会场（工作场）：长官/属下；教授/部长/主任；大夫/护士小姐/白衣天使（chair; dean; Sir/Madam; gentleman; star/fan; master/apprentice）

文化场：辈分（先生/学生；长辈/晚辈/先辈/后进）；教育场（请示/请教/讨教；指导/指正/斧正；赐教/赏赐；点拨/启迪）；宗教场（忏悔/宽恕/赎罪）（excuse/forgive/pardon/humble）

语用学的前期研究者，如莱文森也将敬语（honorifics）纳入了研究范围，认为它是社会语用现象。其实这是一个受到文化态度影响的社会语用现象，唯有文化解释构成最终解释。

从指示语的原型出发，又可以将指示大致分为三类：非言语（手势、头部、视线移动等）、言语以及非言语和言语混合式。从"指示"在希腊语中的含义看，用手势指向某一客体的处所，或用头部带视线转向来指向所谈物体的所在，是十分常用的手法，具有指引或引起注意的作用。通常的方法是言语伴随着手势或身势动作（混合式），例如：

（2）"What's *that* thing?" demanded Sadie, *pointing at* the plastic clip affixed to the vestige of the umbilical cord. (Harry Stein, *One of the Guys: the Wising Up of an American Man* p.182) 赛蒂逼问（那是什么）时，手指着（伴随）贴在脐带上的胶片。

显然，指示是语言与情境（语境）的关联方式；指示语也是表达语境信息的语言（主要）方式；其意义和解释必须参照话语发生时的情境或语境特征。因此，要了解话语的文化指示方式，首先必须了解文化语境的特征。

2. 文化语境及其特征

所谓文化语境，就是焦点话语（或话语内部成分、话语整体、会话、整个交际事件）所激活或凝聚的特定文化信息。文化语境的结构与即刻的、随时变化的情境不同。就即刻情境而言，它的物理属性确定了指示方式的具体可感和明晰性（时间、地点、参与者、话题等都是在社交现场就能感受到的，可以说在很大程度上是共知、共享的）。文化语境则不一样，它在很多时候都不是具体的物理存在，而是特定人群、族群、民族长期生活在一起形成的、对物理或物质存在进行处置或管理的方式；同时，文化又是隐含的、处于可感知层面之下的潜在结构；文化语境也是一个关联的信息网络，彼此之间很难像物理事实那样清晰可辨，所以，它的个体特征很难明说，而只能通过隐喻、象征等手段加以联想；最后，文化语境又是一个系统的心理存在，其核心的思想、信念、价值、态度等世界观的内容为全体成员所共享，但必须通过不断地内化，为个体成员所认同，以指导、约束、解释其行为和话语。

2.1 文化语境的非物质性

文化语境的首要特性就是非物质（物理）属性。文化是一种心理存在，是一个群体、族裔、民族通过自身的历史发展而积累起来的稳定性极强的规范、指导、支配物质生活和社会活动中互动行为及言语交际的设定系统。它是关于物质却又高于物质的心理实在。尽管我们可以发现许多承载文化信息的物质形态（自由女神、巴台农神庙、罗马斗兽场、奥林匹亚山、长城、京杭大运河、教堂、《圣经》《古兰经》、埃及法典、金字塔、狮身人面像等），但这些存在却只是文化的特殊表现形式，因为它们在某种程度上体现或承载或建构着特定民族文化理想和追求，是特定民族或人民在特定时期生活方式或生存方式的写照。文化的承载物是零散的、具体可感的，而文化设定本身则是系统的、相互关联的意识形态设定。比如：平等主义认为，上帝之下，人人生而平等。这是一种美国文化信念。根据基督教的教义，人是上帝创造的，人是上帝的臣民（侍奉上帝），所有人都一样，是兄弟姐妹，所以必须平等相待，不能相互歧视。因此，在社会生活中，每个人都应享有同样的权利和机会。这和"普天之下，莫非王土"的封建主义思想截然不同。文化语境的非物质性存在决定了它的表达方式和指示方式在很多情况下都只能是关联的（非单一）的指称或提及，即提到一个设定，你就会联想到其他相关的设定（平等、基督教、上帝、臣民、自由、机会、公平、民权、性别、年龄、种族、喜好、性格、反歧视等）。物质是文化发生的基础，非物化是文化光芒普照的手段和过程。

2.2　文化语境的潜在性

作为一种非物质的深层结构，文化的结构深深地植根于一个民族、族裔、群体的集体意识之中，大部分内容是潜在的。根据 Edward T. Hall 的冰山模型（Iceberg Model）[1]，文化就像一座冰山，浮在海面上（可以直接感知或经验）只是很小一部分：美术、文学、戏剧、古典音乐、流行音乐、民俗舞蹈、竞技游戏（体育与游戏）、烹饪和服饰等，绝大部分都淹没于海面（水面）之下（主要存在于人们的意识之外，也就是没那么容易意识到）。潜在的文化要进入人们的意识之中，只能融贯到人的社会活动和社交言语行为中。因此，对文化语境特定事项的指示有时也只能是隐含的、通过不同的方式来体现，如：酒桌上宾主的座次体现的礼仪、会议主席台上的座次体现的重要性差异、男女同行谁先谁后体现的特定文化顺序，这些都是思想、观念、联系的语序化。

---

① 转引自 L.Terreni & J.McCallum. 2007. "Considering Culture," in J.Shaules(ed.), Deep Culture: The Hidden Challenges of Global Living, Bristol: Multilingual Matters, p40.

2.3　文化语境的隐喻性

文化语境的潜在性决定了激活方式的隐喻性。为了让人更加容易理解一个文化的特点，人们常常使用隐喻的手法（象形、象征、隐喻、借喻等）将某种文化形象化为特定的形态或物体。比如，曾经有人将美国社会比成 "melting pot"，好像美国就是一个熔炉，其他所有文化来了就必然能够很快地融入主流文化，从而融为一体，这是经典的欧裔美国人的观念；后来又有人把美国比喻成一块 "比萨饼" "马赛克"；最近又有人说美国文化是一个 "色拉碗"（主流文化就像色拉酱，其他的文化就是各种蔬菜、水果等，色拉酱控制整碗菜的味道）。透过隐喻，我们不难发现主流文化与亚文化的深层关系。

2.4　文化语境的内在性

文化隐喻激活的潜在文化从另一侧面说明文化语境是一个存在于文化共同体成员集体意识中的心理结构。每一个有文化意识的个人都会不由自主地按照文化语境的设定系统说话做事，在达成情境特定目的时，确保自己的言行不出文化的 "格"——行动与言语行为、交往行为的文化底线。内在的文化语境是一套集体认同的设定。它包括该文化共同的理念与理想、信念、价值观、态度，以及与上述几项密切关联和一致的行事原则、规则、规范、优选的行事方式和行为特征集、忌讳的行事方式与行为特征集、文化认定的事实集合等。所有这些事项共同作用于个体的文化身份界定：凡是遵从这些事项，并以此作为说话做事、话语理解和解释的参照框架的人，表明他对这些体系有心理认同和自觉意识，也就有了相应的文化身份。在具体情境中，他的文化意识就会发挥强大的指引作用、规范作用、资源作用和规避作用，使其言行不仅不会偏离文化的轨迹，而且还会为文化的繁荣与兴盛做出积极的贡献。比如：

（3）Fox has four children - Sam, 20, twins Aquinnah and Schuyler, 15, and Esme, 8 - and he says one daughter (he doesn't want to say which one) is also a free spirit' a little quirky.

"She's very much like me," says Fox, who is married to actress Tracy Pollan. "She can *end up* being *anything* from Ethel Merman to president of the United States. Maybe both." It's a thought that makes him happy.

Fox says he's not "a complete Pollyanna," but he does believe "that life is *good* and we should *celebrate* that." Despite having Parkinson's disease - he wryly calls it "a *gift* that keeps on taking" - he says he's *fine*. "I can't arrest it, so it does keep on taking, but it *continues* to be a gift because everything it takes, it gives an *opportunity* to *give* something else *back*." (http://ustoday30.usatoday.com/life/books/news/2010-04-12-Fox12STN.htm?loc=interstitialskip)

从这则报道的字里行间不难看出一个有文化的美国人的乐观主义生活态度。一是对女儿的自由精神的高度认同（她也许可以当美国总统）；二是对自身疾病（帕金森氏综合征）的辩证的乐观，认为这已是一种礼物（它不断地拿走你的这样那样，可又不断地回赠给你机会去获取别的东西）。迈克尔-福克斯原本是好莱坞明星，生病以后，他渐渐获得写作的灵感和对生活的乐观态度。关于文化语境的内在性，还可以在法国学者斯波伯（Dan Sperber）等人的自然主义文化语境观中找到印证。

3. 文化指示方式的形式特征

话语对文化语境的指示可以表现为显性、直接的指向和隐性、间接、隐含的示意。直接的指向可以从话语中找到激活文化事项的成分，而间接示意则要通过推理来获取话语与文化特定事项的关联。一般而言，直接指向文化事项相对比较单一，间接示意就要复杂多了。

3.1 直接指向（Direct pointing）

话语对文化语境的直接指向是对话语和文化关联性的显性表达，说明话语的意义在其表面（组合意义）即受到了文化语境的作用。比如：
"周瑜打黄盖——一个愿打、一个愿挨"，是汉语里的歇后语，和三国演义中的历史人物相关联，属于文化事实关联。美国英语中，这样的关联也是随处可见。比如：

（4） He's a *Texas Democrat* all right, but not from the liberal Lyndon Johnson wing of the state party. He's a free trader and deficit hawk with close ties to business and Wall Street. (Robert Reich describes Bentsen in *Locked in the Cabinet*, p.17）

在描述被推荐人本特森时，作者用"德州民主党""党内自由的林顿约翰逊派""预算鹰派"（强硬控制派）和"华尔街"（金融中心）这些各有特殊文化内涵的指示语，用于说明此人的政治倾向性和做事风格，而这样的话语信息的产生离不开上述指示语所激活的文化语境联想。直接指向的条件是：有明确的、合适的文化事项可以关联；有合适的、惯用表达手段可以利用；被直接指向的文化事项一定对话语的信息表达和情境功能发挥有所帮助。又如：

（5） "Oh, she said pleasantly, 'you can talk to me in English.' So she was English - evidently *upper-class*, at that."
"Is my accent that bad?"
"It's not hard to recognize an *American 'r'*." （Harry Stein, *One of the Guys*，p.149）

本来"我"是在讲法语，可那个年轻的小姐让我讲英语，这是为什么？因为我的美国式儿化音"r"让我露馅了。也就是说，明明你是美国人，干吗要硬撑着说法语呢？因此，在本段会话中，女士的最后一句话"听出美国式儿化音并不难"通过儿化音直接指向到对方的文化身份。

3.2　文化语境的间接示意

与直接指称文化语境相对的是隐含的、间接的文化语境指向或暗示。正如前面讨论所示，文化的绝大部分是隐性的、存在于话语背后的信息。因此，指示这类信息只能通过那些具有高度敏感的话语形式来实现，许多是超越词汇层面甚至语句和整个会话的。

（6）（Librarian at SUNY Albany Main Library）

a. How are you *today*?

b. *How* can I *help* you?

c. *You* are *all set*, sir.

表面上看，似乎其他英语国家的人也会说类似的话，但在美国的大学图书馆里听到管理员说出来，尤其是在 How are you 后面还加上 today（今天），就显得不一般了，美国式的热情溢于言表。再说 How can I help you 作为对另一固化的行业招牌话语的替代，同样可以显示美国服务从业人员的行业自信（我一定可以帮到你，只是请你告诉我从何帮起）。众所周知，尽管商业文化并非源自美国，可是就服务业、服务意识和服务水准而言，美国人都将其发挥到了令人佩服的水平。You are all set（搞定）是一句流行的美国俚语，几乎在所有服务场所都可以听到，显示出美国式的爽快。这些话语形式的频繁使用就会使听话者产生一种对美国文化的亲近感，因此，尽管它们并不直接指向美国文化的特定信息，却也不失美国文化语境向导的作用。

如上文所示，文化语境的指示方式多种多样，但比较常见的是：将时空等即刻情境特征投射到文化事项上去，从而使文化的信息易于识别。比如：

（7）a. a nation on *wheels*.

b. *Under God*, *all men* (and women) are created *equal*. In God we *trust*.

c. *Upward mobility* is the theme.

d. You guys are going to stay here.

e. Us-guys, them-guys

第一讲的是生活方式，汽车在美国人生活中的中心地位。第二讲的是美国建国的理念（普天之下，人人平等，因为均为造物主所造），以及美元纸币上印的"我们信任上帝"折射出的金钱背后的信念。第三讲的是美国文化的特点之一：高度的流动性（主流是向上）。第四讲的是对听说者的一种通称（复数），不分性别，这和英国英语不太一样，反映出美国人对听话者近距离指示的随意性。第五更有意思，基于个人主义，美国人的社群分化与不同的文化意识有关。比如，有一种人的生活态度是漫不经心、拖沓，什么事都慢半拍，站在这群人的角度，他们将那些有珍惜时间、按时作息、准时纳税和还款等习惯的人们视为**另类**并加以排斥，而对有相同嗜好的人则视如**同类**，类似的说法折射出彼此间的文化心理间距（cultural distance）。

文化隐喻（折射文化意识的隐喻形式）也是指示文化语境的一种方式，因为从隐喻中人们可以发现一个民族或人群的思维方式。美国社会是一个典型的市场经济社会，什么东西都可以作为商品拿来交换，包括时间。所以，时间就是金钱，是有价值和价格的。美国人说某人说话不当真，会说"You must be kidding""Are you kidding?"Kid 是小孩，作动词就有"把某人当小孩看"的意思，可以表达惊恐、开玩笑、生气等。此处作为现在分词，表示过程，有隐喻的意味。还如："You got a point there. Point"是一个器具的尖端，其实这话里讲的是"有道理"，但道理是不可视的，尖端是可视的，所以，从源域（尖端，可以扎进另一物体）到目的域（道理，可以深入人心）的隐喻说明美国人也喜欢将抽象的事物形象化。又比如：

（8） "There's this very nervous man," she begins, "who's on the verge of a breakdown. His doctor advises him to get away from the city." (Mel Tormé, *The Other Side of the Rainbow* , p.33)

On the verge of（在边缘上），把一个人的精神状态比作一个物体（人）处于另一个物体的边缘，说明"即将、就要、快要"；而breakdown 是机器停止做工（出了严重故障），把人的状态比喻成机器的状态，说明他已经快不行了（撑不住了）。

夸张作为一种修辞格是普遍的，可美国人把夸张发挥到了极致，说明他们的心态之放松，心情之畅达，性格之豪放。比如：

（9）a. So the man says, "Gee, *that*'s not a bad idea. Might do me *a world of* good." (Mel Tormé, *The Other Side of the Rainbow*, p.33)

b. "That there's Ol' Blue，" says George. "*Greatest* huntin' dog in the *world*."（同上）

例（9）a 中的"do somebody good"（对谁有益）是一般的搭配，可以加一个修饰语，但用"满世界的"（world of）实属夸张。可美国人就喜欢用这种程度远远超过实际的修饰词以示其性格的豪放。（9）b 也是如此，本来就一只猎犬，犯得着说它是"最棒的"（greatest）吗？更不用说后面的"in the world"，好像世界上就这么一条狗厉害，无狗能出其右。由此，美国人处事的积极正面态度展露无遗。

与单一的指示手段相对应的是混合或复合的手段，甚至是通过会话结构来指示。像文化隐喻之类的指示方式通常还借助于特定的文化形象，因为特定的形象也可以凝聚许多精神特征。比如，美国的许多名校都有自己的吉祥物，加州大学伯克利分校的人叫自己"Cal Bears"（加州熊），其他学校也有自己的叫法。美国篮球联盟的每个球队都有自己的名号（Chicago Bulls，LA Lakers，Portland Blazers），这些名号不仅可以指示自己的志趣和愿望，也可以将其球迷凝聚到一起，发展出体育文化和进取精神。换言之，动物名称、人物、抽象理念的名称等代表了某种文化特征。

会话以及会话所要求的合作、平等协商的姿态也可以指示美国文化语境。虽然会话无处不在，但不同民族对会话的重视程度、会话中彼此的态度、对会话互动结果的期待等还是存在显著差异的。单一民族的文化与多民族并存的文化在会话中的表现也是不尽相同的。像美国这样多元文化的国家，差异性和平等性使社会互动需要通过会话来实现，因此，美国人尽管话多，但只要有第二人在场，就会说一会儿停下来，让出说话的权利，也会不时地邀请更多人加入会话。对美国人而言会话特别有帮助，可以促进彼此理解，协调社会关系，促进社会合作。因此，即便存在明显的身份差异（上下级、师生、父子、母子），人们仍然选择会话与磋商、友善与合作来处理彼此的差异，达成沟通。比如：

（10）（学校副校长，一位白发绅士与一个故意不学好的学生的谈话）

Mr. Childs: Walter, I *can not stop* you, but I want to *know why* you're doing so poorly.

Walter: There's nothing to know, I don't want to stay in school, That's all.

Mr. Childs: *You*'re only sixteen. What do you *plan* to do?（担心和关心）

Walter: I am going to be a Marine.

Mr. Childs: *Don't you think*, that the Marines might "mess with you" even more than your teachers?

Walter: You *don't understand*, Mr. Childs.

Mr. Childs: (*Reaching across his desk and squeezed* Walter's hand) Good luck.

且让我们看看这位叫查尔兹的副校长是怎样和一个差生说话的。按常规的理解，副校长有权把差生找来训斥一通，说"你怎么搞的"之类的话，可是他没有。他请这位叫沃尔特的同学来，开诚布公地说："我阻止不了你（你不愿学好，谁也管不住你），可是你总可以告诉我你做成这样（学得如此糟糕）的原因吧。"请注意他的措辞，美国老师不能当面说学生愚蠢，只能说"做得很糟"（so poorly）。而当对方说无可奉告时，这副校长只说了"你才 16 岁，你有什么计划？"，而当对方说想当水兵并表示"你不会明白"时，这位校领导也只好说"祝你好运"。因为他只能尊重，而不能干涉他人的决定（美式民主对个人决策力的信任）。所以，整个会话和副校长的言语折射出美国教育肩负的文化理想：把学生作为独立、自主、平等的个体来尊重和塑造。

4. 指示方式与文化的情境化

话语建构的过程既是一个用意与情境的关联与匹配的过程，也是一种文化介入现实活动情境的方式。文化的现实价值在于它对情境中言语行为与交往互动的驱动和参与，指示方式以现实情境化的用意为指南，却又深刻地体现文化的关切。因此，在话语结构中，指示方式成了文化投射的焦点。文化的情境化需要满足几个条件：第一，情境化的言语行为用意对文化有需要；第二，文化体系具有向该用意输出信息的可能；第三，在众多的选择中，文化的选择一定是最适合双方、最有力的因此也是最有效的选择。

4.1 情境需要

情境需要是指说话者作为社会交往者，为了达成某个特定目的，在感到其他形式语力不足或过多时，需要调动文化信息来实现用意和情境效果的匹配。比如：

（11）"*This* Thanksgiving Day, we *reflect on* the compassion and contributions of *Native* Americans, whose *skill* in agriculture helped the early colonists survive, and whose *rich culture* continues to *add to our Nation's heritage*," Obama said in the declaration. （Nov. 23, 2010）

在白宫的演说词中，美国总统是想通过"感恩"来进一步推销他的多族裔团结、共生的理念，因此，他把感恩的焦点集中在早期的印第安人。大家知道，当五月花号载着旧世界的清教徒来到麻省的普利茅斯殖民地的时候，生活环境相当恶劣，是印第安部落的酋长带着一帮人来帮助了这些白人耕种，所以第二年（1621）当白人欢庆丰收的时候，他们把印第安人请过来一道感谢上帝的恩典，同时也感谢他们的慷慨相助。那么为什么奥巴马要用"本土美国人"，而不直接说印第安人呢？因为，他觉得有必要特别提及那些长期被忽视的人群，从而强化融合各个族裔的"美国传统"，一个统一国家的传统。在这个意义上，印第安人是正宗的美国人，黑人也是美国人，大家都一样。他们是先民，他们的文化为国家的文化传统做出了并继续在做巨大的贡献。"我们"感谢他们，是要进一步加强融合和团结，促进国家的进一步繁荣。因此，提及印第安人的方式实际上反映了奥巴马的话语用意——作为总统在感恩节追根溯源、引导公众情感走向的需要。

4.2　文化情境化的可能性

文化情境化的可能性涉及特定情境是否为文化介入的合适情境以及事件和话语主题可否受到文化的关照等方面。也就是说，文化体系内部有没有适合该情境中的话语、行为或互动的相应设定。尽管一般认为，文化的光芒普照大地，可是，文化若要对特定地方产生特殊的关照，就必须确定其特定的输出选项。比如：

（12）　On growing up *biracial* in Long Island: "*Our family* just didn't really *fit in*. I was 9 years old, I had an *Afro*. I was a *lightskinned black girl* with lots of freckles, as I am still today. Some people would be puzzled, 'Well, *what are you?*' There were people who threw out the *N-word* whenever they felt like. It was a wonderful place to grow up, and then every so often, you were *reminded* that you didn't *fit in*." （http://www. nydailynews. com/entertainment/cnn-host-soledad-o-brien-difficult-time-dishing-new-book-big-story-article-1.451040）

本段话语的主人公成长在纽约长岛的一个混血家庭，所以她自幼就是不黑不白，所以，感到不伦不类。在白人占优势的社会里，她的心情自然很复杂，简单地说，就是有点格格不入。在美国英语里就有这样的词语使她感到格格不入，如：fit in（正好合适），the N-word（所有指称黑人的贬义词）。Fit in 不仅仅是身体的，更是文化心态的。因此，当说话人想要表现自己的窘境时，文化习语满足了她的情境需要。

4.3 文化选项为最优选项

在言语交际中，执行同一个意向的往往有多种选项，彼此存在竞争的聚合关系，有些选项更能直接地满足行为用意表面化的需要。那么，文化选项如何才能实现其情境化的功能呢？首先，它必须能够满足情境的需要，并且使情境化的用意主题化更加凸显；同时，它还有文化的优势：使该主题化的用意成为文化合适的用意，也就是说，它不仅能够帮助话语获得最佳的情境效果，而且能够获得最佳的文化效果。比如：

（13）〔福克斯电视节目主持人萨卡利亚（Zakaria）反击美国有线电视新闻网（CNN）主持人贝克（Beck）关于"穆斯林是恐怖分子"的言论〕

"Let's do a bit of math here" said Zakaria, demonstrating his calculations on a chalkboard. "There are 1,570,000,000 Muslims worldwide. Take ten percent of those Muslims and you get 157,000,000. That's how many Muslim terrorists Glenn Beck is suggesting there are in the world." Beck wondered why 'Oh why this wasn't receiving any media coverage?'" Zakaria continued. "Well let me suggest one reason. It is total nonsense. A figure made up by Glenn Beck with absolutely no basis in fact."（http://www.nydailynews.com/news/national/2010/12/13/2010-12-13_glenn_beck_claims_10_of_muslims_are_terrorists_cnns_fareed_zakaria_blasts_him_fo.html#ixzz182LFv5xj）

当今美国社会弥漫着对恐怖主义的恐惧，所以一旦谁和恐怖主义者沾边，立即会引起人们的仇视。在这种背景下，贝克的主观臆测可能带来对全美穆斯林人群的极大伤害，因此，必须针锋相对地反击。那么怎么反击才能奏效呢？你贝克不是说 10%的穆斯林是恐怖分子吗？那就给你做个小小的算术，证明你的话是何等的荒唐。由于美国人喜欢玩数字游戏（文化嗜好、科学倾向），所以，萨卡利亚选择了相应的、也是最适合、最直接和有说服力的方式来提升话语的文化效果，以消除格伦的话造成的仇视穆斯林的态度。

也许人们要问，文化语境指示到底是怎样发生的？关于这一点，曼宁（Manning）指出，语境本身就是一个转移因子（shifter），它的意义和形态都会转移，从即刻情境到社会语境；指示语诸范畴可以机动地使用社会成员共享的文化知识。根据西尔弗斯坦（Silverstein）的观点，曼宁结合他观察多种语言指示形态的经验认为，很多看上去与文化无关的指示词（时间、空间关系指示）其实都是受文化图式化（cultural schematization）作用的。从指示主体视角看，指示就是说话者根据自己的用意去引导听话者注意的一种方式。文化指示就是让听话者或解释者将话语的注意转向文化语境的结果，说明当前话语及行为是具有文化理据或文化用意的。

从以上讨论可以看出，指示方式关注的并不是一个简单的词汇问题，它在多种层次上都是可能的。同时，语境形态是确定指示语对应语境属性的关键参数。指示方式并不是简单地体现语境，而更可能激活会话参与者的语境联想，或帮助搭建会话及言语行为所需要的文化语用平台，为话语释放文化与人际功能提供重要条件。因此，指示方式与文化语境研究已经不是对一个简单的指向关系的研究，而是一项涉及语言和文化之纽带的研究，是话语文化解释的关键所在。

参考文献

Anderson, S.R. & E.L.Keenan. 1985. Deixis.In T.Shopen(ed.), *Language Typology and Syntactic Description: Grammatical Categories and the Lexicon*, New York: Cambridge University Press, pp. 259-308.

Auer, P. 2009. Context and contextualization. In J.Verschuerenn & J.Stman(eds.), *Key Notions for Pragmatics*. Amsterdam & Philadelphia: John Benjamins Publishing Company, pp. 86-98.

Fillmore,C.J. 1982. Towards a descriptive framework for spatial deixis. In R.J.Jarvella & W.Klein(eds.), *Speech, Place and Action: Studies in Deixis and Related Topics*, New York: John Wiley & Sons Ltd., pp. 31-59.

Hanks, W. 1992. The indexical ground of deictic reference. In A.Duranti & C.Goodwin(eds.), *Rethinking Context: Language as an Interactive Phenomenon*, Cambridge: Cambridge University Press, pp. 43-76.

Levinson, S.C. 1983. *Pragmatics*. Cambridge: Cambridge University Press.

Manning, H.P. 2001. On Social Deixis. *Anthropological Linguistics*, (1), pp. 54-100.

Sidnell, J. 2009. Deixis. In J.Verschueren & J.Stman(eds.), *Key Notions for Pragmatics*, Amsterdam & Philadelphia: John Benjamins Publishing Company, pp. 114-136.

何刚，2006，文化语境的建构——拟想的模型，《中国外语》，第 5 期，第 73-77 页。

Interpreting the Cultural Deictic Modes: Instantiated by Contemporary American English Utterances

Abstract: This paper discusses the issue of how cultural context can be indexed. The mode of deictics is proposed on the basis of our research in the variety of indexical expressions in utterances. This paper focuses on deictics in the cultural context of utterances. Through an analysis, we have found that every cultural context has its unique information structure. This is especially true to the American cultural context which is a system of mental information derived from American people's shared life experience and national development processes. The American context also reveals an Iceberg Model of cultural information, a small portion explicit while a larger part remains hidden and implicit. This study also shows that cultural deictic expressions can't occur in a speaker-intention-free fashion. The speaker's cultural predisposition, cultural awareness and culture-related intention can often affect the types of cultural information to activate (pick out) and the way of picking.

Key words: context; deictic mode(s); situated cultural intervention; contemporary American English

此文发表于《浙江大学学报》(人文社会科学版) 2014 年第 6 期

浅谈认知语言学中的范畴理论

胡慧俐

摘　要：范畴理论是认知语言学中一个重要的基础理论。本文从范畴化对人类认知的作用出发，介绍了范畴和原型的基本特性，讨论了范畴和原型在不同语境和文化环境中的变化，探讨了范畴层次化理论在认知和语言使用中的应用。

关键词：认知语言学；原型；范畴；范畴化；认知模型；文化模型；范畴层次化

1. 引言

认知语言学是 20 世纪 70 年代在美国诞生的一个新的语言学流派。作为对乔姆斯基所创立的转换生成语义学为代表的形式主义语言学的反叛，认知语言学更侧重于对**语言和思维**之间关系的研究，抛弃了在此之前占主导地位的语义和句法的研究，转而从认知的角度来寻求解释人类语言普遍规律的途径。人类对语言的使用与人类的思维、体验有着密不可分的关系。传统的语言学认为语言首先是一种交流工具，是对人类思维的反映和表述。而认知语言学则认为语言不仅仅是一种交流工具，也是一种认知工具，除了能够表达思维，还能帮助人类去更好地认识世界，获得新的知识。

那么所谓"认知"是指人感知世界和对世间万物形成概念的方式，

以及在此过程中获得和形成的经验和体验。认知语言学的核心观点就是：语言的创建、学习及运用，基本上都必须能够透过人类的认知而加以解释，因为认知能力是人类知识的根本。在人类的思维过程中有一个重要的步骤，即是对宇宙中的所有物体、事件、现象以及人类的经验和感觉进行**分类**，认知语言学把这个分类的过程称为**范畴化**。而语言正是范畴化这一思维过程中的首要工具。传统的语言学把语言符号称为能指，所表达的意思是所指，而真正指代的内容是独立于语言的参照物。认知语言学则是对语言符号和概念之间的关系进行研究。概念是指"我们对事物及其存在方式的理解"①。简单地说，概念可以指一个单个的事物：比如苹果。也可以指一系列的事物：比如水果。当我们接触到一个新的概念时，要认识它、了解它，我们首先做的就是把这个新概念进行归类。当我们找到合适的语言符号来表述这一新概念时，这个客观范畴就转变成了语言范畴。当然人类的语言还远不能做到表达自然中的一切，但是它在人的认知过程中的作用已经显而易见。

本文尝试对认知语言学中范畴理论进行讨论。首先介绍范畴的内部结构和原型的概念。其次将讨论范畴所受到的语境和文化因素的影响，最后讨论范畴的层次化理论在语言使用和认知过程的应用。

2. 范畴和原型

范畴并不是认知语言学新创造出来的概念。所谓范畴就是具有相同属性特征的成员的集合。早在亚里士多德的时代就开始了对范畴的研究。认知学理论认为人的认知过程就是范畴化的过程。简单地说也就是把我们周围的生物、物体、现象进行归类，把它们组织成便于记忆的词义。

认知语言学对范畴的定义和理解与传统的研究有很大分歧。经典

---

① DELBECQUE Nicole. 2006. L'idée que nous avons de quelque chose, de sa façon d'être dans le monde, Linguistique cognitive, Bruxelles : De boeck.

的范畴理论认为范畴的边界是清晰的，某一成员要么属于这一范畴，要么不属于这一范畴。范畴的每一位成员共享一些属性和特征，它们的地位是平等。而美国心理学家、认知语言学家罗施（Rosch）进行了大量的实验，发现范畴的边界并不是如我们想象得那么清晰，大部分范畴的边界是模糊的。最典型的例子就是颜色和温度。在连续的色谱上，从纯白色到正黄色之间是无数白色和黄色的结合色，那么从哪一点开始我们可以说这不是白色了，而是黄色呢？恐怕每个人的答案都是不同的。再比如水的温度从几度开始可以称为冷，几度开始又可以称为热呢？Rosch 的这一理论不但适用于诸如颜色、温度等连续统一体，也适用于一些轮廓明确的物体。比如杯子，从最瘦长的形状到最矮胖的形状，什么时候我们就不能称其为杯子，而是花瓶呢？什么时候我们又不能说这是杯子，而是一个碗呢？再比如椅子，从最标准的椅子到最原始的树桩或者最简单的一款布垫子再到另外一极最夸张的贵妃椅，什么时候我们就说这不是椅子，是床，什么时候我们说这不是椅子，是块布呢？其实这些日常用品的边界也是模糊的。

罗施还发现，在每个范畴中，总有一个特征最明显的中心成员，也就是说当我们说到一个概念时，大部分人首先想到的那个成员。他有两个著名的颜色和形状实验。他给被试验者看一系列不同的红色。他发现当他请他们指出他们认为最符合红色定义的那个颜色时，几乎所有的人都指出了同一个颜色。当他让他们定义或描述其他红色时，大家几乎都以起先指出的红色为基准来描述。他又给被试验者看一组正方形和正方形的变体所组成的图形，大家毫不困难地指出了最符合正方形这一概念的那个图形，之后人们对变体的图形一律都是以正方形为基准进行描述的：比如正方形缺个角，正方形突出一块。所以罗施得出结论：人们对事物形成的概念是以范畴中的原型为基准。所谓原型也就是范畴中最具典型性，特征最明显的成员。人们从理解这个最好的实例开始理解这个范畴，并理解这个范畴的其他成员。

原型是范畴的典型成员，享有比其他成员更多的属性，位于范畴的核心位置，从原型到范畴的边缘成员，其典型性是递减的，呈辐射状散开。范畴的边界也是模糊的，某一边缘成员可以属于这一范畴也可以属于相邻的范畴。范畴的模糊性和开放性其实是符合"认知经济性"原则，使得我们可以使用较少的认知努力获得尽可能多的信息。随着外部世界的变化，范畴的开放性特征允许新成员的加入，而且范畴的内部结构也并不是一成不变的。比如 20 世纪 90 年代之前说到游戏这个词，大家恐怕多数会想到的是儿童之间的捉迷藏或成人的棋牌类游戏。而之后出现的电子游戏、网络游戏和现在时兴的桌面游戏等，对游戏这个范畴产生了很大的影响。随着网络游戏的普及和发展，它逐渐从边缘位置向中心位置靠近，并成为这个范畴的原型，而以前的传统游戏则退到了边缘位置。所以，认知语言学提出的范畴和原型理论比经典范畴理论有更强的生命力和实用性。

3. 语境和文化

范畴和原型理论在认知科学中得到完善，之后被认知语言学家借鉴用来解释很多语言现象。某一概念所对应的范畴和原型如果用图形表现出来的话，就是以原型为中心，其他成员按照其符合该范畴特性的程度递减向外呈辐射状分布。同一概念的范畴和原型会受到认知模型和文化模型两个因素的影响。

传统的语义分析会认为同一个词在不同的语境中会产生不同的含义。而认知语言学则提出，除了语境，我们之前所获得的和该语境相关的体验和知识也会对某一概念的范畴和原型产生影响。认知语言学家把语境归为心理表征，并把我们已经体验并储存的大量和语境相关的信息称为**认知模型**。比如在 "He opened the door to face a pretty young woman with a dog in her arms."（他打开门，迎面看见一位怀里抱着狗的少妇。）这句话中 dog 所形成的范畴和原型，与没有语境情况下的 "dog" 所形成的范畴和原型是不同的。显然美丽少妇手中抱着的狗更可能是一只宠物狗、贵妇犬，哈巴狗或牧羊犬也说得过去，但是德国猎犬或藏獒的可能性就显得比较低。所以这一语境所产生的范畴原型应该是宠物小狗，而范畴的内部结构也不同于一般的狗的范畴。另一例子 "The policeman lined up with the dogs to face the rioters."（警察带着狗排成一排面对暴徒。）显然，此处所形成的范畴和原型又与上句完全不同了。

之所以这两句话会使我们产生完全不同的范畴和原型，这就跟语境所唤起我们的自身体验有关。在每一次范畴化的过程中，我们都会有意无意地借助我们脑中已有的认知模型，即使在找不到任何相关认知模型的完全陌生的环境中，我们还是会尽力从相似的经验中找到切入点来认识新的事物，获得新的知识。比如一个德国人在英国看板球比赛，他可能就找不到任何可以理解场上所发生的一切的认知模型，但是他还是可以借助之前预存在脑中的有关比赛的常识来慢慢学习这个对他来说完全陌生的运动。

此外，范畴和原型还受到文化模型的影响。认知模型虽然强调的是个人的体验，但是它又是我们所生长的文化环境所决定的。这就是文化模型。认知语言学家做过一个实验，让一组美国人和一组尼日利亚人对食物这个范畴中的 48 个成员根据典型性排序。在美国人那组中排在第四位的披萨饼却排在尼日利亚人的第 41 位。而尼日利亚人排在第三位的山药在美国人那里却排得很靠后。这说明文化模型对范畴的结构有着巨大的影响。

再比如，桌子这个范畴在日本人和西方人的概念中也会存在差异。日本人关于桌子范畴的原型应该是适用于他们席地而坐的那种矮桌，而西方人的桌子原型则是西式的长桌。但是桌子这一范畴也在随着时代的发展而变化。随着电脑的普及，桌子的原型从原来的饭桌越来越趋向于电脑桌。而不同文化环境中对桌子所形成的范畴和原型的差异也会越来越小。

4. 范畴的层次化

在范畴理论的基础上，认知语言学家又提出了范畴层次化理论。刚才提到的范畴和范畴之间的边界是模糊的。这是范畴横向的关系。

在纵向上，从最宽泛到最专业，范畴可以分为至少三个层次：上层范畴、基本范畴和下层范畴。在某些生物领域，甚至可以分为更多的层次。比如水果属于上层范畴，而苹果属于基本范畴，红富士苹果则属于下层范畴。基本范畴是人类认识世界的开始，皮亚杰研究发现，儿童从 0 岁到 3 岁就能掌握基本范畴中的大部分概念。在最初的语言学习中，儿童掌握树木、狗、苹果、裙子这些概念要远早于掌握植物、动物、水果和服装等上层概念，而掌握松树、拉布拉多犬、红富士苹果或迷你裙等下层概念则更要晚得多。所以基本范畴是人类认知的根本。同时基本范畴也是一般情况下，人们对话过程中最经常使用的概念。比如，当人家问你："你在哪里？"你显然不会回答："我在地球上"，而更多地说："我在家里。"如果有人问你："这是什么？"我们也一般会回答说："这是一棵树。"而不会说出它是哪种树。

那么从上层范畴到下层范畴成员的数量会逐渐递增，构成一个树形的网络结构。但是这个网络结构并不是一副完美的拼图。首先，并不是所有的概念都有相对应的语言来表达。其次，并不是所有的分类都是绝对并且唯一的。比如服装作为上层范畴为例，其基本范畴就有裤子、裙子、上衣。而裤子又可以分为牛仔裤、中裤、九分裤、短裤。裙子又可以分为迷你裙、百褶裙等。但是如果从性别的角度出发，分类的结果就会完全不同。服装分为男士服装和女士服装。男式服装中出现的裤子在女士服装中也会出现。而现在越来越流行的中性服装又该怎么分类呢。这种分类的困难在第一种分类方法中也同样存在，比如裙裤到底是裙子还是裤子呢？恐怕不同的人会有不同的分法。所以范畴和范畴之间所构成的网络也并不是有序的、结构整齐的，而是像分子一般发散和模糊的，相互交叉的。

此外，每一种语言都无法逃避的一个致命问题：词汇空缺。也就是说在上述网状结构中还存在不少词汇的空洞。不同的语言所存在的空洞也有所不同。比如英语中的 brother 和 sister 就没有上义词。在法语中也找不到表示遮住上半身的所有服装的总称——上衣。中国人经常说的"买菜"，这个概括所有蔬菜、肉类、海鲜的"菜"在法语和英语中都没有相对应的说法。这些空洞的产生无疑和不同语言群体的文化风俗习惯有关。比如汉语中对亲属关系表述的复杂程度恐怕世上没有一种语言能够企及。所以《红楼梦》中的姐姐妹妹们注定是翻译界的一大难题。而相反，葡萄酒酿造业发达的法国也创造了无数有关酿造工艺、葡萄品种、土质的词汇，这也是汉语中所难以表达的。

5. 结语

综上所述，范畴理论是认知语言学中的基础理论。对经典的范畴理论做出了修改和补充，认为范畴具有开放性和不稳定性等特点，而每个范畴中的原型则是人类认知的基准，或者说出发点。同时范畴和原型又会受到认知模型和文化模型的影响，其内部结构和原型都会随之产生变化。范畴在纵向上又可以分为多个层次，在语言上表现为上义词和下义词。位于中间的基本层次是人类认知和语言学习的出发点，同时也是语言使用中最频繁出现的概念。范畴层次的内部结构并不是有序而紧密的，由于分类的交叉其结构是发散的、模糊的。而范畴不同层次所构成的拼图也并不完整，词汇空缺现象便说明了语言还无法表达自然界中所有的概念，而不同的文化环境所产生的词汇空缺也会有所不同。

范畴理论不仅对人的认知规律做出了很好的解释，而且对人类语言的习得和很多语言现象都有很强的解释性。近年来，随着对范畴及其认知模型本身研究的日益深入，该理论在认知语义学、二语习得、翻译等研究中也发挥着越来越大的作用。

参考文献

Delelbecque, Nicole. 2006. L'idée que nous avons de quelque chose, de sa façon d'être dans le monde, *Linguistique Cognitive*, Bruxelles : De boeck.

成军，2006，范畴化及其认知模型，《四川外国语学院学报》，第1

期，第 65-70 页。

李福印，2008，《认知语言学概论》，北京：北京大学出版社。

刘宇红，2005，《认知语言学：理论与应用》，北京：中国社会科学出版社。

弗里德里希·温格瑞尔、汉斯-尤格·施密特，2009，《认知语言学导论》（第二版），彭利贞、许国萍、赵微，译，上海：复旦大学出版社。

郑银芳，2007，谈认知语言学中的原型范畴理论，《中国成人教育》，第 10 期，第 124-125 页。

Analysis of the Category Theory in Cognitive Linguistics

Abstract: Category is a basic concept in cognitive linguistics. To find out how it works in the cognitive system of human beings, this paper explains the properties of category and prototype and discusses their potential changes in different semantic contexts and different cultural contexts. Based on the discussion, the paper makes an analysis of how the categorization mechanism works in language learning and the cognitive system.

Key words: cognitive linguistics, prototype, category, categorization, cognitive module, cultural module, subcategorization

此文发表于《学园》2013 年第 1 期

高中英语课堂中教师语码转换的
情感因素分析

李辉　王海娉①

摘　要：语码转换是一个比较复杂的社会语言现象，而将英语作为外语开展教学的课堂决定了语码转换的特殊功能，本文通过对上海某重点高中的几位参与教师在课堂上提供的语码转换的译文样本进行实例分析，发现语码转换是外语课堂中师生间情感交流的有效方式。教师通过课堂上角色的变换能够营造一种正式或非正式的氛围，建立一种师生间平等亲密的关系，最终提高外语教学的效果。

关键词：英语课堂；语码转换；情感因素

1. 引言

语码转换（code-switching）是一个比较复杂的社会语言现象，语言学家通过社会语言学、心理语言学、语用学等不同角度对语码转换进行了研究，并取得了丰硕的成果。自从 20 世纪 80 年代以来很多学者对于外语课堂语码转换的研究越来越重视。其中绝大多数的研究主要集中在对两种语码的教学功能上的诠释（Rolin-Ianziti & Brownlie，2002；Krashen，1981；Ellis，1984；Eldridge，1996）。然而，除了语

---

① 上海大学附属学校教师。

码转换的教学功能外，在实际课堂中，外语教师们还经常使用两种语码来达到与学生们情感上的交流，最终促进外语课堂上教学效果的提高。

本文通过对某重点高中的几位参与教师在课堂上提供的语码转换的译文样本进行分析，阐述语码转换如何成为教师在高中外语课堂上进行师生情感交流的有效方式，以及对外语课堂教学所产生的影响。

2. 语码转换的定义

许多国内外语言学家们分别从广义和狭义的角度对语码转换进行了讨论并给出了定义。在广义上，克莱因（Clyne，1991：263）把语码转换定义为，在社会双语文化背景下，两种或更多的语言或语言变体在同一个或连续的话轮中的交替使用的现象。格润（Gearon，1997）认为语码转换是说话者为达到有效的交流目的而采用的一种语言策略。而从狭义上，香港学者林（Lin，1990）则认为语码转换在外语教学中则是指在教授一门外语的过程中目标语（target language）和学生使用的母语（native language）之间的交替转换。可见，语码转换是跨文化交际和学习中一种普遍的社会语言现象。

3. 以英语为外语的课堂环境特点

对于将英语作为外语的初学者和中级水平的学生来说，比起外部世界他们更能在课堂里进行有效的外语学习（Richard-Amato，1988）。在单语的社会环境下，学生很难在课堂之外获得现成的可以交流的外语环境。因此，课堂环境对于外语教学至关重要。

马卡洛（Macaro，1997）在他的研究中总结了外语课堂的几个特点：（1）学生几乎完全依赖教师来学习外语；（2）教师完全支配着上课内容与节奏、师生间的语言互动和管理实际课堂环境。

很明显，教师在外语课堂中的作用至关重要，他/她是课堂上信息的主要提供者和课堂教学的组织者。教师的课堂语言是学生语言输入的一种重要途径。学生在课堂上只能接受来自外语教师有质量的语言输入。在本次调研过程中，我们发现中国的英语课堂实际上带有上述特征。一方面，在儒家传统的教学文化中，中国教师是知识的权威者且掌控着整个外语课堂（Biggs，1996）；另一方面，这种教师的专制并没有影响到课堂上的师生关系并仍然能够维持外语课堂环境的和谐气氛（Ho，2001）。为何中国教师的权威性仍然能维持一种和谐的外语教学课堂气氛呢？卡米利（Camilleri，1996）认为："以英语为外语的老师似乎渐渐地了解了第一语言（母语）和第二语言（目标语）所带有的各自不同的象征价值。在课堂上第二语言（目标语）代表着权威、正式；而第一语言（母语）则代表着是亲切、非正式的意义。"

这些发现（Biggs 1996；Camilleri 1996）促使了笔者想进一步论证中国的外语教师有目的地交替使用两种语言是否有利于师生之间的情感交流，来维持一个和谐的师生关系，从而更有益于课堂教学的开展。

4. 教师的语言态度

近年来关于英语教师在课堂上使用目标语和母语的问题有两种截然相反的观点。很多研究者和教师支持在课堂上单独使用目标语。如埃利斯（Ellis，1984）认为使用母语组织教学或传授语言知识事实上已剥夺了学生接受目标语的输入机会。而埃尔德里奇（Eldridge，1996：303）认为如果学生未经教师的允许开始讲自己的母语，这大体上说明这堂课有问题。这些支持单独（或几乎单独）使用目标语的观点都认为教师将目标语转化成母语将会破坏学生学习的过程。对学生个体而言，通过完全使用目标语的教学会让语境更加真实，也有助于建立学生自己内在的语言学习体系。

然而，在相关研究中仍能听到反对把母语排除出课堂之外的声音。科斯特和西蒙（Coste & Simon，1998，转引自 Macaro，2001）指出把母语从课堂中排除不但不现实，而且也可能剥夺学生进行语言学习的重要工具。纽南和兰姆（Nunan & Lamb，1996）在他们的研究中发现，教师尽可能多地保留目标语很重要，这有利于形成一种和谐的外语学习氛围，同时使用学生的母语来简要地解释语法和词汇、步骤和惯例，会极大推进学习的进程和效果。

总之，在英语为外语的课堂上，教师为了学生的交际需要而进行语言替换（语码转换），这是促进外语习得的有效方式之一。

5. 案例讨论和分析

5.1 研究对象和数据收集

在本研究中，笔者采用了随堂听课和记录、课堂录音、个人采访相结合的数据收集的方法。调查了上海市某重点高中四位英语教师（一位男性和三位女性）在英语教学中的授课情况。样本包括十六个班英语课的录音文本和四位教师的采访记录。他们的名字在本研究中分别被简写成 A 教师，B 教师，C 教师和 D 教师。

5.2 数据分析和讨论

通过研究中对教师交替使用语言的所有案例进行具体分析，发现教师的语码转换不是随意的，而是通过交替使用两种语言来进行有效的师生情感交流。很多例子集中表现在教师表扬或批评学生和鼓励学生使用外语交流两个方面。

5.2.1 表扬或批评学生

案例一：A 教师（上课铃响，教师走进教室）

T: Now, Let's begin our class. Firstly I am happy to tell you a good news…李娜同学获得了本次全校英语听力大赛第一名，让我们一起鼓掌表示祝贺。(The teacher began to applaud.)

Ss: (the whole class followed teacher's action and clapped their hands for congratulation…)

    Ss: (they looked at Li and discussed in Li)她太强了!

    T: (teacher further commented)这次比赛题目很难，很多是来自托福的试题。所以李娜同学非常不容易，大家应该向她学习，平时多加强听力练习。Right, would you please open your book to Page 190…

    在这个案例中，在上课伊始，教师在开始授课之前通过转换到中文来表扬学生（把话题岔到与教学不相关的内容），并解释了学生在难度很高的听力比赛中获得了第一名是很不容易的事。接着 A 教师又转回到英语接着上课。

    当然不是所有的教师都是用中文来表扬学生。下面 B 教师的案例中，我们可以发现教师直接用英语来表扬他们努力学习的行为。

    案例二：B 教师（让学生课上做完形填空练习）

    T: Now, I will give you two minutes to finish the following cloze test on page 106 on your textbook.(About one minute later, she came back to teacher's desk)

    T: Just now, I found some students have already finished these exercises at home; they actually keep the good study habits, well done!

    和 A 教师相比，B 教师是用英语来表扬学生。通过深入研究这两个案例，我们发现课堂上表扬行为通常由两部分组成：简要评价和详细阐述。教师经常使用英语来进行简要评价（比如案例中出现的 well done），但会用中文做进一步说明。A 教师和 B 教师对其在案例中的语言行为做出如下评述：

    A 教师：我转换中文主要是想集中学生的注意力，讲述表扬的内容，同时能让他们感到一种亲切感……

    B 教师：课堂上，英语是一种正式的语言。教师有资格在任何时候表扬或批评学生，使用英语会更加正式一些。而且作为重点高中的学生，他们都能听懂我用英语所做的表扬。

很明显，教师认为在英语课堂上英语是一种比较正式、权威的语言，他们喜欢用英语来客观地"传达"表扬，从而来显示其权威性的地位。此外，教师也认为他们的学生具有中等英语水平，可以完全理解英语中一些简单的表扬词汇。但是，有时教师会通过转换成中文来进一步详细阐述表扬内容，并引起学生的注意。同时，通过转换中文来表扬学生，可以改变说话语气而拉近和学生间的关系。正如 Lin（1990）所认为的，转换到母语能够建立一种亲密的角色关系，可以有效地维持一种相对和谐的氛围。而这对于外语课堂尤为重要。

与此同时，作为另一个课堂上师生情感交流的方式，批评学生的现象也较为普遍。笔者从数据中发现：教师会使用中文来批评学生，以期改善学生的学习态度，规范学生的课堂行为。

案例三：（C 教师在课堂上通过提问学生进行口语拼写练习来检查学生是否复习了新单词）

T: 王其格 (a student's name), Can you try it? … the first one, 'acquire'?

SW: 'acquire', that's 'aq,'Um, 'acq',..(He seemed to be unable to spell this word).

……

T: What are you doing at home? (The teacher spoke to this student in an angry tone) you are supposed to recite these new words after each class…

SW: (he dropped his head and did not make utterance, and the whole class become totally silent)…

T: (after 5 seconds' silence) 你应该课后认真复习新单词，这对英语学习来说很重要啊！Anyway, I will call you next time and I hope you would do it well…

SW: Yes, sir.

在这个案例中，教师先使用英语批评学生消极的学习态度，使课堂氛围有些"尴尬"。接着教师有意识地转换成汉语继续指出学生的不足，但比起英语来说，中文可以减少批评学生的尴尬，让学生略感自在。C 教师对这种转换做出如下评述：

我知道由于学生对母语感觉更加熟悉和亲密，因此我赶紧使用汉语来打破这种尴尬的局面。

事实证明他转换成中文后，学生给出了积极的反馈（比如学生接受了教师的建议，回答道"是的，老师"）。

有时教师的批评不是直接的。他/她可能通过诙谐的母语来婉转地批评学生不当的课堂行为。

案例四：（上课铃响，D 教师走进课堂）

T: Now let's begin our class… (One student was still eating breakfast in the classroom)

T:你吃得好香啊，是否要让大家和你一起分享呢？

Ss: Ha-ha… (This student blushes and stops eating.)

在这段课堂实录中，教师通过转换成中文婉转地批评学生不当的课堂行为（课上吃东西）。不难发现，使用诙谐、幽默的母语对学生进行间接婉转地批评是英语教师控制学生课堂行为的有效方式，有利于营造和谐的课堂学习气氛。

通过对上述案例的研究，可以看出教师在表扬和批评学生时，英语和中文之间的语码转换是经常使用的方法。

5.2.2　鼓励学生用英语交流

许多中国学生在外语课堂学习中显得比较被动，因此有时教师不得不用中文来鼓励学生积极地使用英语和参与到课堂互动当中。

案例五：A 教师（教师把全班分成几个小组，让每一小组根据刚学过的课文进行角色表演）

T: (after ten minutes)…Now, are you ready?　Does any group

volunteer for the first one?

Ss: (no response from the students,)

T: 第一个表演的小组，老师将有额外加分哦！

Ss: (While the teacher was talking about his policy of grading, one student stood up and asks for the first one)…

T: Ok, good…王芳 (student's name), your group first…

这段实录中，教师刚开始使用英语发出指令，但停顿一段时间后，发现仍没有主动要求表演的学生，他便用汉语来鼓励学生参与表演并承诺为主动表演的第一组加分。显然这一做法得到了学生的积极反应，教师接着转换成英语继续他的教学内容。

案例六：B 教师

T: Alright, let's move on to the next paragraph. 李涛, would you please read this paragraph for us.

S1: (Stood up and started to read the text，but his voice was so low and the teacher could hardly hear his reading.)

T: Hey, 李涛, You are a boy, why not your voice is so low, just like a girl.

Ss: (Laughing)

S1: (he looked worried…)

T: Come on, 李涛，老师相信你能读得好，再来一遍吧！

S1: (He nodded his head and raised his voice during his second reading)…

T: It's good now, thank you very much…

在这个案例中，教师用英语开玩笑式地指出学生朗读课文的声音太小。但随后当教师发现她的语言可能不经意地让学生感到不安和忧虑时，她便马上转变成中文来鼓励学生，让他提高朗读的音量。学生在课堂上学习英语不可避免会随时遇到各种问题。当他们意识到自己的错误时，经常会变得忧虑和不安。这会在很大程度上扰乱和教师的交流。

上述两案例说明转变成母语能够达到鼓励学生在课堂上积极参与课堂互动的目的。

6. 小结

语码转换是外语课堂中师生间情感交流的有效方式。比如，它可以用来表扬和批评学生，进而鼓励他们在课堂上积极使用英语交流。

首先，在本研究中笔者发现英语和汉语都可以用于表扬学生。事实上，表扬一般由两部分组成：简要评价和详细阐述。一些教师通常使用英语来简要评价学生的成绩，而之后他们从英语转换到汉语则用于阐释表扬的原因和内容。同时由于母语自身的亲和力，汉语可被看作是外语课堂上的鼓励代码，鼓励学生积极参与课堂互动。

其次，不同于西方其他研究（Gearon，1997；Macaro，2001；Rolin-Ianziti & Brownlie，2002）等，在儒家传统文化影响下的中国大学外语课堂，教师对学生的学习态度和课堂表现的"严格要求"主要体现在较多的批评和较少的表扬。当教师批评学生时，他/她可能首先使用英语，因为他们觉得使用英语能体现其权威的职业角色，也能强调他/她是唯一的课堂掌控者。但是，对于自尊心较强的学生来说，英语批评不是很有效；相比之下，为避免师生之间情感交流失败，而应适当使用中文来表达具有幽默感的话语，以起到课堂上的破冰作用和间接批评的效果。

总之，笔者认为教师在外语课堂上应适当地使用语码转换来改变说话的语气，进而改变角色，拉近师生间的距离，营造一种和谐的课堂气氛以促进外语课堂上的教与学。

参考文献

Biggs, J. 1996. (ed.), *Western misperceptions of the Confucian-heritage learning culture.* In Watkins, D.A. and Biggs, D.A. (Eds.), *The Chinese learner: culture, psychological, and contextual influences.* Hong Kong and Melbourne: Comparative Education Research Center and Australian Council for Education Research, pp. 45-67.

Brown, H. D. 1994. *Teaching by principles: An interactive approach to language pedagogy.* Englewood Cliffs: Prentice Hall.

Camilleri, A. 1996. Language values and identities: Code-switching in secondary classrooms in Malta. *Linguistics and Education*, 8, pp. 85-103.

Clyne, M. 1991. *Community languages-the Australian experience.* Cambridge: Cambridge University Press.

Eldridge, J. 1996. Code-switching in a Turkish secondary school. *ELT Journal,* Volume 50/4, pp. 303-311.

Ellis, R. 1984. *Classroom second language development.* Oxford: Pergamon.

Gearon, M. 1997. *The code-switching practice of teachers of French as a second language in Victorian Secondary Schools.* Unpublished PHD thesis. Monash University.

Ho, T. I. 2001. Are Chinese Teachers Authoritarian? In Watkins D. & Biggs J. (ed.), *Teaching the Chinese learner: psychological and pedagogical perspectives (pp. 99-114).* Hong Kong: Comparative Education Research Center, The University of Hong Kong.

Krashen, S. D. 1981. *Second language acquisition and second language learning.* Oxford, UK: Pergamon.

Lin, A. M. Y. 1990. Teaching in two tongues: language alternation in foreign language classrooms. *(Research Report no.3)* Hong Kong: City Polytechnic of Hong Kong, Department of English.

Macaro, E. 1997. *Target language ,collaborative learning and autonomy*. Clevedon, UK: Multilingual Matters.

Macaro, E. 2001. Analyzing student teachers' code-switching in foreign language classrooms: Theories and decision making. *The Modern Language Journal*, 85,iv, pp. 531-548.

Nunan, D. and Lamb, C. 1996. *The self-directed teacher: Managing the learning process*. Cambridge: Cambridge University Press.

Richard-Amato, P. 1988. *Making it happen-Interaction in the second language classroom: From theory to practice*. New York & London: Longman.

Rolin-Ianziti, J and Brownlie, S. 2002. Teacher use of learners' native language in the foreign language classroom *The Canadian Modern Language Review* 58,3, pp. 402-426.

On Teacher's Code-switching for Affective Exchanges in Senior High English Classroom

Abstract: Code-switching has become a complicated social phenomenon and EFL classroom determines the specific functions of code-switching. The analysis of this article focuses upon the transcribed samples of code-switched passages from the participant teachers' class in one senior high school in Shanghai and identifies code-switching is often used as an effective way to participate in affective exchanges between the teacher and students. Through the shifting of the role, the teacher can effectively monitor the classroom atmosphere (formal or informal), encourage students' participation, and meanwhile maintain a personal relationship with the students that is beneficial for the teaching and learning in the classroom.

Key words: senior high English; code-switching; affective exchanges

此文发表于《中小学英语教学与研究》2012 年第 5 期

教育见习课程对职前英语教师专业发展影响探究①

刘蕴秋　　邹为诚

摘　要：本文采用定性研究的方法分析了英语专业师范生通过见习在教育教学认知与职业态度上的变化，从社会文化视角探讨了影响师范生变化的主要因素：校园环境以及与见习指导教师的互动，目的在于探究教育见习课程对职前英语教师专业发展的影响，为教育见习和职前教师培养摸索经验。

关键词：教育见习；职前英语教师；专业发展

1. 研究背景

教师培养具有很强的实践性，职前英语教师需要在真实的课堂教学环境中认识教学活动，将课本知识内化，形成实践知识。通过与学生、教师、课堂、教学环境等相关因素的互动，在感性体验的基础上，重新认识外语教学理论和实践。随着师范生教育改革的深入，新增的教育见习课程成为师范生进行教学实践的重要组成部分，形成了从教育理论学习到教育实习之间的过渡环节。师范生通过教育见习与实习

---

① 本文为华东师范大学外语学院光华预研究项目"华东师范大学英语教师职前教育中的知识学习与职业态度现状调查研究"的研究成果。

尝试实践体验（practical experience），在美国实践体验是教师教育重要的教学策略（王艳玲等，2011）。关于教育教学实习已有很多相关研究（吴兆旺，2011；郭新婕、王蔷，2009），前者多角度考察了实习教师的教学反思，后者全程跟踪一名英语专业实习生，深入研究实习与教师专业发展的关系。特别是约翰逊（Johnson，2002）采用"参与者观察法"（participant-observation procedures）对实习英语教师 Maja 的实证研究为本文提供了具体的方法论借鉴。

至今，教育见习课程已在某高校英语专业开展两年。检索表明，对教育见习课程的研究还十分鲜见，关于教育见习课程的效果究竟如何大家仍然存有疑虑，本文旨在探究教育见习课程对职前英语教师专业发展的影响以及如何产生影响。因此，本文的研究问题是：通过教育见习师范生对英语教学在认知与观念上产生了哪些变化？导致变化的因素是什么？

2. 研究方法

本文采用定性研究的方法，按照研究目的抽取能够为研究问题提供最大信息量的研究对象（陈向明，2000），以目的性抽样的方式选取 3 批在 A 中见习的英语师范生为研究对象，最终以 16 人撰写的"教育见习听课记录""教育见习记事"和"教育见习总结"为研究的主要数据来源。研究人员作为见习带队教师参加听课观摩及指导教师与见习生的互动交流，既是参与者，也是观察者，在笔记中记录了见习指导教师颜老师（化名）在观课后与见习生的问答互动。研究者对以上数据反复研读，寻找其中的核心概念和逻辑关系，通过归类分析展示师范生见习中在认知与观念上产生的变化及其专业能力发展的过程。

3. 职前英语教师认知与态度的变化

从收集到的数据中我们发现，师范生主要从以下几个方面阐述了自己的认识变化：教师工作、教师专业能力、教师身份、教育理念、师生关系及教学方式方法等。教师认知研究为我们研究教师教学的学习提供了思路（Woods，1996）。舒尔曼（Shulman，1987）和约翰逊（2009）认为，教学中实用的知识包括关于教师自己的知识，包括关于教学内容、学生、课堂活动以及教学环境的知识。他们的研究与我们梳理出的数据基本吻合。因此本文将从教师、教学、学生、课堂活动和教学环境五个方面探寻师范生在见习中经历的认知、情感和职业态度的变化。

3.1 对英语教学相关因素的认识变化

3.1.1 关于教师教学的新认识

如果说以往师范生对课堂教学处在无意识的"观摩学徒期"（apprenticeship of observation）（Bailey et al.，2002），在见习学校耳闻目见真实的课堂教学实施，他们开始着意观察教师的教学行为和课堂活动，对教师工作的性质有了初步认识。

以前一直觉得做老师容易。学得好，自然就教得好。但今天观课发现，面对一群孩子才是真正考验老师的时候。或许自己绞尽脑汁设想的活动，没人响应；又或许，自己引以为傲的讲解，学生不能理解。怎么备课讲课、怎么互动交流，这些都需要认真去思索。（1010TXY）

课上得好坏，与老师备课是否充分、上课对学生的引导高度相关……当老师不能混着过，要认真对待每一次课，更重要的是怎样上课。学会上课是一个很高的目标。（0910GQQ）

传统观点认为，外语水平是外语教师的身份标志（转引自刘蕴秋，2010）。然而见习中师范生发现，语言知识丰富，语言技能好不等于就能教得好。教师还需要对学习者、对教学环境等外语教学相关因素的认识和掌控能力。英语教师的专业性特点恰恰体现在这里。见习使师范生第一次意识到外语教师的专业语言能力与专业教学能力对外语教学缺一不可（吴一安，2004；Larsen-Freeman & Freeman，2008；邹为诚，2009；刘蕴秋，2010）。他们还认识到，教师的教学有可能失败，但通过深入思考，可以从失败的阴影中走出来，所以教师工作的成就感取决于教师是否勤于思考。每一节课，都是一次挑战，因此教师必须认真对待，教学水平的提高需要永无止境的努力。

其实老师的工作是一种思考，要不断地改变、适应，因为学生、教材都会不一样，甚至备完的课和真正进入课堂（也会有变化）。上课本身就是一种思考和创造。（1010TXY）

讲课的是一位毕业不久的青年教师，他准备得十分充分。但作为旁观者，我发现他的课还是存在一些问题。这就提醒我们，作为一名未来的教师，我们应该时刻反思，从他人或自己的实践中总结经验，而不要只把自己关在自己知识的象牙塔中。（0910XD）

师范生在观摩教学时注意到教学是一个动态的过程，存在许多不确定因素，教师要不断适应社会和学生的变化。教师还要经常反思，向别人观摩学习，以他人为镜。近年来教师教育研究一直强调反思是教师专业发展的重要环节（Schon，1983；Schon，1987；刘学惠，2008）。通过观课，师范生由人及己，意识到反思对改善教学的作用，领悟到教师专业发展的真谛。

教师最终要达到的目标是更好地为同学提供英语学习机会。我也深刻了解到，老师不是万能的，真正能够帮助学生的是学生自己。（1010LX）

"教师不是万能的"。教师的工作是"助产士"，是引导者。学习最终发生的基础是在学生身上，而非教师身上。建构主义学习理论（见陈琦、刘儒德，2005）认为，学习是学习者对外部世界的意义建构过程，学习者是学习活动的主人。在外语教学中教师作为一个促进者、指导者、支持者应该最大限度地为学习者创造适宜的学习条件和机会，提高其学习能力，使之不断发展和完善自己。

此外，师范生通过观摩教学见识了 A 中英语教师的专业素养，认识到教师的专业知识水平和专业能力是开展优秀教学活动的基础。

一堂课下来，自己的佩服之情不断上升。高中的英语课可以上得这样多彩而又启发学生思考，对教师的要求该有多高啊。要不是有扎实的专业知识、深厚的教学经验和足够的教学智慧，如何能做到呢？做一名优秀的教师还真不是应付一下就可以达到的。（0910SJJ）

从这一周的见习来看，教师是一个需要不断充实自己、提升自己的职业。每次面对不一样的学生、情境，都是对老师的挑战。老师要有整体的知识架构，这样才能在事先没有预见的情况下，临场不乱。（0910ZYY）

现在的孩子懂得比我们那时懂得多，教师如果不能充实自己，很难教这些孩子。（0910LN）

老师不只是一份养家糊口的工作，更是一种对学生的关爱，这才体现一个老师的价值。（1010TXY）

师范生对教师知识的本质及其运用能力的认识更为具体了。做教师就意味着不断地学习与创新，这既是挑战，也是乐趣。可贵的是，他们对教师职业的认识得到了升华。做教师不仅是一种谋生手段，更是一项培养造就学生的事业，教师在这个过程中找到自己生命的意义和价值。当教师把职业当作兴趣，从"生计的驱使走向生命的自由，从牺牲与付出走向主动创造"的时候，教师就找到了力量的源泉，职业态度就会积极向上。这正是我们培养未来教育家——而非英语教书匠——的重要基础。

3.1.2 教学理念的变化

教师的教学活动无不映衬着他们对教与学的认识，对此师范生在见习观摩中有所体悟，他们感受到了以学生为中心的教学理念。

今天最让我受益的是下午的交流。颜老师说，一个老师走进教室，上讲台并不只是为了完成教案，而是与学生进行一种互动学习。这句话很有道理。（1010TXY）

老师应该时刻谨记从学生的利益出发。在备课过程中，应以学生的需求为前提，在有限的40分钟课堂内，让学生的听、说、读、写都得到最大限度的锻炼。（1010LX）

师范生隐约认识到，上课的时间是属于学生的，这是对传统教学观念的一个反动。他们已经意识到"教学"不等于"讲课","教学"应当意味着"学生活动"。这是非常好的教学理念萌芽。外语教学要使学生的四项技能得到提高和锻炼，写教案、备课就必须针对学生的状况。

3.1.3 对学生和师生关系的重新认识

在大学课堂里，师范生通过文本阅读间接了解学生状况，而见习则为他们提供了直接接触学生，观察他们课堂行为的机会。当师范生直接面对并关注外语教学主体时，他们在对待学生的态度以及师生相处之道上获得了新的领悟。

在 5 天的听课过程中，我收集整理了不少老师的教学技巧、课堂管理技巧。每个老师都会找到一套属于自己的教学风格。有些技巧有时可能用不上，但有一点应该永远不会改变，那就是：热爱自己的岗位，用心去对待每一个学生。（1010YH）

颜老师说："我的学生们的知识远远多于我。"这引起了我的思考，欣赏、尊重学生，才能更好地引导、帮助学生吧。（1010YX）

教学只有进入学生的心灵世界，才能保证不会游离于学生的世界之外，才能懂得学生。与教学技巧相比，尊重、理解、关爱学生更有助于学生的学习和成长。因为教师的尊重可以给予学生充分的自信；理解学生能让学生获得精神上的支持和鼓励；关爱学生，学生才会快乐成长，发展健全人格。

与其他学科相比，外语课堂具有独特性：学生需要使用陌生的语言工具学习目的语及其所传递的内容和信息。外语课堂上，学生往往要面对犯语言错误的风险，所以常常因担心丢面子而不愿发言，结果减少了自己使用语言的机会，久而久之形成恶性循环。因此，在外语课堂上关注学生，还意味着关心他们的外语学习情感目标，教师的热情夸奖和鼓励无疑增强了学生学习外语的自信心，课堂上教师的暗示和即时反馈都可以促进学生的有效学习（邹为诚，2009）。

英语课与其他课的最大不同在于，学生必须通过使用英语来学习英语，老师则要很耐心地聆听，经常用"Very good""Well done"来评价。由于学生对所学语言心生畏惧，感到陌生，老师的鼓励非常重要。

（0910ZYY）

学生是要鼓励的，老师要在课堂上给予学生积极的暗示。学生回答问题后要及时给予反馈。（0910LN）

记得在一堂课上老师是这样鼓励学生的："每一个人都有可能成为天才""要相信自己""我坚信将来有一天你们中的某些人会成为我们的骄傲，我会对我未来的学生说，你们是多么善良、聪明、刻苦又谦逊……"连在场的我们都被老师的话深深打动了。（1010YX）

课堂观摩与课后互动使师范生对情感目标产生强烈的意识，他们变得更细致、体贴、善解人意，联想自己的求学经历，他们懂得了理解学生需求，而且开始关注如何引导调动学生学习的自主性。

3.1.4　对课堂活动的认识

见习中，师范生不仅关注到人的培养，还学习了老师们的教学方法、手段等技能技巧。第一天到校听了指导教师颜老师的课，见习生反响热烈。课堂上颜老师态度亲切，富有感染力，所有的学生都开口说话，人人踊跃表现。在小组讨论环节，学生全都离开了自己的座位，站起来与班级同学一起交流分享，课堂气氛热烈。师范生由衷地钦佩，思索着这堂课的闪光点。

我第一次看到老师与学生搭档完成一个角色扮演，这首先拉近了学生与老师间的距离，其次活跃了课堂，再者激起了学生学习英语的乐趣。之后的调查和访谈也很有特色，使整个课堂动了起来，也培养了学生独立研究问题的能力。（0910WCY）

这堂课还有一个我颇有心得的特点，她让学生听课文——而不是看课文，同时做笔记，然后在 PPT 上给出提示让学生订正完成。我认为这样既节省了时间，又练习了听力，同时也理清了课文的脉络。这对我将来从教很有帮助。（0910WCY）

颜老师强调听说技能，通过精心设计教学活动，让学生在较为真实的环境中使用英语，在师生协作的愉快氛围中学会语言。课堂上，学生不仅可以交流分享，还锻炼了独立判断解决问题的能力。颜老师高效利用课堂时间，锻炼学生的听说能力和综合运用英语的能力。见习生注意到她的教学方法，领悟到其中的道理，在这个过程中构建自己的教学实践知识。对来自偏远地区的师范生来说，这一教学令他们耳目一新。

我来自安徽一个穷僻的农村学校。老师们都是教书匠，只抱着那一本教科书在里面挑单词，挑句型，挑语法来讲，没有"communicative and cultural language"。教室里死气沉沉，学生默不作声，只忙着记笔记。这里的"新"的形式在农村学校特别需要。虽然一些硬件设施（如投影仪，电脑）在农村受到限制，但这里新的教学理念和教学方法却是绝对有适用性的。（0910LN）

曾经的我，孤陋寡闻，认为老师只不过是向学生讲讲课本上的内容，如果要让课堂精彩的话，讲几段笑话，播放段视频，就大功告成了。现在，我总算是大开眼界，一睹真正的教师风采了。（0910LYY）

教育见习开阔了师范生的眼界，他们不仅在教学理念上受到冲击，还看到了多种教学方法在课堂上的实施。反观自己的求学成长经历，这里的教学活动打开了他们的思路，使他们对教学活动和教学行为的认识从单一视角走向多维。

今天听课的两个班整体反应都不是很热烈。以前我一定会简单地归结为老师的原因，老师没有把学生的热情激发出来。现在了解到，除了和老师个人性格有关外，还和班级的文化氛围、课程内容有关……有时学生没有积极的反应，并不代表学生没有参与或老师没有足够的魅力吸引学生。有时老师讲解的内容对学生来说是全新的，学生需要时间消化。即使没能给出热烈的反应，也不意味着学生在整个教学过程中没有收获。（0910ZYY）

师范生意识到教学的目标是帮助学生学会知识技能，因而他们开始关注课程内容与学习效果的关系。教学的实质是知识的获得，而非热闹的课堂气氛。不仅如此，他们对外语教学的特殊性也有了进一步的认识。

我认识到，英语课就其语言本身的特性来说，必须要上得有趣，上得让学生觉得有用，才能调动学生，才能使课堂质量最高化。（0910SJJ）

与母语学习不同，外语学习受到学习者态度的影响。对于大部分学生来说，外语只是学校的一门功课，学习的动力主要是为了升学，为了满足学业的要求，因此学习者往往缺乏学习英语的内在动力。这就要求外语教师在设计课堂教学时，不仅要使活动有趣，还要使学习者感到学习外语有用，提高学习者做"国际公民"的意识，激发他们学习外语的动力。

3.1.5 教学环境

教学环境往往渗透着学校的教育理念，体现了学校的文化风气。英语课堂上实施全英文教学，广泛开展课外活动，融入个人兴趣。这样的校园文化使师范生感受到了学校对学生的人文关怀，对学生全面发展的重视。

A 中选修课非常广泛，社团活动也是一大特色，每个学生都可以依照自己的兴趣加入不同的社团。活动由学生自行操作，老师只加以指点。这让我非常有感触。原以为像 A 中这样的重点学校，一定是学风严肃，学生埋头苦读，老师忙于管教。但从各种社团活动来看，A 中是一所提倡德智体全方面发展的学校。（0910WCY）

学校对学生的人文关怀渗透到英语课堂来，英语课堂也体现着整个学校的文化风气。作为英语老师，不能够只关注直接的教学任务和利益，更应该多为学生着想，不断改进自己的教学。（0910SJJ）

老师必须要为学生提供足够好的英语环境，在保证教学进度的同时，不忽视课堂的趣味性和实用性……高一就开始全英文授课，语法也尽量用英语讲解，这就培养了学生良好的英语语言习惯。这在我是从未有过的学习经历。在我的家乡，即使很好的学校也只是把应试放在第一位。这确实是我以后做老师非常值得借鉴的经验。（0910SJJ）

见习前上的教学法理论知识在见习时能真实地感受到在实际教学中的应用，例如 lead-in, interaction with students (discussion, etc.)。把一个单元的课文讲得生动丰富，保持学生的参与度与积极性，"在做中学"真的能收到比死记硬背更好的效果。（0910LN）

体验了真实的教学环境，师范生敏锐地注意到学校以人为本的教育理念在校园文化中的渗透，理解了人文教化对学生的成长带来的深刻影响。校园文化影响到课堂文化，教师重视英语课堂的趣味性和实用性，注重学生良好的英语语言习惯的培养，而非简单的死记硬背。浸淫在见习学校的校园文化和教学氛围，师范生感受到为学生提供真实的语言环境对英语学习的重要作用，深化了对外语教学理论的理解。

3.2　在职业态度上的变化

经过五天教育见习，师范生在情感上经历了冲击，对外语教学相关因素的认识发生了明显变化，职业态度也与先前有所改变。确切地说，或许他们以前并没有立志做教师，甚或有些不情愿，但教育见习经历坚定了他们从教的信念。

作为第一届国家公费师范生，说实话，其实初衷并不是为了当一名优秀的教师。当时自己对未来的规划也没有好好地想过，加上家人也比较希望我找一份比较稳定的工作，而且公费也减轻了家里不少负担，就这样我糊里糊涂地踏上了师范之路。大学两年一直在学习英语基础知识，基本上没涉及多少师范教育的内容，所以没有重视教师教育，也没有自觉加强道德修养，朝着教师的方向努力的概念。这次见习，虽不能说完全改变了我的想法，但真的是让我产生了当老师并且当好老师的决心。正像我的一个同学所说，我们每天接触到的是世界上最纯洁的灵魂，我们的工作不是对着事、对着文件、对着电脑，而是对着人。在教学这个舞台上，我们可以和孩子同呼吸、共成长，这中间的美妙滋味，只有身处其中的人才能尝到。想到这些都觉得很美好。（0910LN）

这名同学袒露了自己进大学以来的心路历程，代表了一部分师范生的想法，很真实，态度转变也很真诚。对于未知的教学工作，有时年轻的学生会不知所措，不知是否还有更好的机会，难免生出抱怨。然而当他们开始了解教师工作，理解教学，熟悉教学环境，热爱学生，兴趣往往会随之而来。有了这样的态度转变，他们今后的学习会变得更加自觉，更加有目的性。

如果说最直接的收获是什么，我想应该是我的心。我的心更加坚定地要成为一名出色的老师。那一句句简单的"老师好"，顿时使我在情感上得到了满足，这是一帮可爱的孩子，我想要用心去帮助他们一

起学习。（1010YH）

在这里我学到了怎样在内心深处做一名好老师。虽然踏入这里的初衷是为了完成见习任务，但在这几天里，对一线教师有了更深的了解与认同，也用心去领悟了很多做老师的哲理。（0910SJJ）

从进大学那一刻，就注定我将来成为一名教师。两年多过去了，对教师工作我还没有一个清晰的认识。进入大三后，我很幸运地得到了在这所著名高中见习的机会。虽然只是短短 5 天，却也使我学到了很多东西，对将来的教师工作更添了一份向往，未来的蓝图更加清晰了。（1103ZQ）

在回去的路上，同学们还很激动，谈教学，谈老师。我想，其实现在我们心里已经更加坚定了当老师的意志，同时也下定决心当一个好老师，给自己下目标，加压力，现在就要朝着这个方向努力加油。（0910LN）

短暂的见习使师范生在认识和理念上经历了深刻的变化。对一些师范生而言，从教意愿是入学两年来尚未解决的问题，见习使他们热爱上了学生，对教师职业也有了新的认识。见习路途遥远，每天来回近四个小时，然而他们因心向往之而甘之如饴。一位同学写道："这五天的经验是没什么可以代替的，也是多少钱也买不回来的"。见习使师范生对将来的教师职业有了蓝图，看得也更远了，他们不仅仅要做教师，而且还要"当一个好老师"。见习开阔了师范生的视野，他们的心变大了，从教的起点也抬高了。

3.3　小结

经过见习，师范生对外语教学的几个重大问题的认识，如教育理念、教师的专业素养以及学生的学习等都发生了变化，在以学生为本的教育理念基础上达成了对以学生为主体的教学模式的认可。对于从传统教学模式中走出来的师范生，他们经历了一个理念重构的过程。第二，重新认识外语教师专业素质。教师仅有激情和责任心远远不够，还应该具有很高的专业素养和深厚的英语功底（例如准确的英语发音，大量的词汇，广博的英语文化知识）。第三，重新认识学习的发生和发展，强调学生的自主学习和知识构建，重视调动学生的学习兴趣，注重培养学生的学习能力，使之获得持久的发展。可喜的是，师范生一旦获得了这些新知，他们从教的意愿就被激发了出来。一位学生表示："自己有责任将这些先进的理念和方法带回西部，起示范作用。听了这么多老师的课，压力更大，但信心也足了。"

4. 导致变化的因素分析

人类学习理论为我们研究教学学习提供了理论依据。关于人类学习至今已有多种理论视角的研究，如行为主义和认知理论等。约翰逊站在社会文化视角的认识论立场阐释了社会活动对人类学习的意义，认知的发展是一个经由文化、环境、语言和社会交往调节的互动过程（Johnson，2009）。社会文化视角强调人类中介的作用，学习者依据自己先前的经验及所处的社会文化环境对知识进行重构（同上）。社会文化视角对研究教学学习意义重大，它为我们提供了理解构成外语教师教育内容、组织和进程的认识论立场。

从师范生的见习记事和见习总结中可以发现，见习学校的校园氛围和学习环境令师范生震撼，也促成他们新的自我身份的转变。更重要的是，与指导教师的互动帮助他们学到了书本上学不到的知识，解释了他们对教学实践存在的一些疑惑，使他们经历了新的知识的构建过程。

4.1 校园环境的影响

来到 A 中，师范生就为其校园环境、教学氛围和学生们积极向上的精神风貌所吸引。A 中的环境大到校园布局，小到一草一木都渗透着教育对唤起生命自觉的重视，昭示着以人为本，关注人的发展的教育理念。学生的主课在上午完成，下午安排各种有趣的课程，有艺术课、体育课、信息课、劳技课以及选修课。学校的社团活动也很丰富，学生有机会发展自己的兴趣爱好。在感佩学校取得的累累硕果的同时，师范生为教师的付出所感动，而与纯真的学生面对面的现实唤醒了师范生的自我身份意识。他们观察着，感受着，有了做一名优秀的"领航员"的愿望，要将 A 中良好的教学方法、理念带回自己将来执教的学校，帮助更多的学生提高英语学习能力。

在 A 中辉煌的历史中，我被那一批批辛勤的园丁所深深打动。他们把自己的一辈子献给了学生，献给了教育，展览中的累累硕果证明了他们的付出与价值。（0910LYY）

这次很重要的意外收获是，当所有人把你看作老师时，我还真有点做老师的感觉，从开始的不知所措到后来以老师的身份与学生交谈。身份变了，观察问题的角度就不同了。（0910ZYY）

第一天见习给这些来自中国不同地区的师范生带来了巨大的冲击。无论是教学环境、校园气氛、教育理念，还是学生的风貌，都使他们反躬自问，找寻并重新定位自己。有位师范生写道："因今天感触深，整夜辗转反侧，难以入眠，遂起床写下记事。"这个历程或许是兴奋，或许是痛苦，然而由此带来的变化却是脱胎换骨。

做学生 15 年，听了 15 年的课。可这周是第一次以不一样的身份走进课堂。以前是听老师讲什么内容，现在是听老师怎样讲，并且思考老师为什么要这么讲。（0910ZYY）

学生看到我们，热情招呼"老师好"。这让我们颇感意外，也突然有了当老师的感觉。（0910WCY）

第一次听到"老师好"不知所措，可到后来自己以"老师"的身份与学生交谈，这些收获是见习前没有料到的。我第一次体会到了做老师的感觉。（0910ZYY）

"体会到了做老师的感觉。"这是见习给师范生带来的第一个收获。十几年的学习经历使师范生早已习惯了自己的学生定位，见习让他们第一次强烈感受到自己是谁，自己将要成为怎样的人（Tsui，2007）。当师范生离开自己求学的环境，来到真实教学环境面对学生时，内心开始真正理解自己的教学学习者身份。这种内心变化使他们将自己从普通的英语专业学生中跳脱出来，重新定位自己的身份。对于师范生而言这是必要的入职前的心理准备，它意味着师范生将褪去学生的青涩，开始产生对教师身份的认同，今后学习和生活目标更加明确。

4.2　与见习指导教师互动带来的影响

在见习学校，特级教师颜老师负责见习指导，她为师范生精心制定了一周的见习计划，共观摩 12～13 节课，从高一到高三，有很多老师的英语课可以去听。下午颜老师还常常抽空与师范生进行观课后的讨论，这项互动研讨活动使师范生受益良多。

通过一整天的接触，觉得颜老师是一个很好的老师，一心为了教育，从来不开补习班上课，她想的就是怎样教好学生，她喜欢研究，还自己搞些课题。我觉得这才是我立志要做的那种老师。（0910LN）

颜老师向我们讲述了自己的教学经历和对教学的一些见解，真诚地为我们释疑解惑。我非常钦佩她，因为她的敬业精神和她的那种淡定、善解人意的品质，不追逐虚名，特别看重个人精神层次的提高……是我的榜样。（0910LYY）

在互动交流中，指导教师现身说法，讲述了她的教育教学追求。她的经验表明，一个不断提问、反思，敢于挑战自己的教师才会有发展后劲。只有当教师将学生和教学作为自己的事业——而非饭碗，才会全身心投入教学，敬重自己所从事的工作。她还将自己对教学的理解与见习生分享：教学不是为了完成任务，而是与学生共同提高，不断进步。

在与颜老师的交流中，我知道了教案是"活"的，老师在课堂上不能照本宣科地"读"教案。老师在课堂上的思维是跟着课堂、学生一起运转的，所以就没有固定的教案，因为课堂上可能随时迸发出新的想法，这样的想法才是真正适合课堂、适合学生的。（0910LY）

听课过程中师范生发现，"比较凶的老师可以压得住课堂，但是课堂显然比较沉闷。更多的一些和蔼的老师也可以压得住课堂"。一次课堂上，针对没有按时完成作业的学生，任课教师十分严厉。老师立即要求学生到班主任处完成作业，再由班主任签名之后才允许该生重返课堂，而且还要求抄三遍课文。对此师范生与颜老师展开了讨论。

我不知道是否该支持。因为一方面老师是为了学生好，为了学生牢记教训以后及时完成作业。另一方面，老师的做法可能没有顾及学生的感受且浪费了课堂上其他学生的宝贵时间。怎样面对这类学生是一个值得讨论和深思的问题。(0910LY)

有人认为这样的做法是必要的，因为老师必须有一定的威严才能让学生感到压力，及时完成作业。也有人认为这种做法可能会让学生感到难堪，对老师产生厌恶情绪。我认为必要的威信是需要的，如果遇到没有完成回家作业的同学，可以多在这节课上点名要他回答问题，这样既能让他察觉到自己的错误，又能维持住课堂秩序。(0910HDT)

讨论中大家各抒己见，颜老师也分享了自己的观点：一个老师能否管理好班级，并不取决于她是否严厉，而是看她是否走进学生的内心。由此他们认识到，教师不仅要在教学方法上了解学生需求，在课堂管理上也要走进学生的内心世界才能与之沟通。

颜老师的经验告诉我们，任课老师没有必要把自己学科的问题移交给班主任处置，而应更巧妙地解决，比如利用下课时间请同学补作业，或进行面谈。这样的效果一定会比当场责骂好得多。(0910LY)

如颜老师所说，压得住不是因为凶，压不住不是因为不凶……任何人都喜欢真诚的人，学生对老师的要求也不例外。(1010TXY)

这个教学学习机会对师范生十分难得。学生完不成作业是教学中常见的问题，似乎老师怎样做都有一定的道理。拿捏不准时，颜老师帮助他们找到了更为妥帖的方法：首先任课教师应该自己亲自处理这个问题，而且还不能伤及学生的自尊心。这样的教学实践本领只有在与见习指导老师的互动中才能学到。

在交流座谈时，颜老师还解答了师范生关于"公开课"的疑问："公开课就是家常课，因为家常课也应该像公开课那样精心设计。"她的话让师范生心生敬佩，同时也发人深思。

之前我和大多数人一样，觉得公开课有人观摩，有专业人员评点，所以上公开课时，会花更多精力和时间去准备，而平时课准备的时间则较少，花的心思也不太多。颜老师精辟的阐释，让我顿时豁然开朗。(1103YXM)

我当时茅塞顿开，用"醍醐灌顶"来形容也不为过。不是吗？老

师就是应该用心地准备每一堂课，把每一堂课都做成最美味的佳肴来招待学生，这样才能让学生学到最多。（1103ZHF）

"家常课"和"公开课"之分看似是名称问题，实则却隐含着一个预设前提：即对"公开课"要特别关注，格外用心。师范生的疑惑似乎是：如何准备"公开课"？然而颜老师一针见血地指出教学的要义在于学生学到什么，课堂教学不是作秀。

指导老师谈到：做老师最重要的是职业精神。只有当一位老师具有职业精神后，他/她才能成为一个好老师。（0910ZYY）

在互动交流中，指导老师结合课堂观摩适时地将一些教育理念渗透给见习生，此时此地的交流生动鲜活，一句话胜过大学课堂里几节课的理论说教。师范生对教学中的困惑提问的同时，也在努力构建对这些问题的认识，从而收到了非常好的学习效果。

5. 启示与讨论

见习首先使师范生认识自己，发现自己的专业知识与现实职业需求之间存在的差距。见习改变了师范生对教育理念、专业素养和学生学习的认识，它在职前英语教师培养中发挥的作用是显而易见的。此外，真实的教学环境使师范生很快学会了从教师的角度思考问题，激活了他们在课堂上学过的教育教学理论，激发了他们为从教刻苦学习的动力，在教学认知和职业态度上发生了明显的转变。

就教育见习课程而言，见习指导的质量对于师范生从经验中学习极为重要。见习不能走马观花，师范生应抱着寻求答案的心态去听课，不断提问，找寻教师对教学实践的真知灼见。更为关键是，指导教师缜密安排，用心指导，见缝插针地与之勤力互动。在 A 中的教学环境中，双方教师密切配合，形成了促进职前英语教师发展的社会文化环境中的重要条件，其中互动研讨起到了对话中介的作用，解答了师范生的疑惑，这一现场教学机会使见习效果最大化。本文分析了师范生在见习中的认知和职业态度变化及其成因，希望能为今后的教育见习和职前英语教师培养摸索经验，并提供有益的启示和参照。

参考文献

Bailey, K. M. *et al.* 2002. The language learner's autobiography: Examining the "apprenticeship of observation", In D.A. Freeman & J.C. Richards (eds.). *Teacher Learning in Language Teaching.* 上海：上海外语教育出版社。

Johnson，K. E. 2002. The vision versus the reality: The tensions of the TESOL practicum. In D.A. Freeman & J.C. Richards (eds.). *Teacher Learning in Language Teaching.* 上海：上海外语教育出版社。

Johnson, K. E. 2009. *Second Language Teacher Education: A Sociocultural Perspective*, New York and London: Routledge Taylor & Francis Group.

Larsen-Freeman, D. & Freeman, D. 2008. Language moves: The place of "foreign" languages in classroom teaching and learning. *Review of Research in Education,* 32, pp. 147-186.

Schon, D. 1983. *The Reflective Practitioner: How Professionals Think in Action.* New York: Basic Books.

Schon, D. 1987. *Educating the Reflective Practitioner.* San Francisco: Jossey-Bass Publishers.

Shulman, L. 1987.Knowledge and teaching: Foundations of the new reform. *Harvard Educational Review*, 57/1, pp. 1-22.

Tsui, A. B. M., 2007. Complexities of identity formation: A narrative inquiry of an EFL teacher. *TESOL Quarterly*, 41/4, December.

Woods, D. 1996. *Teacher Cognition in Language Teaching.* Cambridge: CUP.

陈琦、刘儒德，2005,《教育心理学》，北京：高等教育出版社。

陈向明，2000,《质的研究方法与社会科学研究》，北京：教育科学出版社。

郭新婕、王蕾，2009，教育实习与职前英语教师专业发展关系探究，《外语与外语教学》，第 3 期，第 28-33 页。

刘学惠，2008，外语教师教育与发展的概念重构和研究进展，见吴一安等，《中国高校英语教师教育与发展研究》，北京：外语教学与研究出版社。

刘蕴秋，2010，论外语教师的知识体系，见邹为诚主编，《中国基础英语教师教育研究》，上海：华东师范大学出版社。

王艳玲、苟顺明，2011，美国反思型教师教育的教学策略：评析与启示，《教师教育研究》，第 5 期，第 71-75 页。

吴一安，2004，优秀外语教师专业素质探究，《外语教学与研究》，第 3 期，第 199-205 页。

吴兆旺，2011，实习教师的教学反思研究，《全球教育展望》，第 6 期，第 52-57 页。

邹为诚，2009，中国基础教育阶段外语教师的职前教育研究报告，《外语教学理论与实践》，第 1 期，第 1-16，19 页。

邹为诚，主编，2010，《中国基础英语教师教育研究》，上海：华东师范大学出版社。

A Study of the Effects of Classroom Observation on the Professional Development of Pre-service EFL Teachers

Abstract: This paper aims to study the effects of classroom observation on the professional development of pre-service EFL teachers.

The authors have explored, with a qualitative research method, pre-service EFL teachers' understanding of teachers, of students, and of teaching as a profession by means of joining their after-observation discussion, studying their journals and reflections in order to find out what they learn from guided observation of classroom teaching, and to identify the changes and development they have experienced in the aspect of cognition and professional attitude through this observation.

Key words: classroom observation；pre-service EFL teachers；professional development

此文发表于《全球教育展望》2012 年第 8 期

对我国日语教育的课堂教学改革之探索

彭瑾　徐敏民

　　摘　要：本研究运用外语教授法理论的研究成果和 **Can-do** 标准，结合教学实践，以培养学习者综合语言运用能力和跨文化交际能力的教学理念为指导，设计了一套课堂教学改革方案，以探讨如何在课堂教学中展开具有实际交际意义的语言活动。

　　关键词：教学理念；教学活动；教授法；Can-do 标准；课程改革

1. 引言

　　我国日语教育的教学理念已经由注重语言知识技能的传授逐渐转向语言交际活动能力的提高。随着教学理念的转变，教学目标的更新和评价体系的完善成为日语教育改革中的重要课题①。如何改善课堂教学，帮助学生在牢固掌握语言知识的同时提高语言交际能力，这是实现教学目标更新的关键所在。课堂教学是第二外语习得的主要途径，与自然习得相比，学生能够得到纠正错误的机会，教师也可以按照学生的能力及需求由易至难循序渐进地调整安排学习内容，但是课堂教学在信息量的输入，语言产出活动以及交流互动方面与自然习得存在一定差距。那么如何在保持课堂习得优势的同时，在课堂教学中展开

---

　　① 关于"教学目标的更新和评价体系的完善"的论述详见彭瑾、徐敏民，『JF 日本語教育スタンダード 2010』与我国日语教育改革[J]日语学习与研究，2013：2。

接近自然习得环境、具有实际交际意义的语言活动呢？本研究围绕上述课题，运用外语教授法理论的研究成果和 Can-do 标准，提出了课堂教学实践中的具体教学改革方案，并结合学习者对于课堂教学改革的反馈意见，论述新的课堂教学改革方案和传统的日语教学模式之间的差异，以探索日语教学改革的新思路。

2. 传统的日语教学模式及存在的问题

传统的日语精读课程的教学模式一般分为三个阶段，即："语言知识的学习→会话·文章的说明理解→检验语法熟练度的练习"。这一教学模式的问题主要体现在三个方面，即学习目标偏重知识传授、课堂教学以教师为主导，教学内容与实际交际活动脱节。

我国现行的综合日语基础教材多以语言知识的习得为主要教学目标，因而教材中会话部分的内容一般都会依附于语法需求，练习部分的设计也以帮助学习者熟练掌握语法形态和含义为目的。但是，语法的含义和功能并非一一对应，一个句型往往拥有多种语法功能。传统的语法教学把主要精力放在语法形态和含义的学习上，其结果是学生在运用目标语言进行语言活动时，经常会出现语法形式和含义正确，但是语法功能使用不恰当的误用。这类误用比起语法形态和含义的错误，会给社交活动带来更大的障碍。那么如何在实际教学活动中克服上述问题，实现提高语言交际能力的学习目标呢？我校日语系在一二年级日语教学中，使用与日本高校的教师共同开发的引入 Can-do 标准的综合日语教程①，并且尝试在精读课和会话课采用同一本教材，在教学中运用教授法理论的研究成果，设计了一套课堂教学的改革方案，以下结合具体教学活动案例展开论述。

---

① 使用教材是徐敏民、丸山千歌主编《新界标日本语综合教程》(1)（复旦大学出版社，2013年），本论文所有教案均以该教材为依据而设计。

3. 课堂教学改革方案

我们以教授法理论和 Can-do 标准为依据而设计课堂教学改革方案。所谓"Can-do"就是以"我能够完成什么（课题）"这样的句子来表述学习者的外语能力，它可用于客观把握学习者的外语熟练程度，确立学习目标，评价和检验学习成果。日本国际交流基金"みんなのCan-do"网站上提供了六个水平等次（A1～C2）四类语言活动（信息产出、接受理解、交流互动和表述策略）的具体活动内容信息，教师可直接选择其中的项目用于确定教学目标，也可参照 Can-do 的设定标准，设计符合学习者需求的个性化"My Can-do"。参照 Can-do 标准设定的学习目标具有交际意义，而语言知识的学习则是围绕着完成交际活动即达成学习目标而进行的。

教授法理论的研究成果早在新中国日语教育刚刚起步的时候，在课堂教学活动中就已经得到运用，并且收到了较好的效果。例如 20 世纪 50 年代起步于美国的听说法给我国的日语教学带来了深远的影响，尤其是"反复操练法"①至今仍然活跃于我国日语教育的课堂教学中。虽然机械的反复操练存在过于单调、难以直接连接实际语境等诸多缺陷，但是以归纳学习的方法对语法句型的说明及操练，对于成年二语习得者而言，仍然不失为行之有效的方法。随着二语习得研究的深入，教授法理论的研究成果也不断推陈出新，把这些研究成果有效运用于课堂教学，无疑对于丰富教学手段、实现教学目标具有积极意义。以下将结合具体的教学案例详细阐述如何参照 Can-do 标准设定学习目标、运用教授法理论的研究成果展开课堂教学活动。

3.1 信息产出活动：讲演及发表（A2）

表 1 是信息产出活动"讲演及发表"的具体教学案例。

---

① 反复操练法包括"代入、替换、问答、扩大"等练习形式。

表 1 信息产出活动"讲演及发表"

设定教学目标（Can-do）

（教师与学习者共有学习目标）

↓

知识输入阶段（インプット活动）

（提示语法知识→导入词汇语法）

↓

知识输出阶段（アウトプット活动）

（句型练习→会话练习）

↓

实际演示阶段（パフォーマンス活动）

（导入范文→完成讲稿→小组练习→课堂发表）

↓

回顾与自我评价（ふりかえり）

（学习目标与教学评价的一体化）

3.1.1 教学目标的设定

　　教学目标是教师和学习者共有的努力方向，目标的设定将左右教学活动的展开。只有明确目标才能鼓励学生加强自主学习。日本国际交流基金发表的《JF 日语教育标准 2010》附加了 15 个在日语教学活动中可供参考的活动课题①，为我们把教学目标由以往的知识传授转向语言活动能力的培养和提高，提供了具体的内容框架。

　　本教案教授对象为入门期的一年级学生，参照 Can-do 标准为这一教学活动设定的 My Can-do 的水平等级为 A2，具体内容如下。

　　信息产出活动"讲演及发表"（A2）

　　在来自全国各地的学生聚会上，能够就自己家乡的生活环境的变化以及环境问题等，偶尔看一下事先准备好的笔记，进行简短的发表，

---

　　① 15 个活动课题的内容详见『JF 日本語教育スタンダード 2010 利用者ガイドブック』国際交流基金 P16

并能回答关于发表内容的简单提问。

3.1.2　知识输入阶段

在进入语言活动前，教师首先要给学生输入完成这一学习目标必须掌握的知识，即词汇、语法、句型等。教师要改变以往"一言堂"的授课方式，选择适合学生认知能力、具有明确语境的语言材料，通过播放影像录音资料、展示图片照片、阅读短文等方法，把新的语言知识以具象的形式提示给学生。在调动既有语言储备的基础上，让他们尽可能自我发现该语言表述的语法规则及该语法的形式、含义与功能之间的联系。引导学生按照自我理解的方式对将要学习的语法构筑一个使用规则，然后通过实际操练以及教师的提示指导来修正自我理解规则的偏差。自然环境下的二语习得者之所以能够较好地掌握目标语言就是因为充分运用了自我发现和自我修正的策略，这一策略在课堂教学活动中也应该加以利用，这样做既可以让学生加强思考，同时也可提高他们自主学习的热情，帮助他们温故而知新，保障知识的连贯性。这种"诱导发现"式的学习，可以帮助学生把输入的语言逐渐转化为内在知识。

在完成语言知识的习得之后，可适当导入与教学目标相关的社会文化知识及谈话结构等内容，例如本课可向学习者介绍日本生活环境的变化等相关内容。

3.1.3　知识输出阶段

在传统的日语教学模式中知识输入阶段成为整个课堂教学活动的重点，但是改革后的教学活动中，知识输入成为后阶段活动展开所必需的语言能力准备阶段。如表 1 所示，知识输出阶段作为连接知识输入阶段和实际演示活动的中间桥梁，对于学习目标的达成起着关键作用，教师应该尽量围绕学习目标来设计活动内容。以上述信息产出活动为例，可设计以下活动[①]。

---

① 句型练习及会话练习内容及插图均引自徐敏民、丸山千歌主编《新界标日本语综合教程（1）》（复旦大学出版社，2013 年）第 251 页。

（1）文型練習：イラストを見ながら、この町の変化をペアで話しましょう。

イラストＡ：昔の町
◎街路樹や花が多かったです。
◎建物が低くて少なかったです。
◎お店が少なくて、車も少なかったです。　…

イラストＢ：今の町
◎今の町は街路樹や花が少なくなりました。建物が増えました。

◎店がたくさんできました。

◎道路が広くなりました。町の雰囲気がにぎやかになりました。

◎人も車も多くなりました。空気が汚くなりました。環境問題が心配です。…

句型练习的目的在于检验知识输入阶段对于语法词汇知识的掌握情况。要求学生看着插图主动产出信息，单句的产出为完成学习目标迈出了第一步。

（2）会話練習：例にならって、「故郷の変化」について、グループに分けてお互いにインタビューをしてみてください。そして、その回答を次の表に入れなさい。

モデル会話：

王：李さんの故郷はどこですか。

李：上海です。

王：上海は大都会ですね。

李：そうですね。人も車もますます多くなりました。

王：高い建物も多いですね。

李：ええ、5年前から高層ビルがたくさんできました。

王：交通も便利になったでしょう。

李：はい、便利になりました。昔はよく渋滞しましたが、今地下鉄ができました。道路も広くなりました。

王：ところで、王さんの故郷はどこですか。…

名前	故郷	故郷の変化
李敏	上海	人も車もますます多くなりました。 高層ビルがたくさんできました。お店も増えました。 交通も便利になりました。 昔はよく渋滞しましたが、今地下鉄ができました。 道路も広くなりました。

会话是由单句逐渐向着独自完成一段具有实际内容、构思相对完整的课堂发表的过渡练习。学习者在按照要求完成这段采访的过程中，听、说、写三方面的技能都能得到锻炼。

教师应把信息输出阶段的练习设计成具有"信息间隙"的课堂活动，因为社会交际活动的目的之一便是填补彼此所拥有的信息量之间的差距。在课堂教学中应该尽量避免纯粹为了练习语法而设计的没有实际交际意义的语言活动。

3.1.4　实际演示阶段

学习者通过知识输出阶段由单句到简短会话的准备后，教学活动便进入实际演示，即检验学习目标达成度的阶段。演讲是本教案设定的实际演示活动。在构思演讲稿之前，教师可向学生提供参考范文，也就是传统日语教材中的课文。在学生进行发表演讲的过程中，教师在不影响语言活动展开的前提下，要适度容忍他们在语音、语调及表述等方面出现的错误。第二外语的习得是通过教学活动将显在知识转化为潜在知识的过程，教师的适当反馈可以帮助学生缩短习得过程，可是过于严厉的反馈也可能激起他们在第二外语习得过程中心理上的抵触情绪。为了提高学生的学习兴趣，增强自信心，就要尽可能降低他们的"情意过滤"因素，减少运用目标语言时可能产生的抵触态度①。语言知识的学习是支持语言交际活动的基础，可并非语言习得的终极目标，因此在不影响语言活动进行的前提下，为保障其流畅性，同时也为了降低学生的"情意过滤"因素，课堂教学过程中，教师对于学生的误用，应该采取适度宽容的态度。

课堂发表完成后，教学活动并未结束，教师要让学生参照教学目标，对自己的发表进行回顾和总结，即自我评价。学生之间也可进行相互评价，找到问题点，以确立新的学习目标。

---

① 引自鎌田修・川口義一・鈴木睦，『日本語教授法ワークショップ（増補版）』—東京凡人社，P. 134。

3.2　交流互动活动：交流信息（A2）

表 2　交流互动活动"交流信息"

定教学目标（Can-do）

（教师与学习者共有学习目标）

↓

知识输入阶段（インプット活動）

（提示语法知识→导入词汇语法）

↓

知识输出阶段（アウトプット活動）

（句型练习→会话练习）

↓

实际演示阶段（パフォーマンス活動）

（导入范文→扮演角色会话ロールプレイ→完成课题タスク）

↓

回顾与自我评价（ふりかえり）

（学习目标与教学评价的一体化）

　　表 2 是交流互动活动"交流信息"（A2）的课堂教学活动案例。教授对象仍为入门期的一年级学生。知识输入、知识输出阶段的要点与前一案例基本相同，限于篇幅不再赘述，在此仅就实际演示阶段进行简单介绍。

　　交流互动活动在课堂教学的实际演示采取扮演角色会话和完成课题两种形式。扮演角色会话主要是以两人为单位的互动交流，既可测试学生对语言知识的掌握程度，又可检验他们灵活运用习得知识的能力。课题以小组为单位、利用课余时间由小组成员协同完成。任务内容必须是具有实际交际意义的活动。相比于传统的教师主导的日语教学，小组活动更注重学生在教学活动中的主体性和学生之间的互动交流。全班结成若干成员相对固定的学习小组，组员之间要商定阶段学习的达成目标，为了达到共同的目标而签下"契约"①，并依照"契约"及时反省自己的学习状况，修正学习策略。小组活动不仅可相互促进，共同提高，还将学习活动延续至课堂之外，对于缺乏自然习得环境的二语习得者而言，集团学习是延伸课堂教学的最佳选择。

上述"信息产出活动"和"交流互动活动"虽然在实际演示阶段采取的练习手段有所不同，但其教学活动的展开方式有着共同点。首先两者都是具有实际交际含义的具体活动，其次对于语言知识的导入和语言活动的展开都采取了"螺旋性积累提升"模式，即同一知识点在不断重复的过程中逐渐增加难度，将即时习得的知识转化为阶段性习得的一种能力提升模式。知识输出阶段的活动（单句→简短会话→实际演示）便是依照这一理念进行设计的。

螺旋性积累提升不仅可用于词汇、语法的学习以及以课为单位的教学活动的设计，还可运用于整个课程的教学目标的设定。Can-do 标准中同一类型的活动在不同等级均有相应的水平界定，以产出活动"演讲和发表"为例，在国际交流基金"みんなの Can-do"网站可以找到从 A2—C2 六个等级的"演讲和发表"活动，所以 Can-do 标准的递增式等级设定，为螺旋性积累提升贯穿于从课程设计到每课教学活动的安排提供了有利条件。

4. 改革后的课堂教学活动与传统的教学模式之差异

通过对上述教学案例的说明分析，不难发现改革后的课堂教学与传统的教学模式相比较，在教学目标，教学方法和教学活动展开方式等方面有着诸多不同，主要体现在以下四个方面。

---

① 引自鎌田修・川口義一・鈴木睦，『日本語教授法ワークショップ（増補版）』—東京凡人社，P.82。

4.1　学习目标的转变

学习目标由语言知识的传授转向交际能力的提高，这一转变可以推动我国日语教学的课程设置以及课堂教学的改革，对于专业日语教学大纲的修订也具有启示意义。

4.2　教学目标与教学活动、学习评价的一体化

教学目标与教学活动的一体化，要求教学活动围绕着教学目标展开，避免了教学活动的盲目性，使得课堂教学更加充实有效。目标与评价的一体化则可以保障语言习得过程的一贯性，提高学习者学习积极性和自主学习的能力。

4.3　教学活动的双向化

改革后的教学活动中，教师不再是课堂教学的主导者，而是展开教学活动的策划者。教师把更多精力用于设计教学活动和帮助学生完成课堂内互动。这一角色的转变不仅能够活跃课堂气氛，而且还促进了教师和学生以及学生之间的交流互动。

4.4　听说读写四种技能的同步提高

按照上述教学活动案例展开教学活动的过程中，听说读写四种技能经常得以同时使用。例如在演讲时，需要用到写与说的技能，在角色扮演会话中需要用到听与说的技能，由小组协同完成的课题中听说读写四种技能更是缺一不可。这样的教学活动能将听说读写四种技能"统合"起来，成为一门真正意义上的综合日语课程。

我国传统的精读、会话、听力、阅读各自分开的课程设置，存在着同一知识点重复出现、语言知识导入顺序不同步、话题重叠等诸多问题，学习效率不高。因此精读与会话课程一统化的改革尝试，给我国日语教学课程设置的改革也带来了启示。

5. 学生对教学改革的反馈意见

　　我系把新的教学理念引入初级日语教学课堂所进行的一系列改革已经有近两年时间，任课教师们认为这批学生在语言交际能力方面较之以往的学生有了明显提升，那么学生们是否认可这样的改革呢？为此我们对二年级两个班级的 37 名学生进行了问卷调查，以下对问卷调查的结果做一汇总分析。

　　在有关"课程关联性"的调查项目中，如图 1[①]所示，几乎所有被调查者都认为精读课与会话课之间的关联性很强或比较强，有近 65% 的学生认为相比于会话课，采用不同教材的听力课与精读课之间的关

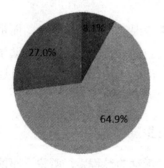

图 1　课程关联性

联性显得不足。由此可见使用同一本教材或相互内容衔接的一套教材，将精读、听力和会话课统合为综合日语课，可以避免各课程间知识的重叠及教学的重复。学生对此表示认可，在今后的课程改革中有必要进一步进行研究探索。

---

① 文中图 1 至图 5 笔者按照问卷调查所得数据自制而成。

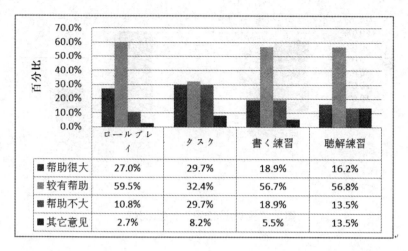

	ロールプレイ	タスク	書く練習	聴解練習
■ 帮助很大	27.0%	29.7%	18.9%	16.2%
■ 较有帮助	59.5%	32.4%	56.7%	56.8%
■ 帮助不大	10.8%	29.7%	18.9%	13.5%
■ 其它意见	2.7%	8.2%	5.5%	13.5%

图2 「ロールプレイ」「タスク」「書く練習」「聴解練習」的作用

图 2 中出现的数据是学生对课堂教学中涉及的扮演角色会话等四项教学内容的具体评价。有九成以上的学生对于"角色扮演会话""完成课题"和"写作练习"在教学中的作用予以肯定,"听力练习"部分也有八成以上的学生表示对自己有帮助。由此可见,在加强语言知识习得的基础上,重视信息输出和实际演练的课堂教学改革得到了学生的普遍认可。

改革后的课堂教学在得到肯定的同时,也出现了一些值得我们思考的调查数据。例如,有关课堂教学时间安排如图 3 所示,认为老师在词汇语法和课文说明的教学上分配时间最多的学生基本各占一半。尽管学生们肯定了课堂教学中实际演练部分对于提高日语综合能力的作用,可是没有一个学生认为老师在上述三环节的教学中最注重实际演练。这就说明虽然改革后的课堂教学把知识输出和实际演练视作实现学习目标的主要教学环节,希望教师投入更多精力,但是在实际的教学中,大多数教师还是会把比较多的时间用于语法词汇和课文的教学,从中不难看出重视知识传授、教师主导的课堂教学模式仍然在延续中。

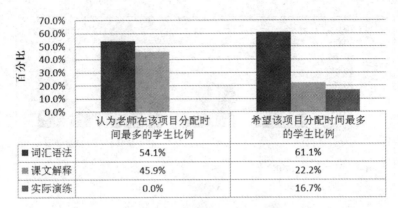

图 3 "教学时间分配"人数比例表

图 3 所显示的另一组数据更加引人深思。有六成以上的学生希望老师把主要精力用于语法词汇的教学，希望重视实际演练人数的百分比在三个项目中位居最低数值。这说明重视知识传授的教学模式不仅在教师中，在学生中也已根深蒂固。理念的转变如果不先于方法的更新，那么再先进的教学方法最终只不过是"新瓶装陈酒"，难有成效。因此，在探索以学生为主体的教学改革的同时，不仅对教师，还应该对学生灌输外语教学改革的必要性，使得教与学的两端都对教学改革的目的及意义有一个比较全面的认识，以此为前提的课堂教学才能真正收到实效。

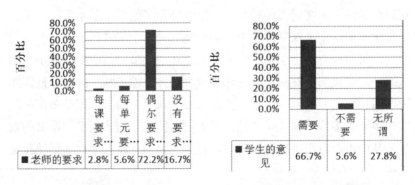

图 4 老师对于自评的要求   图 5 学生对于自评的要求

图 4 和图 5 是有关自我评价的调查内容。数据表明只有少数老师会在每课或每单元的学习后让学生进行自我评价，实际上有近七成的学生认为作为教学活动的一个环节，自我评价是非常需要的。由此可见，虽然我们在教学改革方案中提出要加强自我评价的设想，但由于实际操作经验的缺乏，教师多会选择回避自我评价这一环节。作为教学改革的一个重要课题，如何在教学中引入自我评价体系，让自我评价成为促进学习者自主学习能力的有效手段，还有待进一步探索研究。

6. 结语

本研究运用外语教授法理论的研究成果及 Can-do 标准六个水平等次的衡量尺度，从教学目标的设定着手，在实际课堂教学中改变以往重知识轻能力的教学模式，尝试把教学重心置于知识输出，设计了一套以提高学生交际能力为主旨的课堂教学改革方案。通过学生对课堂教学改革的意见反馈，笔者对教学改革进行了重新审视，对于外语教学活动中缺一不可的四要素"学生、教师、教材、教授法"之间的密切关联有了进一步认识。"以学生为主体"、注重培养综合语言运用能力和跨文化交际能力的教学理念要在实际教学中真正得以贯彻，在改革课堂教学的同时，还必须改变教师和学习者持有的"以传授知识为主"的传统外语教学观；在尝试课程改革的同时，有必要同步进行新教材的开发。只有做好每一个环节的衔接，日语教育改革才能真正落到实处，收到应有的效果。

参考文献

鎌田修·川口義一·鈴木睦. 2007.『日本語教授法ワークショップ（増補版）』凡人社，82-134.

青木直子·尾崎明人·土岐哲. 2010.『日本語教育学を学ぶ人のた

めに』世界思想社.

　　小柳かおる. 2010.『日本語教師のための新しい言語習得論』スリーエーネットワーク.

　　国際交流基金. 2010.『JF 日本語教育スタンダード 2010』.

　　国際交流基金. 2010.『JF 日本語教育スタンダード 2010 利用者ガイドブック』, 16.

　　彭瑾、徐敏民，2013，『JF 日本語教育スタンダード 2010』与我国日语教育改革，日语学习与研究，第 2 期，第 69-76 页。

　　徐敏民、丸山千歌，主编，2013，《新界标日本语综合教程（1）》，上海：复旦大学出版社，第 241-245 页。

Insights into Reforms of Japanese Language

Classroom Teaching in China

Abstract: The research is based on the achievements and theories of foreign languages teaching methodology and Can-do Standard. A series of reform plans on classroom teaching have been designed with both the integration of teaching practice and the instruction of the notions of cultivating learners' comprehensive language application and cross-cultural communicative abilities in attempts to examine the communicatively effective language activities in class room teaching.

Key words: teaching concepts, teaching activities, teaching approaches, Can-do standard, curriculum reform.

此文发表于《日语学习与研究》2014 年第 3 期

中国英语学习者语块认知加工优势研究

桑紫林

　　摘　要：语块的认知加工因兼具整体认知的经济性与结构语义理解的复杂性而不易探索。本实验研究主要通过测量中国英语学习者对语块短语和非语块短语语法判断的速度与错误率，考察他们处理语块言语的方式。结果表明，在英语言语认知加工中存在语块主效应，语块呈现出显著的处理优势；习语语块的提取速度显著低于非习语语块，表明语块内部的复杂性对其认知经济性有干扰；高水平组处理语块的速度显著快于低水平组，因而更趋向采用于整体提取认知方式。

　　关键词：语块；认知加工；优势 ；反应时 ；错误率；语言水平

1. 前言

　　语块（formulaic sequence）的认知处理近年来受到学界关注，研究角度不一，取得了丰硕的成果。母语习得研究（Brown，1973；Clark，1974；Nattinger and DeCarrico，1992；Dabrowska，2000）表明，语块在语言习得中处于中心地位。二语习得研究认为语块能够促进二语习得（Wood，2001、2004、2006；Schmitt & Carter，2004；Weinert，1995；Wray，2000、2002；Yorio，1980；Howarth，1998；Ellis，1984、1994等）。同时，语块的语用和社会功能研究也得到了相应的发展，许多语言学家（如 Wray & Perkins，2000；Wray，2002；Kecskes，2000；

Scher &Adolphs，2006；Overstreet & Yule，2001 等）指出语块在促进社会交际方面起着不可或缺的作用。神经语言学的研究表明，语块和通过语法生成的新语句的语言处理机制不尽相同，前者主要由右脑负责（Wray，2002；Van Lancker，2001、2004）。心理语言学研究则是紧扣语块的言语处理的经济性，语块由于其块状模式，使得其在言语理解和产出中更为便捷快速，这一观点已在许多研究中得到部分的验证（Jiang & Nekrasova，2007；Schmitt，2005；Conklin & Schmitt，2007；Schmitt et.al.，2004；Schmitt and Underwood，2004；Underwood，Schmitt and Galpin，2004）。

对语块的研究可以从多个层面展开，目前，国外研究二语语块认知主要通过三个学科层面进行：语法学层面、语料库语言学层面、心理语言学层面，这三个层面彼此互补（王立非等，2006：17）。但是从国内二语习得研究资料统计看，研究者更加关注语块对于语言教学，尤其是词汇教学所产生的影响（段士平，2008；严维华，2003，2008；原萍等，2010；马广惠，2009）。对其认知处理方式的探讨略显不足，语块的认知机制研究未受到应有的重视。

2. 研究背景

心理语言学理论认为，以语块为单位加工语言可以节省工作记忆中有限的认知资源，提高言语信息的加工速度与贮存能力。波利和西德尔（Pawley & Syder，1983）明确地指出了语块的言语处理经济性，认为语块处理之所以更加便捷是因为它们以整体的形式在大脑中表征和处理，因此是储存在长时记忆中的，不需要各个单词逐个处理，因此节省了时间。康克林和施密特（Conklin & Schmitt，2007）和江和内克拉索瓦（Jiang & Necrasova，2007）都指出语块处理的经济性源于其作为一个整体的记忆单元直接提取，中间没有句法操作。但是，语块的整体存储和提取这一观点目前仍是假设，尚在理论探讨阶段，相关的实证性研究较少，只是获得了部分验证。

学者们主要从言语产出或理解两个角度进行语块处理的研究。从言语产出角度进行研究的，主要有科尔莫斯（Kormos，2007），伍德（Wood，2001、2004、2006），切诺韦思（Chenoweth，1995），范兰克尔（Van Lancker，2001、2004）等人。他们的共同结论是：语块无论在书面语体还是口语体中对语言产出都具有促进作用，尤其是在口语的流利性方面，验证了语块的自动处理体系理论。在言语理解方面，施密特、格朗德吉和阿道夫（Schmitt，Grandage & Adolphs，2004）采用让受试（母语非英语）在有限时间内复述听到的英语内容的方法。其使用的材料是通过语料库检索来的高频词丛，将其嵌入篇章中；其设计理念是如果这些词丛是整体表征的，那么受试的口语输出这些词丛应该是准确流利的。但是测试结果证实，多数词丛至少对非母语者来说，并非整体储存和提取的。其不尽人意的结果可能与实验材料选择有关，在该实验中多数词丛都是开放性的，因此受试可能会进行句法分析从而肢解其成分，导致准确性和流利度丧失。除此之外，康克林和施密特（2007），江和内克拉索瓦（2007）以及施密特（2004）也就言语处理发表了各自的研究报告，但是这些研究结论不一致。

研究者们大都采用采集客观数据的实验工具。安德伍德、施密特和加尔平（Underwood, Schmitt, and Galpin，2004）使用视觉追踪技术（Eye-tracking Paradigm）检验语块的整体储存这一假设。他们认为，如果语块是整体表征的，那么受试就有可能会预测到该语块中的末位词（Terminal Word），从而在这个词上的注意力会减少，注视该词的次数和长度（number and length of eye fixations）都会相对较少。因此他们把注视次数和长度作为主要分析数据。操母语者的实验结果完全证实了这一假设，但是非母语者的数据只能部分支持这个结论（Jiang & Nekrasova，2007）。笔者认为，他们的这种实验设计理念适合采用结构比较封闭、语义具有合成性的习语做实验材料，不适合非习语语块，所以他们大量使用习语作为实验材料的做法有一定的片面性。另外，习语的掌握与使用是操母语者和非母语者在语言方面的最大差异之一，这也可以解释为什么结论不完整了。为了能够获得更为可信的数据，实验材料应该包括类别更为丰富的语块，语块结构上的变异程度应该更为灵活。

施密特和安德伍德（Schmitt & Underwood，2004）则使用了自控速度阅读方法（Self-paced Reading），他们认为同一个词在语块中的阅读时间要更短，因为语块是整体储存和提取的，不再需要额外的认知努力去分割、分析它。他们在实验中的目标词仍然是末位词，但是同时该词出现在许多控制短语中，位置一样。结果是，实验没有发现该词在语块中和控制短语中的阅读时间差异，对操母语者如此，对非母语者也是一样。Jiang & Nekrasova（2007：435）认为实验结果不一致，部分是由于实验材料的选择不当。

康克林和施密特（2007）再次使用了自控速度阅读方法，但是语块材料是嵌入到篇章的，这样上下文可以支撑语块的字面意义（如 a breath of fresh air=breathing clean air outside）和习语意义（如 a breath of fresh air= a new approach），他们还选择了一些非语块表达形式，他们认为语块的整体表征会得出这样的阅读时间次序：语块（习语意义）<语块（字面意义）<非语块表达形式。实验结果证明了这一推论。另外，他们指出："到目前为止，对于语块听觉处理的优势，还没有直接的证据"（Conklin & Schmitt，2007：13）。因此实验的范围尚需要扩大。

江和内克拉索瓦（2007）采用了在线短语判断任务（online phrase judgment）来研究语块的言语处理。他们认为，语块整体表征观意味着其处理过程不涉及任何语法分析，因而会导致处理经济便捷。同时，他们强调在有限时间内让受试判断语法，由于句法分析需要额外的认知努力，非语块可能会导致更多的判断错误。因此错误率和反应时间就作为实验分析的数据，也确实证实了先前的语块整体储存观的假设。他们的结论为：相对于非语块，以英语为母语或非母语的受试对语块的语法判断更快、更准确（Jiang & Nekrasova，2007：440）。但是他们的研究材料完全排除了习语，只采用一些相对封闭的语块形式，受试对该类短语相对比较熟悉，因而反应快，所以其结果不能概括全部语块的处理情形。

可见，语块言语处理研究由于涉及复杂的心理认知机制，现有结论并不完善，语块的整体提取和表征假设有待在更宽的范围内和不同的层次上得到验证。本研究意在对中国的英语习得者的语块处理方式进行考察。

3. 研究设计

3.1 研究问题

该研究要回答的问题如下：

第一，语块在英语处理中是否存在判断速度快与准确率高之主效应？

第二，英语学习者处理习语语块与非习语语块的速度与错误率是否存在显著差异？

第三，语块的提取速度和错误率与英语学习者语言水平是否相关？

3.2 实验对象

共 52 名英语学习者参与本研究，按照他们英语学习时间长短和专业分为高水平组和低水平组，每组 26 人。高水平组都具备或正在攻读英语语言文学硕士学位；低水平组为上海某综合性大学的非英语专业一二年级学生。两组受试的有关情况请参看下表。

3.3 研究材料

本研究中测试材料包括 30 条语块短语，30 条非语块短语，30 条不符语法规则的短语。

本研究涉及 30 条语块短语中有 10 条习语语块（如：the last straw）和 20 条非习语语块（如：in the first place）。30 条非语块短语参照江和内克拉索瓦（2007）的做法，用词频和词长相似的词替换语块短语中的某一单词，生成 30 条符合语法规则的有意义的非语块短语，比如用 to break the cup 代替习语语块 to break the ice，用 there is no paper in…代替非习语语块 there is no point in…。再用同样方法生成 30 条不符合语法规则的短语（如：to late usual as），用作填充与参照。

表 1　实验对象信息

组别	是否英语专业	平均年龄	英语学习时间	起始年龄	出国经历		性别	
					有	无	男	女
高水平	是	31 岁	20 年	11 岁	21 人	5 人	8 人	18 人
低水平	否	19 岁	10 年	9 岁	1 人	25 人	13 人	13 人

为了避免实验中可能出现重复效应，将语块短语和其对应的非语块短语分为 A 和 B 两个列表，比如，如果语块短语 as a result 归入列表 A，而其对应的非语块短语 as a woman 则归入列表 B，反之亦然。不符合语法规则的短语分别归入两个列表。这样，每个列表就包含 15 条语块短语（含 5 条习语语块和 10 条非习语语块），15 条非语块短语，15 条不符合语法短语。

3.4　实验过程

3.4.1　实验方法

该研究采用在线判断法，即要求受试尽可能快地判断出某一短语是否在语法和意义上可接受。该方法强调时效，因此对于要考察的语块效应具有针对性。也就是说，如果语块效应存在的话，判断语块短语时，受试会直接跳过语法分析过程，因此反应时会更快。

3.4.2　实验工具

本研究利用 DMDX 软件随机呈现列表中的短语并记录受试的判断反应时和结果，将两个列表各 45 个条目写入 DMDX 可接受的程序，在计算机上运行。如果受试判断可以接受，按下电脑上的←键；如果不能接受，则按下电脑上的→键。

3.4.3 实验操作

实验前，受试填写个人信息，接受实验指导，并且做 15 个测试练习项目以熟悉试验环境。实验开始后，受试在最短的时间内完成一个列表中所有 45 个项目的判断，高分组和低分组各有 50%的人完成列表 A，50%人完成列表 B。所有数据由实验者用一对一的方法直接向受试采集，历时两周完成。

3.4.4 数据处理

实验结束后，收集所有受试的反应时和错误率数据，作为因变量，进行统计前对原始数据进行了如下整理：如果短语判断错误，其反应时不纳入分析范围；删除反应时间低于 400 毫秒和高于 4000 毫秒的数据，以避免受试不看材料随意按键或使用较长时间进行充足语法分析的数据进入统计分析。删除量为总数据的 5.8%。

4. 结果与讨论

4.1 语块在反应时和错误率上呈现主效应

表 2 显示的是受试在判断不同类别短语的反应时和错误率的方差分析结果。结果表明，短语类别在判断反应时上主效应显著（$F_{(2, 87)} = 15.378$，$p < .05$）；短语类别在判断错误率上的主效应显著（$\chi^2 = 22.852$，$p < .05$）。另外，事后多重比较检验（Post Hoc Multiple Comparison）LSD 结果表明，三种短语反应时的两两比较 p 值均小于.05，表现为受试判断语块用时最少，不符合语法短语用时最多。错误率由于不成正态分布，采用了多独立样本非参数检验，无法进行事后多重比较。但对语块与非语块的错误率用 Mann-Whitney U 两独立样本非参数检验，结果显示 $z = -4.79$，$p = .000$，两者错误率差异显著，语块短语的错误率显著少于非语块短语。

语块短语的判断反应时显著低于非语法语块，表现出语块认知加工式的经济性优势。这个结果能从一个角度证实语块呈整体存储和提取的假设：由于存储时呈现块状，因此在提取时无须语法分析，可减少认知努力，节省认知资源，加快判断速度，体现了语块提取的效率优势。用于参照的不符合语法语块判断所需时间最多，表明学习者的大脑已经建立了英语语法图式，打破语法图式的短语激发大脑对相应语法条目的搜索、通达、提取和判断，因而显著延长了判断时间。效应幅度 η2 值.26 表明，从整体上看，语块类别这一变量的效应幅度在"有限"范围内（张少林，2009），这个统计量指出，语块类别虽然有极其显著的统计学意义上主效应，在我国英语学习者的实际英语使用过程中，重要性有限。这个结果可能与固定语块在英语中的数量有限，出现频率不高有关系。

表 2　不同类别短语的反应时方差分析和错误率 Kruskal Willis 检验

判断类别	短语类别	N	均值	标准差	标准误	F	p	η^2
反应时	语块短语	30	1362	393	71	15.378	.000	.26
	非语块短语	30	1544	334	61			
	不符合语法短语	30	1849	298	54			

判断类别	短语类别	N	均值	标准差	均秩	χ^2	p	
错误率%	语块短语	30	2.08	7.47	29.08	22.852	.000	
	非语块短语	30	7.78	7.35	58.67			
	不符合语法短语	30	4.84	5.25	48.75			

　　语块判断的错误率显著低于非语块，也间接证明了语块呈整体存储和提取的正确率更高，亦体现了语块处理的效果优势。

4.2　习语语块的处理速度显著慢于非习语语块但错误率无差异

　　习语是一类特殊的语块，为了考察中国英语学习者在处理习语语块和普通语块时的差异，本研究对语块进行了再分类，分为习语语块和非习语语块。表 3 呈现了两类语块反应时 t-检验和错误率 Mann-

Whitney U 检验（曼·惠特尼秩和检验）的结果。结果表明，英语学习者判断习语语块的速度显著慢于非习语语块（t=7.493，p＜.05）对比表2与表3的反应时平均值，可以看出，受试对习语语块进行判断，平均需要反应时 1689 秒，高于判断非语块短语的反应时 1544 秒（表2）。可以说，对中国英语学习者而言，语块短语整体处理的优势与正确率主要是由对非习语语块的认知判断体现的。习语具备语义合成性，其实际意义与字面意义相去甚远，因此受试在辨别习语语块时，字面意义的干扰导致受试需要耗费更多的认知努力，因而导致判断反应时更长；另外，相对来说，习语语块在英语学习者的语言输入中的频率远远低于非习语语块，因此英语学习者对非习语语块更为熟悉，判断反应时自然也就更快。效应幅度因 d 值高达 1.47，这种"强"（张少林，2009）效应幅度证实在实际英语应用过程中，我国英语学习者对英语习语的掌握的确比较弱，而且这种对习语语块的掌握弱于非习语语块的趋势在高低水平组中是一致的（图 1）。这一结果提示我们，不论对本科生还是研究生，都应该加强英语习语的输入和学习指导。

表3　习语语块和非习语语块反应时 t-检验和错误率 Mann-Whitney U 检验结果

判断类别	语块类别	N	均值	标准差	均秩	t	p	d
反应时	习语	52	1689	433	60	7.493	.000	1.47
	非习语	52	1170	249	345			
判断类别	语块类别	N	均值	标准差	均秩	z	p	
错误率	习语	52	0.027	. 069	52.11	-.213	.832	
	非习语	52	0.017	. 038	52.89			

就判断错误率而言，习语语块和非习语语块之间无显著差异（z=.213，p＞.05）。究其原因，大概是由于这两类语块只是在语义上存在显著区别，内部结构上并无差异，所以在判断短语在语法结构上的可接受性测试中未呈现显著差异。不过，在判断错误率发生的趋势上，高低水平组似乎相反（图 2）。低水平组判断习语的错误率高了对非习语的判断，而高水平组则与之相反，显示低水平组对习语的了解甚少。

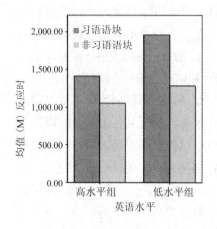

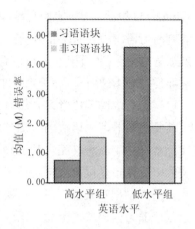

图 1　习语与非习语语块反应时比较　　**图 2　习语与非习语语块错误率比较**

4.3　英语语言水平主效应显著

语言水平是该实验设计中的受试间变量，其对任务判断的反应时和错误率的影响是我们关注的问题之一。为了检验英语水平效应是否存在于语块分类的理解判断中，两个水平组受试对语块与非语块短语的判断反应时与错误率分别接受了 t-检验和 Mann-Whitney U 检验，结果见表 4。

高水平组在判断习语语块和非习语语块的反应速度均显著快于低水平组，说明高水平组有较强的语块概念，语块信息整体提取的几率比较大，因而认知加工的速度快。与此情形相配的是，高水平学习者在提取语块时的错误率显著地低于低水平英语学习者。这是因为随着语言水平的逐步提升，语块不仅在语言输入中的频率加大，其整体记忆的优势也越发明显，学习者对语块的区别性特征更为敏感，因而提取效率更高，这也表明语块在高水平英语学习者中呈整体存储的程度更高。这种语块整体记忆的方式，不仅使高水平者在阅读过程中提取速度快，而且提取正确率高。反之，低水平者的语块概念不强，没有把语块作为整体记忆并提取。不仅在短语判断上耗费时间，出错的几率也比较高。

表4　高低水平组判断习语语块和非习语语块反应时

t-检验和错误率 Mann-Whitney U 检验结果

语块分类	语言水平	N	均值	标准差	标准误	t	p
习语反应时	高水平组	26	1415	315	62	-5.893	.000
	低水平组	26	1964	356	70		
非习语反应时	高水平组	26	1055	207	41	-3.730	.000
	低水平组	26	1285	238	47		
错误率	语言水平	N	均值	标准差	均秩	z	p
习语错误率（%）	高水平组	26	.77	3.92	24.00	-2.012	.044
	低水平组	26	4.62	8.59	29.00		
非习语错误率（%）	高水平组	26	1.54	3.68	25.44	-.611	.541
	低水平组	26	1.92	4.02	27.56		

　　但在非语块短语判断的错误率上，高低水平组没有显著差异。这主要是因为本研究中选择的非习语语块在学习者语言输入中的频率较高，两个水平组受试对它们都颇为熟悉；另外，该实验环境中，时间要求紧迫的实验条件可能会使得提取效率不得不补偿提取速度，导致反应时上的显著差异抹平了判断错误率上的差异。

5. 结论

　　本次研究的结果证明，与非语块相比，英语学习者加工语块时总体呈现出言语处理优势，高水平者对语块整体认知加工的程度更高。但语块处理经济性这一结果的数据主要是由非习语语块加工速度支撑的，习语语块的结构复杂性制约了其加工速度，因而其经济性在我国英语学习者中未得到支持。语块自身的结构与语义特殊性决定了英语学习者在对其认知处理过程中，整体认知经济性与结构分析复杂性两者并存，并且呈以此消彼长的动态关系。语块广泛存在于各类口头与

书面语篇之中，所以，对语块的认知处理速度与语义理解正确性是影响英语学习者阅读与听力理解水平的重要因素

本次实验结果虽然以我国英语学习者为实验对象，验证了语块认知加工趋向于整体处理的假设，但实验数据表明的仅仅是语块言语处理的结果，认知过程中的某些重要因素，如语块处理优势的触发点等，仍然不得而知。因此，需要更多后续实验研究，采用更加深层次的设计，采集客观认知过程数据，从各个角度验证语块言语处理的经济高效特性，为帮助我国英语学习者建立语块整体处理方式提供认知机制的支持。

参考文献

Brown, R. 1973. *A First Language.* London: Allen & Unwin.

Clark, R. 1974. "Performing without competence". *Journal of child languag,* 1. pp. 1-10.

Chenoweth, N.A. 1995. "Formulaicity in essay exam answers". *Language sciences* 17(3), pp. 283-297.

Conklin, K., & Schmitt, N. 2007. "Formulaic sequences: are they processed more quickly than nonformulaic language by native and nonnative speakers?". *Applied linguistics* 29(1), pp.72-89.

Dabrowska, E. 2000. "From formula to schema: the acquisition of English questions". *Cognitive linguistics* 11. pp.83-102.

Ellis, R. 1984. "Formulaic speech in early classroom second language development". In J. Handscombe, R. A. Orem, & B. P. Taylor (eds.). *On TESOL '83.* Washington, DC: TESOL.

Ellis, R. 1994. *The Study of Second Language Acquisition.* Oxford: Oxford University Press.

Howarth, P. 1998. "Phraseology and second language proficiency". *Applied linguistics* 19 (1), pp.24-44.

Jiang, N., & Nekrasova, T. 2007. "The processing of formulaic sequences by second language speakers". *The modern language journa.* 91(3). pp.433-445.

Kecskes, I. 2000. "A cognitive-pragmatic approach to situation-based utterances". *Journal of pragmatics 32.* pp.605-625.

Kormos, J. 2007. *Speech Production and Second Language Acquisition.* London: LEA.

Nattinger, J., &J, DeCarrico. 1992. *Lexical Phrases and Language Teaching.* Oxford: Oxford University Press.

Overstreet, M., & Yule, G. 2001. "Formulaic disclaimers". *Journal of pragmatics 33.* pp.45-60.

Pawley, A. &Syder, F.H. 1983. "Two Puzzles for linguistic theory: native-like selection and native-like fluency". In J.C.Richards & R.W.Schmidt (ed.) *Language and Communication* (pp. 126-138). London: Longman.

Schauer, G., & Adolphs, S. 2006. "Expressions of gratitude in corpus and DCT data: vocabulary, formulaic sequences, and pedagogy". *System 34.* pp119-134.

Schmitt, N., & Carter, R. 2004. "Formulaic sequences in action: an introduction". In Schmitt (ed.) *Formulaic sequences: acquisition, processing and use.* Philadelphia: John Benjamins, pp.1-22.

Schmitt, N., et al. 2004. "Are corpus-derived recurrent clusters psycholinguistically valid?". In N. Schmitt (ed.) *Formulaic sequences: Acquisition, processing, and use.* Philadelphia: John Benjamins, pp. 127-151.

Schmitt, N. (ed.) 2004. *Formulaic sequences: Acquisition, processing, and use.* Philadelphia: John Benjamins.

Schmitt, N. 2005. "Formulaic language: fixed and varied". *ELIA 6.* pp.13-39.

Underwood, G., et al. 2004. "The eyes have it: an eye-movement study into the processing of formulaic sequences". In N. Schmitt (ed.) *Formulaic sequences: Acquisition, processing, and use* (pp. 153–172). Philadelphia: John Benjamins.

Van Lancker, D. 2001. "Preserved formulaic expressions in a case of transcortical sensory aphasia compared to incidence in normal everyday speech". *Brain and language* 79. pp.38-41.

Van Lancker, D. 2004. "When novel sentences spoken or heard for the first time in the history of the universe are not enough: toward a dual-process model of language". *International journal of language and communication disorder* 39 (1). pp.1-44.

Weinert, R. 1995. "The role of formulaic language in second language acquisition: A review". *Applied Linguistics* 16. pp.180-205.

Wood, D. 2001. "In search of fluency: what is it and how can we teach it?". *The Canadian modern language review* 57(4). pp.573-589.

Wood, D. 2004. "An empirical investigation into the facilitating role of automatized lexical phrases in second language fluency development". *Journal of language and learning* 2(1). pp.27-50.

Wood, D. 2006. "Uses and functions of formulaic sequences in second language speech: an exploration of the foundations of fluency". *The Canadian modern language review* 63(1). pp. 13-33.

Wray, A., & Perkins, M. 2000. "The functions of formulaic language: an integrated model". *Language and communication* 20. pp.1-28.

Wray, A. 2002. *Formulaic Language and the Lexicon.* Cambridge: Cambridge University Press.

Yorio, C. 1980. "Conventionalized language forms and the development of communicative competence". *TESOL Quarterly* 14 (4). pp.433-442.

段士平，2008，国内二语语块教学述评，《中国外语》第 4 期，第 63-68 页。

马广惠，2009，英语专业学生二语限时写作中的词块研究，《外语教学与研究》第 1 期，第 54-60 页。

王立非、张大凤，2006，国外二语预制语块习得研究的方法进展与启示，《外语与外语教学》第 5 期，第 17-21 页。

严维华，2008，语块在语言输入和输出中的优势，《外语教育》第 1 期，第 99-105 页。

严维华，2003，语块对基本词汇习得的作用，《解放军外国语学院学报》第 6 期，第 58-62 页。

原萍、郭粉绒，2010，语块与二语口语流利性的相关性研究，《外语界》第 1 期，第 54-62 页。

张少林，2009，效应幅度：外语定量研究不能忽视的测度值，《外语教学理论与实践》第 3 期，第 69-72，98 页。

A study of cognitive advantage in formulaic sequence processing among Chinese learners of English

Abstract: Formulaic sequences processing, due to its coexistence of integral cognitive economy and structure and semantic comprehension complexity, is difficult to measure. This experiment explores the formulaic sequence processing mechanism employed by Chinese learners of English through measuring their reaction time and error rate in judging the grammaticality of formulaic and nonformulaic sequences. It is found out that formulaic sequences provide an unequivocal processing advantage over nonformulaic sequences in terms of processing speed and accuracy, that within formulaic sequences, idiom processing speed is slower and accompanied with more errors than that of non-idioms, showing the negative influence of structure complexity on processing, and that the main effect exists in the variable of language proficiency, with higher level learners having a tendency of processing the formulaic sequence as a whole with shorter response time and fewer errors.

Key Words: formulaicity; cognitive processing; advantage; reaction time; error rate; language proficiency

此文发表于《外语教学理论与实践》2013 年第 2 期

论表示目的的"テ形从句"及其定位

吴红哲

    摘　要：用テ形连接构成的复句，根据分句间的语义特点可以理解为各种不同的关系。这方面的研究已经很多，但对テ形从句表示目的的语言现象没有给予足够的重视。本文明确主张テ形从句可以表示目的，并对テ形目的从句的谓语动词类型、句法语义特点进行详细的探讨。

    关键词：目的从句；同时性；同一主体；意志性

1. 问题的提出

    众所周知，テ形可连接两个分句构成复句。但テ形不像「から」、「ので」等其他接续形式那样表示某一特定的逻辑关系，因此，由テ形连接而构成的复句根据分句的语义特点可以理解为各种不同的关系。这方面的研究已经很多，如大鹿（1986）、森田（1989）、语言学研究会（1989）、仁田（1995）等，对テ形连接可能实现的各种用法已经较详尽地进行了描述。尽管研究者之间在用法的分类标准以及所使用的名称等方面存在着异议，但大家普遍认为复句中テ形可以表示并列、附带状态、手段方法、先后顺序、原因理由等关系。

    然而，我们通过观察大量实例发现有些复句中的テ形从句很难归类为上述各种用法分类中的任何一类，并且这种用法并不少见。试看

下面例句①:

(1)（頼朝は）政子が長男万寿を懐妊したとき、<u>安産を祈って</u>、八幡宮から由比ケ浜に通ずる<u>参道を作った</u>。(BCCWJ 语料)

(2)サダム・フセイン元大統領が米軍に<u>拘束されたことを祝って</u>、市民が銃で<u>「祝砲」を乱射した</u>。(BCCWJ 语料)

(3)このニュースが中国に届くと、<u>二十一か条条約に抗議して</u>北京大学の学生三千人が天安門に集まり、五月四日から街頭に出て<u>デモを行った</u>。(BCCWJ 语料)

(4)そこで<u>本物を探して</u>名古屋の<u>農家をたずねた</u>スタッフが、「おたくの卵はブロイラーじゃないですよね」と、相手に質問してみた。(BCCWJ 语料)

我们认为上述例句中的テ形从句可以理解为表示目的，这一点从不改变句意的情况下可以用最具代表性的表示目的的「ために」来替换得到佐证。在这类テ形连接的复句中，前一个分句和后一个分句可看作构成［目的－方法］这一逻辑关系，即：前置的「安産を祈る」、「拘束されたことを祝う」、「二十一か条条約に抗議する」、「本物を探す」表示目的，而后置的「参道を作った」、「祝砲を乱射する」、「デモを行う」、「農家をたずねる」是为达到这一目的而采取的方法手段。而且，这类テ形复句的前后项顺序转换后句意保持不变，原来的目的分句、方法分句仍然表示目的和方法。如例句（1′）—（4′）。

(1′)<u>参道を作って</u>、<u>安産を祈る</u>。
　　　　方 法　　　　　目 的

(2′)<u>礼砲を乱射して</u>、<u>拘束されたことを祝う</u>。
　　　　方 法　　　　　目 的

---

① 本文所使用的例句绝大部分来自日本国立国语研究所『現代日本語書き言葉均衡コーパス（少納言）』，以下简称 BCCWJ 语料，并在例句末特别标示。为方便起见，部分例句在不影响原意的前提下进行了适当的删减。

（3´） デモを行って、二十一か条条約に抗議する。
方法 目的

（4´） 農家をたずねて、本物を探す。
方法 目的

这在テ形从句的各种用法中是一个独特的现象。我们知道除表示并列的テ形从句外，在其他用法中如果转换前后项的顺序，句意都会发生变化。基于以上语言现象，本文将类似例句（1）-（4）中的テ形从句认定为目的从句，并在详细探讨其特点的基础上，进一步探讨テ形目的从句的定位问题。

2. 先行研究及问题点

就笔者管见所及，在诸多先行研究中只有语言学研究会（1989）对表示目的的テ形从句有所涉及，认为「第二なかどめの位置に『さがす』『もとめる』というような動詞があらわれてくるとき、あるいは『しようとする』『しようとおもう』という動詞のかたちがあらわれてくるとき、第二なかどめは定形動詞によってさしだされる動詞の目的を表現するようになる」（语言学研究会 1989:39），并举出以下四个例句。

（5） 夜おそくまで、血眼になった補給部将校は受け持ちの梱包をさがして波打際をはしりまわっていた。

（6） 三人は日陰をもとめて、岩山のしたの松林の方へあるきだした。

（7） 日課を終わった後、三吉は家の方へ帰ろうとして、また鉄道の踏み切りをこした。

（8）「いいえ、これあたしのお古よ。この冬着ようとおもって、洗張をしたまま仕立てずにしまっといたの」

例句（5）、（6）的用法是本文所关注的表示目的的用法。但遗憾的是，语言学研究会（1989）只注意到「さがす」「もとめる」这一种类型，并没有观察到可以表示目的的其他动词类型，而且对它的特点也未进行进一步的论述。至于例句（7）、（8），这里的"目的"意义是源于「～ようとする」、「ようと思う」中的动词意向形，而不是「帰る」、「着る」动词的テ形本身，很显然这与例句（5）、（6）中テ形从句表示目的的现象需要区别对待①。

那么，目前为止研究者对本文所要探讨的这类テ形从句是如何看待的呢？据笔者的前期调查，先行研究中所使用的例句里几乎看不到类似（1）-（4）这一类型的例句，所以也很难判断它的归类。这类テ形从句之所以在先行研究中没有得到足够的重视，也许是因为构成这类从句的动词数量相对有限，但我们认为与这类テ形从句的前后项之间在时间顺序上有不同于其他用法有关。

一般认为，在テ形复句中「動的動詞の場合は、先の連用形による接続でも、並んだ順にそのことが生起する（した）意味が伴うのがふつうであるが、テ形による接続ではいっそうその感じが強くなる。とくに主格が同一の場合そうなる」（寺村，1991:219）②。仁田（1995）在论述"附带状态"时指出，前项和后项所表示的事态需要存在于同一时间段，但同时也指出「もっと言えば、二つの事象が「C1シテC2」のあり方で連結される時、その連結の順序にしたがって、事象「C1」と事象「C2」の間に、先行・後続の時間的関係を与えるのが、シテ形接続のもっとも基本的で無標な解釈であろう（そうでない意味を表すには、「C1」に、「C2」との同存を読み取りうる手掛かりが付与されなければならない）」（仁田1995:104）。渡边（1994）则认为，在テ形接続中テ形的语义功能在于「前件の事象が実現しているという認識に基づいて、後件の事象を語ること」（渡边，

---

① 仁田（1995:118-119）也谈到「しようとする」、「しようとおもう」表示目的的起因用法。
② 寺村（1991:219-221）把动词分为「動的動詞」和「静的動詞」，前者包括动作动词和变化动词。

1994：399) ①。

　　的确，绝大部分情况下テ形复句的前后项在时间顺序上是先后关系。尤其是前后项均为行为主体可控的意志动词且同一主体时这种现象更为明显。试看以下例句。

　　(9) 見たところ五十五六の品のいい小奇麗な老婦人が静かに坐って煙草を喫っていた。[仁田 1995：93 例 (2)]

　　(10) 李先生は、気が向けば台所へ入って包丁をふるう。

[仁田 1995：105 例 (3)]

　　(11) もし医者が留守で、行ってすぐ手術の用意ができないと困ると思って、電話を先にかけてもらうことを頼んだ。

[仁田 1995：113 例 (13)]

　　(12) 彼女は女中を買収して、私の顔を隙見したのだから。

[仁田 1995：119 例 (38)]

　　上述例句中，例句 (9) 为 "附带状态" 用法，表示动作主体在「煙草を喫う」时的＜し手容態＞；例句 (10) 为 "先后顺序" 用法，表示先「台所へ入る」，然后「包丁をふるう」；例句 (11) 为 "原因理由" 用法，表示「～困ると思った」这一主体的判断是「頼む」的理由；例句 (12) 为 "方法手段" 用法，表示动作主体通过「女中を買収する」的手段来达到「私の顔を隙見する」的目的。不管哪一种用法，前项都先于后项发生。即便是普遍认为具有＜同時性＞特点的 "附带状态" 用法也是如此。比如在例句 (9) 中，先「坐る」然后在这一动作结果持续的状态下进行「煙草を喫う」动作。因此，在这些句子的分句间插入表示前后顺序的接续词「それから」后句意基本保持不变。但也有一些例句中，前后项似乎可以理解为同时关系。试看以下例句。

---

① 包括在附带状态用法中，越过动词所表示事态的起点即视为「実現」。

（13）a. 石橋を叩いて渡る。

     b. 指を折って、数を数える。

例句（13a）、（13b）中，虽然第一次「石橋を叩く」、「指を折る」的动作开始点应该是先于「渡る」、「数を数える」，但本文将整个「石橋を叩く」、「指を折る」这一反复动作与「渡る」、「数を数える」看做同时关系。据此，我们把表示目的以外的テ形复句的前后项时间关系概括为：[前项≥后项]。

而本文认为可以表示目的的テ形复句，在时间顺序上恰恰与之相反。例如：

（14）サダム・フセイン元大統領が米軍に拘束されたことを祝って、市民が銃で「祝砲」を乱射した。[=例句（2）]

（14´）#祝砲を乱射した。それから、拘束されたことを祝った。

（15）そこで本物を探して名古屋の農家をたずねたスタッフが、「おたくの卵はブロイラーじゃないですよね」と、相手に質問してみた。[=例句（4）]

（15´）農家をたずねた。それから、本物を探した。

例句（14）可以理解为在「祝砲を乱射する」的同时，实现「拘束されたことを祝う」这一目的。但在例句（15）中，必须是先「農家をたずねる」然后才能「本物を探す」。因此，插入「それから」后前者句意发生变化[例句（14´）]，而后者句意保持不变[例句（15´）]。综上，我们把表示目的的テ形复句的前后项时间关系概括为：[前项≤后项]。

3. テ形目的从句的谓语动词类型

通过对实际调查中收集到的实例进行分析发现，出现在テ形目的从句的谓语动词有一定的倾向性，本文将它们分为以下几个类型。

3.1 「祈る」类

此类有心理动词中与表示积极意愿有关的少数几个动词，如「祈る」、「祈願する」、「祈念する」等。

（16）長篠の戦役で没した数多くの将兵の冥福を<u>祈って</u>、静かに手を合わせた。（BCCWJ 语料）

（17）日本の大晦日には、大掃除の末に、蕎麦のような長寿を<u>祈願して</u>年越し蕎麦を食べる習慣がある。（BCCWJ 语料）

（18）六月二日、幕府は火事の厄払いを<u>祈念して</u>、宝暦から明和へと改元した。（BCCWJ 语料）

心理动词所表达的是内心的状态或活动，在通常情况下不必借助外在的行为表现出来，如「考える」、「信じる」等。但「祈る」类心理动词虽然只表示心理活动，但往往会伴随外在的表现形式。如例句（16）中，以「手を合わせる」的行为来表现出「冥福を祈る」的心理活动，这时从句表示目的，主句表示实现这一目的的方法手段，即：分句间成立[目的-方法]关系。

纵观テ形从句的先行研究，学者们广泛关注的是心理动词中非意志性的心理状态或心理变化动词表示"附带状态"或"原因理由"的用法。如：「油断していたぼくらは相当に<u>あわてて</u>応戦したが～」（仁田1995:97），「妙に<u>いらいらして</u>、眠れないから、～」（仁田1995:111），而没有关注到「祈る」类意志性心理动词充当テ形从句谓语的情况。当然，「祈る」类有时可以用「ながら」替换，显示出与"附带状态"用法的相似性，这一点我们将在后面详述。

3.2 「祝う」类

此类动词数量较多，这类动词的共同特点可以概括为：表示对某一事态的对待活动或态度表明。其中，有些是积极的对待活动或态度

表明，如「祝う」、「記念する」、「称える」、「歓迎する」、「表彰する」等；有些是消极的对待活动或态度表明，如「抗議する」、「対抗する」、「雪ぐ」、「避ける」、「防止する」等。下面我们看其中几个例句。

　　(19) 三年目の今回は、二十一世紀の最初の年を<u>記念して</u>、二千一本の松を植える予定です。（BCCWJ 语料）

　　(20) 地元のリトアニア政府は九一年末に、人道的な行為を<u>称えて</u>首都ビリニュス旧市街の北西郊の新興地域にスギハラ通りという通り名を贈っている。（BCCWJ 语料）

　　(21) バブル崩壊後の九〇年代後半からは、銀行の貸し渋りに<u>対抗して</u>、企業が社債を発行して資金を調達する傾向が強まった。（BCCWJ 语料）

　　(22) ソ連の赤軍将兵は、その父兄がかつてそこで受けた国民的屈辱を<u>雪いで</u>、仇をとったのだ。（BCCWJ 语料）

　　这一类动词我们认为与「祈る」类非常接近，尤其是表示积极的对待活动或态度表明的「祝う」、「記念する」、「讃える」、「歓迎する」、「表彰する」等动词。以「祝う」为例，其词义为「めでたい事があったとき、それを喜ぶ気持ちを言葉などで表す」（『スーパー大辞林』三省堂 1995），词义上它由心理状态「喜ぶ気持ち」和其外在的行为表现形式「言葉などで表す」构成，把心理状态或活动及其外在表现形式包含在其中，而「祈る」类只表示心理活动。

3.3　「探す」类

　　这一类除语言学研究会（1989）提到的「さがす」、「求める」外，还有「訪ねる」等极个别的少数几个动词。

　　(23) アイスクリーム売りは、汗をかいて冷たいものをほしがってる子どもたちを<u>探して</u>、また別の公園にむかったんだろう。（BCCWJ 语料）

(24) 冬木は販路を求めて、東京中を走り回った。（BCCWJ 语料）

(25) そこで黒澤監督と私と二人連れで、彼を訪ねてハリウッド
へ行きました。（BCCWJ 语料）

在「探す」类中，主句谓语有其特点：它必须是与移动相关的动
词。如果主句谓语动词为表示起点、终点（「出る」、「発つ」、「寄る」、
「入る」等）或方向（「行く」、「来る」、「向かう」、「赴く」等）的移
动动词，那么就可以用表示移动目的的格助词「〜に」来替换。如：

(23´) 冷たいものをほしがってる子どもたちを探しに、別の公
園にむかった。

(25´) 黒澤監督と私と二人連れで、彼を訪ねにハリウッドへ行
った。

通过以上所举例句的分析，テ形目的从句的句法语义特点可以概
括为：

①前后项的行为主体为同一主体，且前后项谓语动词均为意志性
动词，是行为主体可控的事态；

②前后项事态的时间关系是[前项≤后项]，且前项谓语动词表示
抽象动作，后项谓语动词表示具体动作。

关于第一点，尽管本文所给出的有些例句并没有明确出现行为主
体，但我们可以从上下文语境判断出前后项为同一行为主体可控的事
态，本文不再赘述，在此我们着重探讨第二点。テ形目的从句有三个
类型，即：「祈る」类、「祝う」类、「探す」类。如：

(26) 長篠の戦役で没した数多くの将兵の冥福を祈って、静かに
手を合わせた。[=例句 (16)]

(27) 三年目の今回は、二十一世紀の最初の年を記念して、二千
一本の松を植える予定です。[=例句 (19)]

(28) そこで黒澤監督と私と二人連れで、彼を訪ねてハリウッド

へ行。[=例句（25）]

　　前面已经谈到，表示目的的テ形复句中前后项的时间关系有两种可能。一种是同时关系[如例句（26）（27）]，一种是后项先于前项[如例句（28）]，本文把这种时间关系概括为：[前项≤后项]。那么，这里的[前项≤后项]这一时间关系又有什么特点呢？通过上述例句的分析不难发现，可以理解为表示目的的テ形复句的一大特点是：实施后项动作即意味着实施前项动作，这时前项谓语动词表示抽象动作，而后项谓语动词表示具体动作。以例句（26）—（28）为例，实施后项「手を合わせる」、「松を植える」、「ハリウッドへ行く」等具体动作，即意味着实施前项所表示的「没した数多くの将兵の冥福を祈る」、「二十一世紀の最初の年を記念する」、「彼を訪ねる」等抽象动作。

　　通常情况下，我们的行为都有其目的或意图，而这类テ形复句中，从句正是表示主句所表示的行为目的，主从句之间构成[目的-方法（行为）]关系。

4. 与"附带状态"的关系

　　表示目的的テ形复句中前后项的时间关系是[前项≤后项]，而其他用法中前后项的时间关系是[前项≥后项]，也就是说，两者都有表示同时关系的情况。下面我们通过对同时满足同一主体、意志性、同时性的テ形复句进行比较，弄清テ形目的从句与其他相关用法之间渐次重叠、连绵渐变的关系。

　　根据语言学研究会（1989）、仁田（1995）、吉永（1993）等研究，以下各句为同时满足同一主体、意志性、同时性的テ形复句。

　　（29）彼はラッパをふいて、新聞を売りにくるような女のあるような在郷くさい町はずれへきていた。（语言学研究会，1989：17）

　　（30）家鴨は～忙しく足を動かして、上流の方へ泳いでいった。

[仁田，1995：99 例句（27）]

（31）板敷きを<u>踏んで</u>、目指す方向へ渡った。[吉永，1993：2 例句（19）]

（32）雄鶏の憎らしい表情を見ると、里子は小屋の金綱を<u>ぎしぎしゆすぶって</u>、雄鶏を<u>おどかした</u>。（语言学研究会，1989：19）

（33）祖母は手を<u>叩いて</u>、拍子を取った。[吉永，1993：2-3 例句（18）]

以上テ形复句在仁田（1995）、吉永（1993）的研究中没有区别对待，一并归入到"附带状态"中表示主体动作的用法。它的特点是，从句所表示的动作主的反复性可控动作，与主句所表示的动作共存于同一时间内。但如果关注主句的谓语动词，例句（29）—（31）和例句（32）—（33）之间还是有区别的。

例句（29）—（31）的前后项谓语动词由[具体动作-具体动作]构成（以下称 A 类），而例句（32）—（33）由[具体动作-抽象动作]构成（以下称 B 类）。我们认为其中一项由抽象动词构成的 B 类与本文所探讨的表示目的的テ形从句有着某种相似性。前面已经谈到，テ形目的复句有别于其他用法的一大特点是，前后项顺序转换后句意保持不变，原来的目的分句、方法分句转换顺序后仍然表示目的和方法[见例句（1′）—（4′）]。在此，我们对同样表示[方法-目的]关系的 A、B 两类例句（34a）、（35a）进行前后项顺序转换，得出例句（34b）、（35b）。试比较：

（34）a. 忙しく足を動かして、上流のほうへ泳いでいく。

b. 上流のほうへ泳いでいって、忙しく足を動かす。

（35）a. 金綱をゆすぶって、雄鶏をおどかす。

b. 雄鶏をおどかして、金綱をゆすぶる。

我们发现，此时例句（34b）句意发生变化，转换顺序后已经不能构成[目的-方法]关系，而例句（35b）虽然有些歧义，但仍有理解为为

了「雄鶏をおどかす」而采取「金綱をゆすぶる」这一方法手段这样一种[目的-方法]关系的可能性，可接受程度也相对高一些。

再来看下面的例句。此类テ形复句在先行研究中几乎被忽略，但我们在实际调查中收集到为数不少的实例。它的特点是，前项谓语经常出现「からかう」、「批判する」、「非難する」、「促す」、「忠告する」等抽象的发话动词，而后项由「～と言う」引出具体的发话内容（以下称 C 类）。

(36) その時は、すごく大変だったのですが、監督を始め、先輩やスタッフは私をからかって「少しはクラクラしてきたか？」と言っていました。（BCCWJ 语料）

(37) たまたま同じ強い点を持っている人同士が集まって、その分野において弱い人たちのことを批判して「あんなことをするなんて私には考えられないことです」と一人が言った。

（BCCWJ 语料）

我们认为上述 C 类例句中的テ形从句，已经更加接近于本文所探讨的表示目的的用法，结构上完全相同，前后项谓语动词都是[抽象动作-具体动作]结构。此类テ形复句，如果把后项的具体发话内容「～と言う」替换成相关的具体行为，就很容易理解成表示[目的-方法]关系。下面举两个实例：

(38) アレンは自分を拒否した大学をからかって、シティ・カレッジの女子学生という設定にしている。（BCCWJ 语料）

(39) チャールズ・チャップリンは、機械文明の進歩を批判して、『モダン・タイムス』を製作した。（BCCWJ 语料）

通过以上分析我们看到，表示目的的テ形复句与"附带状态"中的主体动作用法在同一主体、意志性、同时性等方面有着相似性，并以其中的 B 类以及 C 类为中介，在用法之间形成渐次重叠、连绵渐变的一个连续的类型。

5. 结语

"テ形从句"可以表示目的，这一点长期以来一直为日语研究界所忽视。本文明确主张"テ形从句"可以表示目的，并对テ形目的从句的谓语动词类型、句法语义特点进行了详细的探讨。主要结论如下：

（1）可以出现在テ形目的从句的谓语动词有：「祈る」类、「祝う」类、「探す」类。

（2）表示目的的テ形复句中，前项为抽象的可控动词，后项为具体的可控动词；实施后项动作，即意味着实施前项动词。

（3）テ形目的从句在同一主体、意志性、同时性等方面与"附带状态"中表示主体动作的用法有相似之处，并以其中的 B 类以及 C 类为中介形成一个连续的类型。

参考文献

大鹿薫久，1986，『て』接続考，《叙説》12 号，219-228。

森田良行，1989，《基礎日本語辞典》，東京：角川書店。

言語学研究会・構文論グループ，1989，なかどめ－動詞の第二なかどめのばあい－，《ことばの科学 2》，東京：むぎ書房，11-47。

仁田義雄，1995，シテ接続をめぐって，《複文の研究（上）》，東京：出版くらしお，87-126。

寺村秀夫，1991，《日本語のシンタクスと意味Ⅲ》，東京：黒くろしお潮出版。

渡辺文生，1994，接続形式「～テ」の意味に関する一考察，《山形大学紀要（人文科学）》，13/1，392-402。

松村明，1995，《スーパー人辞林》，東京：三省堂。

吉永尚，1993，付帯状況を表すテ形動詞について，《園田語文》

第 7 号, 1-13。

A Study On The TE Clause of Purpose

Abstract: The semantic relations between the Clauses linked by TE can be understood in different ways. Though there have been quite a number of studies on this phenomenon, the TE clause has not been given much attention as a grammatical means to express purpose. This paper is aimed to provide a detailed typological description on the predicate verb in the TE clause, including its syntactic and semantic features.

key words: clause of purpose; synchronization; same subject; volition

此文发表于《日语学习与研究》2014 年第 3 期

基于语料库的中国大陆与本族语学者英语科研论文模糊限制语比较研究

——以国际期刊《纳米技术》论文为例

徐江　郑莉　张海明

摘　要： 本文通过自建语料库，对比分析了中国大陆学者与英语本族语学者发表在国际期刊《纳米技术》上的英文科研论文中使用模糊限制语的异同。研究显示，中国大陆学者模糊限制语使用比例总体略高于本族语学者，除结论外论文其余各部分中国学者使用模糊限制语比例均超出本族语学者，但引言部分没有显著性差异。中国大陆学者使用的四小类限制语仅有间接缓和型使用比例低于本族语学者，程度变动、范围变动、直接缓和三种类型使用频率二者没有显著差异。两个语料库模糊限制语均以实义动词和情态动词比例最高，名词最少。两类学者使用频率最高的模糊限制语有较多重叠，但有些词在使用频率和用法上呈现显著差异，中国大陆学者还有误用和跨语体使用等问题。

关键词： 模糊限制语；科研论文语料库；中国大陆学者；英语本族语学者

1. 引言

模糊限制语普遍存在并使用于人类所使用的语言。语言表述有时客观上没有必要精确或无法精确，有时主观上为了使语言更加委婉得体或更有利于言者自我保护，人们都会使用模糊限制语，因此模糊限制语常被视作一种重要的交际策略（Brown & Levinson，1987：145）。

作为特殊的书面交流形式，学术论文中的模糊限制语也受到了我国学术界的广泛关注。应该说对学术论文中模糊限制语的研究已经不少，但这些研究有的是对英语科技语体中的模糊限制语表现形式、理据及分类的探讨，如赵英玲（1999）、杨慧玲（2001）；有的主要从英汉对比角度考察两种语言科技论文中模糊限制语的差异性，如王舟（2008）、刘珍（2003）；有的侧重于母语迁移对中国学者英语科技论文中使用模糊限制语的影响，如刘珍（2003）；有的主要考察学术论文摘要部分中国与本族语学者模糊限制语的使用异同，如王舟（2008）、冯茵等（2007）；有的从语篇语用和人际意义角度对学术论文中的模糊限制语进行了研究，如黄小苹（2002）、徐润英等（2009）。关于中国大陆与本族语学者在英语学术论文中模糊限制语使用情况对比研究目前尚不多见。从知网查询结果来看，仅有余千华等（2001）做过此类研究，但余千华等主要就模糊限制语中特定的词加以统计，并没有对模糊限制语进行分类统计，也没有对比分析模糊限制语在论文各个部分的分布情况。同时他们考察的是本族语者在英美人士主办、主审的四种英语原版科技期刊上发表的论文和中国大陆科技工作者在中国大陆主办、主审的四种英语科技期刊上发表的英语论文，期刊分别涉及数学、物理、化学或医学和水利工程等。研究表明，期刊类别（Namsarvaev，1997）和学科门类（徐润英等，2009）等都会影响论文中模糊限制语的使用，所以这两个因素可能会对该研究产生不可忽视的影响。为了避免由于期刊和学科不同而可能存在的自身语言差异性，笔者从专门研究纳米技术的国际性刊物《纳米技术》2006—2007 年所发表的论文中选取了大陆学者和本族语学者撰写的各 40 篇学术论文组成小型语料库，通过对比分析中外学者在模糊限制语的使用频率、类型、文中分布以及用法等方面的异同，以期对我国英文学术写作教学及其实践提供参考。

2. 模糊限制语的分类及其表现形式

模糊限制语是莱科夫（Lakoff）最早提出的一个概念，他把模糊限制语定义为"把事情弄得模模糊糊的词语"（Lakoff，1972）。在相当长的一段时间里，语言学界对模糊限制语的研究主要集中在语义层面，直到 20 世纪 80 年代，研究视角才开始逐渐拓展到社会语言学、语用学和语篇分析等领域，对模糊限制语的界定范围也随之扩大。从现有研究来看，模糊限制语已经从词汇、语法结构扩大到了语篇。

不同学者对模糊限制语也提出了各自不同的分类标准。陈林华、李福印（1994）按照语义特征将模糊限制语分为程度模糊限制语、范围模糊限制语、数量模糊限制语、质量模糊限制语和方式模糊限制语。海兰德（Hyland，1996a）从语用角度，根据使用者背后的深层动机，把模糊限制语分成缓和命题内容与现实之间关系的内容导向模糊限制语和以作者为中心，保护作者可能受到否定或挑战的读者导向模糊限制语。但迄今为止比较有影响力的仍是美国语言学家普林斯等（Prince et al.，1982）从语用角度对模糊限制语的划分。按照他们的观点，模糊限制语可以分为两大类，即变动型模糊限制语和缓和型模糊限制语。前者可以改变话语的真值条件，属于语义范畴，而后者只是体现言者对话语内容所持有的态度，而不会改变话题内容，属于语用范畴。变动型模糊限制语可以再分为程度变动型和范围变动型。程度变动型指根据已知情况对原有话语意义做某种程度的修正，范围变动型则给原话语定出一个变动范围。缓和型模糊限制语也可以进一步划分为直接缓和型和间接缓和型。前者表示言者对话题的直接猜测或所持态度，后者通过引用他人的看法或观点间接性地表达自己对某事情的态度。

3. 研究设计

3.1 研究问题

本研究拟主要回答以下问题：①中国大陆学者与本族语学者使用模糊限制语总量及其在论文中的分布位置是否存在差异？②两类学者使用的模糊限制语类别是否存在差异？③两类学者在模糊限制语的用法和质量方面是否存在差异？

3.2 语料及其处理

本研究自建语料库基于 IOP 中国高等教育文献保障系统（CALIS）本地站点获取的 2006—2007 年发表在专业杂志《纳米技术》上的 80 篇论文构成，中国大陆学者论文和本族语学者论文各 40 篇。学者身份通过作者单位并结合姓名特征加以认定，不同国家合作完成研究论文也被剔除，最终本族语学者分别来自美国、英国、澳大利亚和加拿大。

表 1　数据库论文构成情况

学者类型		论文篇数	正文总词数（不含摘要）	
中国大陆学者（CS）		40	105,078	
本族语学者（NS）	美国	20	65,397	125,113
	英国	11	30,188	
	澳大利亚	6	21,750	
	加拿大	3	7,778	
总计		80	230,191	

硬科学学术论文通常采用 IMRAD 格式，即由 Introduction，Methods，Results 和 Discussion 构成。斯克尔顿（Skelton，1988）研究发现，硬科学学术论文中模糊限制语分布不均，各部分使用频率从高到低依次为讨论（包括结论）、引言、结果与方法。为了确保研究的效度，我们在选取论文时严格要求文章必须具有清晰的引言、实验结果、讨论和结论四个部分。

表 2　两类论文各部分词数统计

类别	引言	实验	结果与讨论	结论
中国大陆学者	17,431	17,116	65,616	4,915
本族语学者	23,645	22,129	71,534	7,805

为了便于统计，我们将两大语料库分为全文语料库和分解语料库。分解语料库由两大全文语料库论文各自分解为引言、实验结果、讨论和结论的四个子语料库组成。此外，我们将这些语料又使用 TreeTagger2.0 进行词性标注处理，形成标注语料库。

3.3　语料分析方法

通过多次通读 80 篇论文，确定文中所使用的模糊限制语并结合相关研究提供的模糊限制语，最终形成自己的模糊限制语集合，对论文中的模糊限制语进行逐一的穷尽性检索，并使用 SPSS 进行相关系数统计分析。

由于某些模糊限制语词项有多词性和多词义性质，在使用检索软件 Antconc3.2.4 统计时就可以根据需要选用标注或未标注语料。比如统计程度变动型模糊限制语 most 或 much，则可以将标注语料导入统计软件，直接输入 most RBS 或 much RB 加以统计，统计范围变动型限制语 most 或 much 则可统计 most_JJS 或 much_JJ 的数量。我们没有使用词形还原技术，这是因为语境对认定模糊限制语具有决定性的作用（Mauranen，1997），某些属于缓和型模糊限制语的动词，其使用形式对其归类有着决定性的作用。比如 assume, believe, calculate, conclude, deduce, detect 等谓语动词与第一人称主语 I/we 搭配使用，则属直接缓和型，而与非第一人称主语搭配或使用被动语态结构则属间接缓和型。保留其文中原有词形对模糊限制语类别的认定至关重要，既未加词性标注也没词形还原的语料更便于阅读。所以统计这类词的模糊限制语数量时，我们则先将生语料导入检索软件，使用软件的高级检索功能，将动词的各种曲折变化形式纳入统计范围，形成统计数据 1。然后观察含有该词的所有句子，根据语境判断除了 I 和 we 之外，还有哪些同现词会使其成为直接缓和型模糊限制语（如 conclude 出现在 lead us to conclude 中，us 就与 I 和 we 具有了同等重要的识别功能）。在此基础上再将其前面的同现词限定为 I、we 和其他具有同等重要识别功能的同现词，形成统计数据 2。数据 2 就是直接缓和型数据，数据 1 去除数据 2 相关词的词频后就是间接缓和型的词频数据。为了避免检索软件自动检索误认所导致的统计数据污染问题，我们对所有搜索结果还需语境分析加以确认，剔除那些词形相同但并非模糊限制语的词频。例如下句中的 calculate 表示"计算"而非"估计"，所以不是模糊限制语。

The conductivity of the handsheet was <u>calculated</u> by measuring the current-voltage characteristics using a Keithley measurement system and is given in figure 11.

4. 研究结果与讨论

4.1 模糊限制语在两类论文中的总量及其分布

表3 模糊限制语在两类论文各个部分分布情况统计表

（相对数按 1,000 词计算）

类别		变动型模糊限制语				缓和型模糊限制语			
		程度变动		范围变动		直接缓和		间接缓和	
		绝对数	相对数	绝对数	相对数	绝对数	相对数	绝对数	相对数
大陆学者	引言	57	3.27	121	6.94	193	11.07	159	9.12
	实验	5	0.29	90	5.26	48	2.80	18	1.05
	结果与讨论	284	4.33	458	6.98	998	15.21	669	10.19
	结论	21	4.27	15	3.05	97	19.74	34	6.92
	合计	367	3.49	684	6.50	1336	12.71	880	8.37
本族语学者	引言	84	3.55	170	7.19	301	12.73	119	5.03
	实验	34	1.54	32	1.45	77	3.48	54	2.44
	结果与讨论	229	3.20	444	6.20	849	11.87	896	12.53
	结论	36	4.61	28	3.59	133	17.04	100	12.81
	合计	383	3.06	674	5.39	1360	10.87	1169	9.34

表4 组统计量

学者类型	N	均值	标准差	均值的标准误
中国学者	40	81.6750	9.23313	1.45989
本族语学者	40	89.6500	23.14564	3.65965

　　两数据库对比显示，中国大陆学者所使用的模糊限制语形符总数为3,267词，在文中所占比例为31.09/千词，本族语者使用总量为3,586词，比例为28.66/千词。前者高于后者，且具有统计显著性（p=0.048）

（见表 5）。

表 5　独立样本 T 检验

模糊限制语总量	方差方程的 Levene 检验		均值方程的 t 检验						
	F	Sig.	t	df	Sig.（双侧）	均值差值	标准误差值	差分的 95% 置信区间	
								下限	上限
假设方差相等	33.031	.000	-2.024	78	.046	-7.97500	3.94009	-15.81911	-.13089
假设方差不相等			-2.024	51.106	.048	-7.97500	3.94009	-15.88466	-.06534

　　从模糊限制语的分布位置来看，虽然两类学者在结果与讨论部分使用模糊限制语的绝对数量均为最高，但若按模糊限制语在论文各部分使用的相对数计算，则有所不同。中国学者使用模糊限制语相对数降序排列为：结果与讨论>结论>引言>实验，而本族语学者分别依次为：结论>结果与讨论>引言>实验，除引言部分没有显著差别外（p=0.068），结论、结果与讨论和实验部分均具有统计显著性（p 值分别为 0.016，0.003 和 0.049）。变动型和缓和型模糊限制语在两类学者论文各部分出现的多少排列顺序也不尽一致。两个语料库缓和型模糊限制语降序排列一致，依次为：结论>结果与讨论>引言>实验，但变动型则有所不同。大陆学者论文降序排列依次为：结果与讨论>引言>结论>实验，而本族语学者论文降序排列为：结果与讨论>结论>引言>实验。除结论和实验部分没有显著差异外（p 值分别为 0.165 和 0.191），结果与讨论部分以及引言部分均具有显著性差异（p 值分别为 0.002 和 0.001）。

　　在模糊限制语的使用数量上，本族语学者除论文结论部分使用的模糊限制语总体比例高于大陆学者外，其余各部分使用总体数量均低于中国学者。若将变动型和缓和型细分为程度变动、范围变动、直接缓和、间接缓和四类加以分析，中国大陆学者使用的各类限制语仅有间接缓和型使用比例低于本族语学者，且具有统计显著性（p=0.048），其他三种类型使用频率虽高于本族语学者，但不存在显著性差异（程度变动、范围变动和直接缓和三类限制语的 p 值分别为 0.061，0.222 和 0.471）。

中国大陆学者使用模糊限制语数量反超本族语学者可能是由两大因素促成：一是中国学者的学术地位。尽管麦尔斯（Myers，1989）认为，任何人，无论其地位如何，都必须以其学科领域谦逊的仆人身份进行写作，但马尔卡宁和施罗德（Markkanen & Shroder，1997）认为，模糊限制语使用数量与作者在该领域的地位、潜在的读者以及作者的性格密切相关。中国学者使用模糊限制语数量较多可能源于其处于国际学术话语弱势地位，陈述观点时必须小心谨慎，更多地利用缓和手段削弱强加色彩和断言程度，给读者以谦逊的印象，从而使自己的观点更加容易为审稿人和读者所接受。二是文化因素。中国传统文化强调人际的和谐，特别好'稳'，不可'冒失'（何刚、张春燕，2006），主张说话处事要留有余地。反映在学术论文中可能就是大量使用模糊限制语，将表达猜疑或保留态度的话尽量说得缓和一些，把接近正确但不敢肯定完全正确的话题说得得体一些。

4.2　模糊限制语词类比较

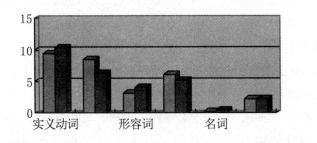

（按每 1,000 词计算）

图 1　模糊限制语各词类相对数量

从词类来看，两类学者使用的模糊限制语总体均以实义动词和情态动词频率最高，名词最少。变动型模糊限制语也以副词最多，形容词次之，短语第三，实义动词最少。程度变动模糊限制语中，本族语者和中国学者使用的几乎都是副词，形容词极少；范围变动模糊限制语两类学者均以形容词、副词和短语为主，但大陆学者以副词使用频率最高，为另两类模糊限制语的两倍以上，而本族语者以形容词使用数量最多，且形容词、副词、短语使用数量比较均衡。

两大语料库中使用的缓和型模糊限制语按词类绝对数量来看基本一致，使用最多的为实义动词，情态动词第二，其余依次为形容词、短语、名词和副词。但大陆学者论文中实义动词和情态动词数量接近，本族语者实义动词总数超过情态动词近 70%。直接缓和型模糊限制语中，中国学者使用情态动词总数为 891，占直接缓和型模糊限制语总数的 66.69%，本族语者使用情态动词总数为 784，占直接缓和型模糊限制语总数的 57.65%；实义动词类缓和型模糊限制语中国学者共使用 993 次，占缓和型模糊限制语总数的 44.81%，本族语者共使用 1287 次，占缓和型模糊限制语总数的 50.89%。形容词在两个语料库中的缓和型模糊限制语中所占比例仅相差 2 个百分点，没有显著差异（p=0.238），但直接缓和语中国学者使用的近乎一半是-like 派生词（如 cable-like、flower-like 等），而本族语学者论文中仅有 15 例。如果剔出这一部分形容词，中国学者所使用的形容词性缓和型模糊限制语数量仅有 87 个，占缓和型模糊限制语总数的 3.92%，而本族语学者形容词总数则为 226，占缓和型模糊限制语总数的 8.94%，是大陆学者的 2 倍以上。

大陆语料库中实义动词与本族语者一样为模糊限制语中使用比例最高的词类。按照海兰德和米尔顿（Hyland & Milton，1997）的观点，副词本身可以表达清晰的级差概念、句法功能简单，句中位置比较灵活，对于使用英语尚不太自信的非本族语者来说副词使用起来相对比较容易。而实义动词虽然也能够显性、甚至比副词更加精确地表达作者对命题内容的承诺以及对信息来源可靠性的自我判断，但认识性动词①的恰当使用不仅需要仔细挑选词汇，而且还需考虑时态、语态等相关问题，使选用实义动词变得更加复杂往往令作者却步。这一论点和我国学者使用实义动词情况并不相符。尽管我国学者使用的副词比例较高，但实义动词使用频率和本族语者一样在所有词类中是最高的。那么我国学者使用认识动词比例如此之高，原因何在？林同济（1980）、刘丹青（2010）认为汉语是一种动词型语言，其主要特征是"汉语句子中动词出现的频率惊人地高"（林同济，1980）。因此，母语迁移极有可能是我国学者英语论文中动词性模糊限制语数量较高的原因。前人研究也为这一假设提供了支持。尼克拉（Nikula，1997）发现以英语为第二语言的芬兰人在讲英语时更多地使用与他们母语有相近含义的模糊限制语；刘珍（2003）发现，在中国科技工作者写的英语科技文章中出现频率较高的模糊限制语，其相应的汉语表达形式在汉语的科技文章中出现的频率也较高。艾杰默（Aijmer，2002）也认为瑞典人在英语书面语中过多使用某些情态动词可能源于母语影响。

两个语料库形容词和名词使用频率没有显著性差异（p 值分别为 0.327 和 0.683），这说明我国学者对形容词和名词的模糊限制语功能有了相当的了解。例如将认识性动词和认识性形容词转换成名词加以表述就是名词化过程。研究表明，以名词化为典型特征的概念语法隐喻在增强科技语篇的技术性和理性色彩的同时，也使语篇具有了客观性，因为语法隐喻手段在对经验成分名词化时，事件的参与者及其事件的逻辑关系均被"隐喻"出语篇之外（董宏乐，2003），造成一种施事缺席的效果，从而最大限度地保护说话人。

①即能够表达作者对命题内容的确信程度、对陈述的真实性的承诺程度，以及某事可能性的判断等的动词，如 believe，think，infer，know 等；能够表达此类情态的形容词就是认识性形容词，如 possible，probable，(un)likely 等。

4.3　模糊限制语类别比较

4.3.1　变动型模糊限制语比较

表6　变动型模糊限制语分布情况统计表

（相对数按 1,000 词计算）

排序	大陆学者		本族语学者	
	程度变动型	范围变动型	程度变动型	范围变动型
	词项（绝对数/相对数）	词项（绝对数/相对数）	词项（绝对数/相对数）	词项（绝对数/相对数）
1	very（91/0.87）	about（144/1.37）	Very（58/0.46）	Some（63/0.50）
2	much（36/0.34）	Several（65/0.62）	highly（49/0.39）	About（56/0.45）
3	greatly（30/0.29）	some（60/0.57）	relatively（36/0.29）	several（54/0.43）
4	relatively（28/0.27）	various（47/0.45）	significantly（30/0.24）	approximately（48/0.38）
5	most（27/0.26）	many（44/0.42）	much（30/0.24）	various（40/0.32）
6	significantly（24/0.23）	usually（33/0.31）	even（23/0.18）	around（35/0.28）
7	obviously（19/0.18）	almost（32/0.30）	too（21/0.17）	many（34/0.27）
8	highly（16/0.15）	in the range（30/0.29）	slightly（20/0.16）	less than（26/0.21）
9	mainly（14/0.13）	around（28/0.27）	most（14/0.11）	generally（24/0.19）
10	quite（12/0.11）	nearly（20/0.19）	in particular（13/0.10）	most（23/0.18）

变动型模糊限制语中，中国大陆学者使用的程度变动语共有 367 个，占变动型模糊限制语总量的 34.92 %，种类有 29 个词项，范围变动语有 684 个，占变动型模糊限制语总量的 65.08%，种类达 31 个词项，而本族语学者使用的程度变动语有 383 个，占变动型模糊限制语总量

的 36.23%，有 29 种词项，范围变动语为 674 个，占变动型模糊限制语总量的 63.77 %，种类多达 41 种。两类学者使用程度变动型和范围变动型模糊限制语的比例上没有显著差异（p 值分别为 0.061 和 0.222），中国学者使用的程度变动语种类和本族语学者一样丰富，但范围变动型种类却不及后者。

虽然两类学者使用频率最高的 10 个程度变动语中有 5 个相同（very, highly, relatively, significantly, much），但仅有使用频次最多的 very 排序一致，且大陆学者使用 very 的频率远超本族语学者，是其 1.89 倍，具有显著性差异（p=0.021）。其余 4 个词中，much、relatively、significantly 二者基本持平，但 highly 使用频次大幅低于本族语者，只有本族语者的 38.46%，具有显著性差异（p=0.004）。这与 Atai & Sadr（2008）对波斯语本族语者和英语本族语者英语研究论文中模糊限制语使用情况对比研究结果基本一致。Atai & Sadr 发现，英语本族语者使用最多的副词性模糊限制语为 highly 和 relatively，而波斯语本族语者使用 significantly 频率最高。

中外学者使用最多的前五个范围变动型模糊限制语中有 4 个词完全相同（about，several，some，various），只是排序略有不同；中国学者使用相对频次均高于本族语者，其中尤以 about 最为突出，是本族语者的 3 倍，具有显著性差异（p=0.006），其余三个词没有显著性差异（p 值分别为 0.412，0.081 和 0.277）。

二类学者使用变动型限制语词类没有明显差异：程度变动型基本均为副词，形容词极少；范围变动型限制语中形容词和副词使用都比较均衡，不过中国学者使用的范围变动型短语数量明显低于本族语者（p=0.000），表达方式也不及后者丰富。比如表达数值在某一范围内变化时两类学者都使用了与 range 有关的短语。中国学者仅限于使用 in the range of、ranging from…to …, in the range from … to …, a wide range of, within the range, in the range +数词；本族语学者则使用了 in the range of, ranging from … to …, a range of, range of, wide ranges of, a wide range of, an extensive range of, a diverse range of, a huge range of, range between…and…,within the range of, in the range +数词, in the +名词

+range+数词。表达方式的有限性反映出中国学者缺乏语言变化的能力。

此外，quite、almost 等是日常会话型模糊限制语，属于非正式语体词，正式语体的学术论文中一般很少出现（Hinkel，2004：323）。在本族语者论文中，quite 没有出现，almost 虽有使用，但频率仅为 0.13/千词，但大陆学者使用频率最高的前 10 个变动型模糊限制语中就有这两种。

4.3.2 缓和型模糊限制语比较

4.3.2.1 缓和型模糊限制语实义动词比较

表 7　缓和型模糊限制语实义动词类型

分类	揣测性动词			证据性动词			推理性动词			总计		
	绝对数	缓和比①	认动比	绝对数	缓和比	认动比	绝对数	缓和比	认动比	绝对数	缓和比	认动比
CS	367	16.56	48.35	335	15.12	44.13	57	2.57	7.52	759	34.25	100
NS	366	14.47	38.94	508	20.09	54.04	66	2.61	7.02	940	37.17	100

表 8　缓和型模糊限制语最常用实义动词

（相对数按 1,000 词计算）

排序	大陆学者				本族语学者			
	词项	绝对数	相对数	认动比	词项	绝对数	相对数	认动比
1	indicate	131	1.25	17.26	observe	264	2.11	28.09
2	observe	114	1.08	15.02	find	126	1.01	13.40
3	find	102	0.97	13.44	indicate	124	0.99	13.19
4	see	75	0.71	9.88	demonstrate	68	0.54	7.23
5	suggest	55	0.52	7.25	suggest	57	0.46	6.06
6	demonstrate	52	0.49	6.85	see	53	0.42	5.64
7	reveal	47	0.45	6.19	reveal	39	0.31	4.15
8	propose	36	0.34	4.74	propose	29	0.23	3.86
9	detect	30	0.29	3.95	assume	25	0.20	2.66
10	estimate	22	0.21	2.89	estimate	24	0.19	2.55

---

① 缓和比=在缓和型模糊限制语中所占百分比；认动比=在认识动词中所占百分比。

　　排在前 10 位的缓和型模糊限制语实义动词基本相同，但在使用频率上存在一定的差异。海兰德（Hyland，1996b）将认识性动词分为揣测性动词、证据性动词和推理性动词。揣测性动词表明对命题的真实性存在猜测成分，如 suggest, speculate, believe, indicate 等。例如，"Thus, we *propose* that this insert is the major site of interaction with the membrane." 证据性动词一类是表示作者命题具有合理的依据，如基于自己的感知、理解或者他人的报告等，如 appear, seem, observe，detect 等，另一类是那种使获得证据的方式或知晓过程变得模糊的动词，如 seek, attempt 等。例如，"We *sought/attempted* to investigate this by studying the regulatory properties of PEPc kinase." 推理性动词则表明判断是基于推理得出，而非揣测，如 calculate, infer, deduce 等。例如，"On the basis of the elemental depth profile and our structural model, we may *infer* that the depth of the SiO2 nanoislands is ~40 nm."

　　中国大陆学者使用最多的是揣测性认识动词 indicate，占认识动词的 17.26%，高于本族语者的 13.19%，但没有显著性差异（p=0.143）。本族语学者使用最多的是证据性认识动词 observe，占认识动词的 28.09%，几近中国学者使用比例的 2 倍，具有显著性差异（p=0.002）；中国大陆学者使用的揣测性动词、推理性动词和证据性动词分别占认识动词总数的 48.35%，7.52% 和 44.13%，而本族语学者使用的认识动词中，这三类动词使用比例分别为 38.94%，7.02% 和 54.04%，但仅有证据性动词具有显著性差异（p=0.002），揣测性动词和推理性动词则不具显著差异（p 值分别为 0.976 和 0.397）。中国学者最偏爱使用揣测性动词，其次是证据性动词；本族语学者则恰恰相反，证据性动词远远超过揣测性动词。这与海兰德（1996b）的研究结果不尽一致。海兰德发现本族语学者使用三类动词显现出如下特征：对揣测性动词的偏爱胜过推理性动词，对揣测性和推理性动词的偏爱胜过证据性动词。中国大陆学者对三类动词的偏好模式更加接近 Hyland 的判断。由此看来，中国和本族语学者一样不仅依靠试验证据而且还倾向于使用谨慎的语用策略论述、支持自己的观点，但本族语者更加强调让事实说话的严谨科学态度。

中国学者与本族语学者在实义动词的使用上也表现出明显差异。虽然大陆学者用词和本族语者同样呈现多样化，如在表达"表明"之意时，中国大陆学者同样使用了本族语学者使用的揣测性动词 indicate，suggest，demonstrate，reveal，illustrate，imply 等，但在具体用法上有差异。以 indicate 为例，本族语者 1/3 以上都是作状语的 indicating 形式，且其中近 1/3 与主句谓语动词 observe，see 或 detect 搭配使用（例1—2），indicate 以谓语形式用于 which 引导的定语从句仅有 3 例（例 3）。

例 1：A similar silicide peak was also <u>seen</u> on the nanowire regions, <u>indicating</u> the existence of a Pt-Si phase, but with an increased transmittance.

例 2：Only a weak blue emission at 420 nm was <u>observed</u> from the as-deposited film sample, but after annealing for 5 min a deep red emission at 780 nm could be <u>detected</u>, <u>indicating</u> that preliminary segregation and crystallization of Si QDs occurred in the film.

例 3：A linear relationship between current and voltage was obtained, <u>which indicated</u> that an ohmic contact was formed between the CNT film and the highly conductive polymer composite.

中国大陆学者也使用了 131 次 indicate，但以作状语的 indicating 形式出现比例不足 1/4，且仅有 2 例与 see 或 observe 搭配使用，还有近 10%以谓语动词形式在 which 引导的非限定性定语从句中出现（例 4）。

例 4：No changes in surface morphology were observed on either bare or MHA/Au(111) substrates (data not shown here), <u>which indicated</u> that a mechanical scratch could not result in the formation of patterns.

　　两类学者使用证据性动词差异也较大。笔者考察了两个语料库中使用最多的三个证据性动词 observe、find 和 see，发现两类学者在 observe 的用法上比较接近，本族语者共使用被动形式 113 次，占使用总数的 42.80%，大陆学者共使用 49 次，占总数的 42.98%。但另外两个词则表现出一定的差异。本族语学者使用 find 共 144 次，被动形式 89 次，占 61.81%，与 we 搭配使用的主动形式共 12 次，占 8.33%；大陆学者共使用该词 118 次，65 次为被动形式，占 55.08%，与 we 搭配使用的主动形式共 15 次，占 12.71%，是本族语学者的 1.5 倍。see 的使用差异性最大。大陆学者共使用 75 次，44 次为被动形式 seen，31 次为主动形式，其中使用 we can see 共 17 次，one can see 使用 2 次，it is easy/hard/clear to see 结构 5 次，而本族语学者使用动词 see 共 53 次，49 次为被动形式 seen，仅有 4 次为主动形式，其中 we see，one can see 和 one would expect to see 使用各 1 次，大陆学者使用较多的 we can see 和 it is easy/hard/clear to see 均没有出现。这说明中国学者在使用认识性证据动词时比本族语者更倾向于使用主动形式和 "we+动词" 这种具有主观色彩的表达方式。

　　在认识性动词中有一类动词——半助动词两类学者都有使用，但数量有较大差异。例如 appear 和 seem 在本族语学者语料库各出现 16 次，我国学者语料库分别使用 1 次和 6 次。tend to 本族语学者使用 24 次，中国学者使用 9 次。这三个半助动词占本族语学者使用全部认识性动词的 5.96%，而仅占中国学者全部认识性动词的 2.11%，具有显著性差异（p=0.001）。

　　这表明中国学者虽然能够运用本族语学者经常使用的认识性动词，但尚未意识到这些词汇在学术语篇中存在一些特定的使用习惯和搭配限制，大陆学者语言可能存在隐性不地道现象。

4.3.2.2 情态动词比较

表 9 情态动词使用对比

（相对数按 1,000 词计算）

大陆学者				本族语学者		
排序	词项	绝对数	相对数	排序	绝对数	相对数
1	can	390	3.71	1	379	3.03
2	could	167	1.59	4	62	0.49
3	will	101	0.96	3	109	0.87
4	may	75	0.71	2	114	0.91
5	would	57	0.54	5	57	0.45
6	should	53	0.50	6	26	0.21
7	might	44	0.42	7	22	0.18
8	must	4	0.04	8	15	0.12
共计		891	8.48		784	6.27

中国学者与本族语学者使用情态动词总频率分别为 8.48/千词和 6.27/千词，总体没有显著性差异（p=0.202）。

除 could 和 may 外，两类学者其他情态动词使用频次排序完全一致，若将这两个词的位置互换，则排序完全相同。就个体而言，本族语学者使用最多的三个情态动词依次为 can，may，will，这也正是巴特勒（Butler，1990）研究确认的本族语学者专业科学论文中使用频次最高的情态动词，且排序相同。阿泰和萨德尔（Atai & Sadr，2008）研究发现，英语本族语学者使用最多的情态动词为 can 和 may。这一方面表明这三个词是以英语为母语的硬科学研究者使用最频繁的情态动词，另一方面也说明大陆学者某些词使用频次过高或过低。统计显示，大陆学者使用的情态动词中，may 和 must 都低于本族语学者，且具有显著性差别（p 值分别为 0.016 和 0.000）；could 使用频率为本族语学者 3 倍以上，might 也是本族语学者的 2 倍多，具有显著差别（p 值分别为

0.000 和 0.017）。这与艾杰默（2002）对瑞典高级学习者研究结果基本吻合。艾杰默发现瑞典高级学习者使用情态动词的比例无一例外地都超过本族语者，尤以 will，might，should，have to 和 must 最为突出。

国内学者使用 could 和 might 频次远超本族语者的主要原因估计是对情态动词的误用。中学是我国学生集中学习情态动词的主要阶段，大学基本不再涉及，然而中学英语教学由于教材等原因往往只是有选择性地对情态动词的用法进行讲解（程晓堂、裘晶，2007），加之情态动词用法复杂，很难通过感悟习得，这就可能导致学生对情态动词用法了解不够全面而出现误用。在两大语料库中，笔者确实发现国内学者有较多误用情态动词的情况：

例 5：Comparing the morphologies of the microwave-assisted sample [figures 1(a) and (c)] with those of the control sample[figures 1(d) and (e)], we could draw a conclusion that the use of microwave treatment was helpful for the maintenance of theTiO2 nanorods originating from the solution.

例 6：It could be easily concluded that UV radiation can excite the electrons in the W clusters, making it easier to lose electrons when exposed to oxygen, which was the main motivity of the self-erasing process.

例 7：In summary, we have described a facile surfactant directed chemical polymerization method to prepare size-controlled PPy/TiO2 coaxial nanocables, which might open new opportunities in a myriad of applications, such as energy storage systems, nanophotoelectric devices, fuel cell membranes, antibacterial coatings and catalysis.

显然，在以上三例中，大陆学者都试图得出自己有相当把握的结论，但由于不了解 could 和 might 表达的可能性极弱而误用，使结论的力度大大削弱。而与我国学者误用 could 和 might 降低情态量值形成鲜明对比的是，本族语学者不仅在下结论时都倾向于使用 can 和 will，以显示自己对结论的信心（例 8—10），有时甚至在前后使用过去时的情况下仍使用 can，以提升情态量值（例 11—12）：

例 8：It <u>can be concluded</u> from these observations that the method of incorporating MWCNTs into the P(3HB)/Bioglass® compositefilms has been successful since no preferential segregation ofMWCNTs in the matrix was observed.

例 9：<u>The following conclusions can be obtained</u> from this study.

例 10：In summary, we believe that this work <u>will advance the ability</u> to fabricate epitaxialQD arrays of arbitrary complexity, with application tonovel nanoelectronic architectures.

例 11：From several TEM images, the size of the Genanocrystals *was determined* to be between 4 and12 nm. Crystal lattice fringes from clearly resolved individual Genanocrystals <u>can be seen</u> and these *were analysed* using a fast Fourier transform (FFT), shown in figure 2(c).

例 12：When zeolites containing more than 11 CuCl per primitive unit cell *were irradiated* with a very low intensity, thin wires composed mainly of silver *were obtained*, consistent with the greater ease of reduction of silver than copper. In some areas lattice fringes <u>can be observed</u>. However, when these materials *were irradiated* with a stronger beam, thicker wires appeared that were too thick to obtain high resolution images.

海兰德和米尔顿（1997）认为，用 might 表达可能性似乎太弱而无法表达说服意图，从而使作者显得"模棱两可、缺乏自信或者幼稚可笑"。此外，might 一般更多用于英语口语，而非书面语（Holmes，1988）。这可能是 might 受到本族语学者冷遇的两大主要原因。might 的数量远超本族语者表明中国学者对 might 的用法和语体特征缺乏了解。

由此可以看出，尽管大陆学者使用情态动词总体接近本族语学者，但在使用某些词的质量上与本族语学者尚有差距。

4.3.2.3　间接缓和型模糊限制语

本族语学者使用的间接缓和型模糊限制语表达形式比中国大陆学者丰富，更加具有变化。例如在提及前人研究成果时，大陆作者使用较多的主要为 sb. reported，reported by sb.，in sb.'s work，previous report/study/work，reported/described/used previously，agree with，in (good) agreement with，according to 等，而本族语学者除这些表达方式外，还使用 in the work of sb.，earlier results of sb.，earlier reported work，earlier report，as reported earlier，agree well with，in excellent agreement with 等。而且我国学者使用较多的 according to（54 次）在本族语学者语料库中出现频次并不高，仅有 10 次，具有显著差别（p=0.000）。尽管两类学者表达"众所周知"的手段均呈现多样性，不仅有 is known, it is well-known that，还有 is well-recognized/ well-established/ well-documented that 等，但大陆学者还大量使用了 as we know 这种形式，本族语学者并无一例。因为这样的说法本身在学术论文中显得"缺乏依据，易于受到质疑"（Hinkel，2004：325）。

5. 结论

本研究主要结论为：

（1）中国大陆学者论文语料库所使用的模糊限制语在文中所占比例总体高于本族语学者语料库；除结论外，论文其余各部分中国学者使用模糊限制语比例均超出本族语学者，但引言部分没有显著性差异。中国大陆学者使用的四小类限制语仅有间接缓和型使用比例低于本族语学者，程度变动、范围变动、直接缓和三种类型使用频率二者没有显著差异。

（2）两个语料库中所使用的模糊限制语均以实义动词和情态动词频率最高，名词最少。在认识性实义动词中，揣测性动词和推理性动词两个语料库没有显著性差异，但证据性动词具有显著差异，本族语学者使用频率高于中国学者；尽管情态动词使用比例两个语料库没有显著差异，但部分情态动词我国学者有误用现象。

（3）中国大陆与本族语学者科研论文使用最多的变动型和缓和型模糊限制语词项大体一致，但在使用频次和具体用法上存在差异。

（4）中国大陆学者科研论文中使用了部分口语体模糊限制语，有跨语体使用问题，语体意识有待加强。

参考文献

Aijmer, K. 2002. Modality in advanced Swedish learners' written interlanguage. In S. Granger, J. Hung and S. Petch-Tyson (eds.) *Computer Learner Corpora, Second Language Acquisition and Foreign Language Teaching*. Amsterdam & Philadelphia: Benjamins, pp. 55-76.

Atai, M.R. & L. Sadr. 2008. A cross-cultural genre study of hedging devices in discussion section of applied linguistics research articles. *Journal of Teaching English Language and Literature Society of Iran* 7, pp. 1-22.

Brown, P. & S. Levinson. 1987. *Politeness: Some Universals in Language Usage*: Cambridge CUP.

Butler, C. 1990. Qualifications in science: Modal meanings in scientific texts. In W. Nash (ed.) *The Writing Scholar: Studies in Academic Discourse*. Newbury Park, CA, Sage.

Hinkel, E. 2004. *Teaching Academic ESL Writing*. Mahwah, N.J.: Lawrence Erlbaum Associates.

Holmes, J. 1988. Doubt and certainty in ESL text books. *Applied Linguistics* 9, pp. 21-44.

Hyland, K. 1996a. Writing without conviction? Hedging in scientific research articles. *Applied Linguistics* 4, pp. 433-454.

Hyland, K. 1996b. Talking to the academy: Forms of hedging in science research articles. *Written Communication* 13/2, pp. 251-281.

Hyland, K & J. Milton. 1997. Qualification and certainty in L1 and L2 students' writing. *Journal of Second Language Writing* 2, pp. 183-205.

Lakoff, G. 1972. Hedges: A study in meaning criteria and the logic of fuzzy concepts. *Chicago Linguistic Society Papers*. Chicago: Chicago University Press.

Markkanen, R. & H. Shroder. 1997. Hedging: A challenge for pragmatics and discourse analysis. In R. Markkannen & H. Schroder (eds.) *Hedging and Discourse: Approaches to Analysis of a Pragmatic Phenomenon in Academic Texts*. New York: Walter de Gruyter.

Mauranen, A. 1997. Hedging in language reviewers' hands. In R.Markkannen & H. Schroder (eds.) *Hedging and Discourse: Approaches to Analysis of a Pragmatic Phenomenon in Academic Texts*. New York: Walter de Gruyter.

Myers, G. 1989. The pragmatics of politeness in scientific articles. *Applied Linguistics* 10, pp. 1-35.

Namsarvaev, V. 1997. Hedging in Russian academic writing in sociological texts. In R. Karkkanen and H. Schroder (eds.) *Hedging and Discourse: Approaches to Analysis of a Pragmatic Phenomenon in Academic Texts*. New York: Walter de Gruyter.

Nikula,T. 1997. Interlanguage view on hedging". In R. Markkannen & H. Schroder (eds.) *Hedging and Discourse: Approaches to Analysis of a Pragmatic Phenomenon in Academic Texts*. New York: Walter de Gruyter.

Prince et al. 1982. On hedging in physician — physician discourse. In R. J. Di Pietro (ed.) *Linguistics and Professions*. Norwood: Ablex.

Skelton, J. 1988. Comments in academic articles. In P. Grunwell (ed.) *Applied Linguistics in Society*. London: CILT, The National Center for Languages.

陈林华、李福印，1994，交际中的模糊限制语，《外国语》，第 5 期，第 55-59 页。

程晓堂、裘晶，2007，中国学生英语作文中情态动词的使用情况，《外语电化教学》，第 12 期，第 9-15 页。

董宏乐，2003，概念语法隐喻理论对阅读教学的指导意义，《国外外语教学》，第 4 期，第 37-41 页。

冯茵、周榕，2007，学术论文摘要中模糊限制语的调查与分析，《外国语言文学》，第 2 期，第 108-112 页。

何刚、张春燕，2006，试论文化语用原则，《修辞学习》，第 5 期，第 34-38 页。

黄小苹，2002，学术论文中的模糊限制语的语篇语用分析，《四川外语学院学报》，第 4 期，第 85-88 页。

林同济，1980，从汉语词序看长句翻译，《现代英语研究》，第 1 期，第 16-23 页。

刘丹青，2010，汉语是一种动词型语言，《世界汉语教学》，第 1 期，第 3-17 页。

刘珍，2003，模糊限制语与母语迁移，《宁夏大学学报》（人文社会科学版），第 3 期，第 106-109 页。

王舟，2008，英汉学术论文摘要中模糊限制语的对比研究，《华中科技大学学报》（社会科学版），第 6 期，第 59-63 页。

徐润英、袁邦株，2009，社会科学论文中模糊限制语的人际意义研究，《外语教学》，第 6 期，第 33-36，53 页。

杨慧玲，2001，科技论文中的模糊限制语，《四川外语学院学报》，第 1 期，第 84-87 页。

余千华、秦傲松，2001，英语科技论文中的模糊限制语，《华中科技大学学报》（社会科学版），第 4 期，第 121-123 页。

赵英玲，1999，英语科技语体中的模糊限制语，《外语与外语教学》，第 9 期，第 15-17 页。

A Corpus-based Contrastive Study of Hedges in

Mainland Chinese and Native Scholars' English

Scientific Research Articles

Abstract: The article reports on a corpus-based contrastive study of hedges used in English research articles by mainland Chinese and native English scholars that appeared in the journal Nanotechnology. The results show that the mainland Chinese scholars' articles have a slightly higher percentage of hedges as a whole and only the Conclusion Section in their writing contains a lower frequency of hedging expressions than their counterparts' when four sections of the articles by the two categories of scholars are examined separately, but there is no statistically significant difference between the Introduction Sections. With the exception of attribution, no statistically significant difference is found between the two groups in the frequency of three of the four sub-categories of hedges, namely adaptor, rounder and plausibility. Parts of speech of the hedges are examined and lexical and auxiliary verbs are identified as the most frequently used in the two corpora and nouns as the least. It is also found that a large number of most frequently used hedges in the articles by both Chinese and native scholars overlap but many of them differ remarkably in frequency and how they are used and some are even used by the mainland Chinese scholars incorrectly or in wrong registers.

Key Words: hedges; scientific RA corpus; mainland Chinese scholars; native English scholars.

此文发表于《外语教学理论与实践》2014 年第 2 期

基于语料分析的汉语口语人际隐喻研究

杨延宁

　　摘　要：语法隐喻现象出现的根源在于人类语言中语义层和语法层的分离。这种分离导致特定语义和语法表达之间的一一对应关系被破坏，出现了很多不同于该语义原始状态的语法表达形式。因而，语法隐喻可以被简单定义为在语义上同源的一组语法表达形式。这一语言现象同语言的概念功能和人际功能都密切相关，可以被划分为概念隐喻和人际隐喻两大类型。概念隐喻主要出现在书面语中，而人际隐喻则主要同口语有关。语法隐喻在书面语和口语中有不同的表现形式。在口语中比较常见的语法隐喻现象包括以疑问句的形式表达肯定的含义。在书面语中常观察到的以词组来表达小句甚至复句的语义，同样属于语法隐喻的范畴。从语法隐喻理论被提出至今，已超过 30 年。其间，大量的研究都针对书面语中的语法隐喻展开，对口语中该现象的使用特征鲜有触及。已有语法隐喻研究的另一个特点是聚焦于英语，对其他语言中该现象的研究相对较少。本研究尝试弥补这两方面的不足，以汉语口语为研究对象，开展针对性的人际隐喻研究。由于这方面研究的缺乏，本文首先对汉语口语中的语义表达体系和对应的语法实现方式进行细致的梳理，并以此为基础建立汉语人际隐喻的识别和分类框架。为保证研究结论的可靠性，本文以大型汉语口语语料库为分析对象，并依据研究需要对语料进行了更细致的划分。其目的在于找出对话中话题的改变和交流双方社会地位的不同，对人际隐喻的使用特征有何种影响。语料分析的过程划分为两步。第一步利用已建立的识别和分类框架来确定语料中各类人际隐喻的分布特征。第二步则以此为出发点，分析各分布特征形成的内在原因。研究表明汉语口语中的人际隐喻分布表现出很强的不均衡性，部分类型的使用频率远高于其他类型。另一方面，人际隐喻的使用同话题的改变和交流双方社会地位的变化有密切关系。

关键词：语法隐喻；汉语口语；语料库

1. Introduction

Grammatical Metaphor (GM) is a phenomenon automatically arising from the interaction between meaning and wording in a language. In the development of human languages, the realization of meaning by wording evolves first as the patterns in which a semantic meaning is congruently mapped onto a grammatical expression. For example, the semantic meaning of command is congruently realized by an imperative clause. The congruent pattern is not the only form of realization because a language has the inherent power of realigning the mapping between semantic meanings and grammatical realizations. For instance, the meaning of command can be realized by an interrogative clause or even a declarative clause. In other words, there is the possibility of metaphorical realization of a particular meaning in a language. Therefore, GM is "the phenomenon whereby a set of agnate forms is present in the language having different mappings between the semantic and the grammatical categories" (Halliday and Matthiessen, 1999, p7). There are two types of GM occurring respectively in the expressions of ideational meaning and interpersonal meaning. Ideational GM is mainly deployed in prototypical written texts – like scientific, administrative and legal texts, while interpersonal GM is frequently observed in spoken discourses – like casual conversations and service encounters.

This article addresses how and why interpersonal GM is used in spoken Chinese. It first presents a framework for the identification and categorization of interpersonal GM in Chinese. Based on the framework, the article ascertains how different types of interpersonal GM are distributed in spoken Chinese, revealing the deployment of grammatical resources in the interaction between meaning and wording. The distribution is obtained by analyzing a spoken Chinese corpus composed of various types of dialogues. The realization of semantic meaning in a language must be investigated by considering its social context. This article thus explores the relationship between interpersonal GM in spoken Chinese and its immediate context of situation (register), demonstrating how the GM deployment in spoken Chinese is affected by the topic of conversation and the social status between speaker and addressee.

Within the field of Systemic Functional Linguistics (SFL), many studies of GM have been carried out in the past three decades (e.g. Halliday, 1994; Halliday and Matthiessen, 1999; Ravelli, 1985). While these studies provide a wealth of information about different aspects of GM, they have been limited in two aspects. Firstly, these studies investigate the features of GM with the focus on the most thoroughly investigated language of English. There has been relatively less research describing in depth the phenomenon of GM in other languages. Secondly, these studies have not sought to explore systemically the use of interpersonal GM. In other words, previous GM research is confined to the analysis of GM in written texts. Despite its greater potential of remapping meaning and wording, spoken discourses have not received as much attention from previous GM studies as written texts. This article fills these gaps by undertaking a comprehensive study of interpersonal GM in spoken Chinese.

The exploration of interpersonal GM in spoken Chinese faces two major difficulties. Firstly, there has been very little research on interpersonal GM both theoretically and empirically. This gives rise to the difficulty of discussing the phenomenon on the basis of a less rigid theoretical framework. This study thus develops a framework for the identification and categorization of interpersonal GM in spoken Chinese by examining the semantic and lexicogrammatical systems in the language. Secondly, a research on interpersonal GM must be carried out by analyzing a corpus of spoken language, which is difficult to collect, transcribe and code. A reliable and manageable corpus of spoken Chinese is thus needed to enable the detailed analysis. This study investigates the profile of GM deployment with a large corpus of spoken Chinese developed in mainland China. The corpus is used not only as the language material for analysis but as the major source of examples to illustrate different subtypes of interpersonal GM in Chinese. The authentic examples of GM from the corpus are indicated with the word 'authentic' in square brackets. A smaller corpus formed by discourses extracted from the large one is manually analysed to show the GM features not exposed through the automatic search of the large corpus.

As pointed out by DeFrancis (1984), the term "spoken Chinese" suffers from a lack of precision in view of the wide varieties of speech that are usually subsumed under this name. The Chinese spoken in various parts of China is quite different in pronunciation, although they write in the same way as in standard Chinese (Mandarin). For example, "九" sounds like "gau" when pronounced in Cantonese, but the same Chinese character is pronounced as "jiu" in standard Chinese. In addition to pronunciation, Chinese dialects are different in vocabulary and grammar to a certain extent. This study focuses its analysis on the use of GM in Mandarin Chinese which is the most widely used Chinese variety in China. With this in mind, the Chinese corpus selected is a corpus of spoken Mandarin. The spoken Chinese hereinafter refers to spoken Mandarin if not specially noted. In addition, the following abbreviations are used in this article to represent some frequently used grammatical classes in Chinese:

Asp.: Aspect markers (*le, zhe, guo*)
Partic.: Particles (e.g. *a/ya, ne, ma, ba*)
Clas.: Classifier (e.g. *ge, zhong*)
Sub.: Subordinating particle *de*

In the next section, the framework for the identification and categorization of interpersonal GM in Chinese is presented. Section 3 explains how the Chinese corpus is selected and analyzed. Section 4 discusses the distribution of two types of interpersonal GM, namely metaphor of mood and metaphor of modality, in spoken Chinese. The relationship between GM deployment and register variables is examined in Section 5.

2. Identification and Categorization of Interpersonal GM in Chinese

2.1　Identification of Interpersonal GM in Chinese

The conceptualization and understanding of GM vary in different phases of GM studies, which in turn result in various working definitions of GM. In addition, the differences between ideational GM and interpersonal GM increase the difficulty of identifying GM. The development of GM studies is thus briefly reviewed here to clarify the motifs of GM identification in spoken Chinese.

GM is interpreted in the first phase of GM studies as the counterpart of lexical metaphor (Halliday, 1985; 1994). It is claimed that the phenomenon is a kind of metaphor which is grammatical rather than lexical. Halliday (1985) thus makes an attempt to extend the boundary of metaphor, which is usually understood as a lexical phenomenon, to the grammatical field. As pointed out by Romero and Soria (2005), this interpretation of GM gives rise to some difficulties in the understanding of the nature of GM mainly because "metaphor" is used as a metaphorical extension of the term. It is suggested that the concept should be renamed as "marked morphosyntactic variation" (Romero and Soria, 2005: 156).

In the second phase of GM studies, the phenomenon is described in terms of the interaction between the semantics and lexicogrammar in a language (Halliday, 1998; Halliday and Matthiessen, 1999). According to Halliday and Matthiessen (1999), the emergence of GM is related to the natural development of the content plane in a language. Initially, the content plane is formed by semantic and lexicogrammatical strata coupling in congruent patterns. The content plane of a language evolves by extending the congruent patterns between semantic and lexicogrammatical strata. The disruption of the congruent patterns between the two levels of content plane opens up the possibility of metaphorical expression. The remapping of the semantics on to the lexicogrammar thus becomes the motif of GM identification in this phase of GM studies.

The third phase of GM exploration follows previous GM studies by taking stratal remapping as the criteria for identifying metaphorical expressions. However, Halliday and Matthiessen (2004) propose that GM systematically expands the meaning potential by creating new patterns of structural realization. In other words, metaphorical modes of meaning are motivated by the need to expand meaning potential. This clarification of the inherent motivation of GM enhances the understanding of the nature of GM.

The discussion above shows that the realignment between semantics and lexicogrammar and the expansion of meaning potential should be treated as the two motifs of GM identification in Chinese. More importantly, the two motifs of GM identification are the common foundations of ideational GM and interpersonal GM. Ideational GM and interpersonal GM are distinctive with respect to the direction of grammatical movement. The general tendency for ideational GM is to 'downgrade' the grammatical category realizing a particular semantic unit (Halliday and Matthiessen, 2004). In contrast, interpersonal GM is characterized by its tendency to upgrade the categories of grammatical realization.

Despite their differences in grammatical movement, both ideational GM and interpersonal GM arise from the remapping between semantics and lexicogrammar. Furthermore, both of them are deployed for the purpose of expanding the meaning potential of a language (Halliday and Matthiessen,

2004). To be more specific, the metaphorical realizations of semantic units in ideational dimension increase the meaning potential of construing our experience of the world. The metaphorical realizations of mood system provide new meaning potential for negotiation between speakers of a language. The metaphorical realizations of modality systems expand the methods of making interpersonal assessment (Halliday and Matthiessen, 2004).

In order to develop the framework for identifying interpersonal GM, this study needs a detailed description of how semantic and lexicogrammatical categories are remapped in spoken Chinese. The congruent and metaphorical realizations of interpersonal meanings in spoken Chinese are differentiated for this purpose. Interpersonal GM is accommodated into grammatical system in the expression of mood and modality (Halliday, 1994). The differentiation is thus conducted along the two lines: metaphor of mood and metaphor of modality.

Metaphor of mood is concerned with the expression of speech functions in a language. It is easy to define that the speech functions of statement, command, and question are congruently realized by the moods of declarative, imperative and interrogative in Chinese. However, the congruent realization of offer is less determinate because both declarative and interrogative clauses in Chinese are the unmarked expressions of the speech function. As claimed by Halliday (1994: 95), "for offers there is no distinct mood category at all". In this case, the congruent realizations in the mood system for the options in the speech function network are summarized in Figure 1.

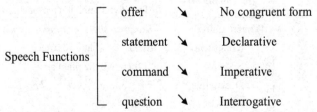

Figure 1   Congruent realization of speech functions in Chinese

In addition to their congruent realizations, the speech functions in

Chinese are frequently construed by their metaphorically expressions. The transfers from congruent to metaphorical realizations are shown with their examples in Table 1.

Table1　The transfer from congruent to metaphorical realizations

Speech functions to be construed	Grammatical transfer	Examples
Offer	No transfer	
Command	1) Imperative (congruent) ↓ Interrogative (metaphorical) ↓ 2) Imperative (congruent) ↓ Declarative (metaphorical)	*He　yi　bei　shui.* drink one Meas. water "Drink a cup of water." *Yao　he　bei　shui　ma?* want drink Meas. water Ma "Would you like a cup of water?" *He　yi　bei　shui.* drink one Meas. water "Drink a cup of water." *Zhe　you　yi　bei　shui.* here exist one Meas. water "There is a cup of water."
Statement	3) Declarative (congruent) Interrogative (metaphorical)	*You daoli.* exist reason "It is reasonable" *Nandao　meiyou　daoli?* do you think　not exist　reason "Don't you think it's reasonable?"
Question	4) Interrogative (congruent) ↓ Declarative (metaphorical)	*Hangban shenme　shijian daoda?* flight　what　time　arrive "When will the flight arrive?" *Wo　xiang　zhidao　hangban　de daoda shijian.* I want know flight Sub. arrival time "I want to know the arrival time of this flight."

There are four categories of modality in a language, namely probability, usuality, inclination and obligation (Hallday, 1994). Halliday and Matthiessen (2004) claim that modality is congruently realized by the grammatical elements within a clause. Based on previous research on the modality system in Chinese (Wang, 1959; Chao, 1968; Lü, 1982; Zhu, 1996), the congruent realizations of modality system in Chinese are presented in Figure 2.

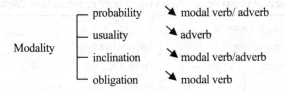

Figure 2   Congruent realizations of modality system in Chinese

According to Halliday (1994), the metaphorical realization of modality is coded as a projecting clause in a hypotactic clause complex. Projecting clauses cannot be used for expressing every kind of modality in Chinese. It is observed that the meanings of usuality and inclination are not construed in the form of projecting clauses in Chinese. According to previous studies of modality (Palmer, 2001; Tsang, 1981), usuality and inclination are distinguished from probability and obligation in that these meanings typically relate to the subject of a clause instead of to the speaker. On the other hand, probability and obligation in most cases relate directly to the speaker of a clause. In sum, usuality and inclination are "semantic domains where the speaker cannot readily pose as an authority" (Halliday, 1994: 358). In this case, the projecting process concerned with the attitude of the speaker is not applicable to the expressions of usuality and inclination.

In addition to projecting clause, two special structures are used for the metaphorical realization of modality in Chinese, i.e., structures of *shi...de* and *you* .... The two structures could be translated into English as 'it is ...'

and 'there is ...'. However, they are not projecting clauses because they cannot instate another clause as a locution or an idea. The two structures, especially *shi...de*, are widely deployed for the expression of every category of modality in Chinese. With the consideration of all these points, the grammatical transfers involved in metaphorical realization of modality in Chinese are presented in Table 2.

Table 2　Grammatical transfers involved in metaphor of modality in Chinese

Modalities to be construed	Grammatical transfer			
	Cong. realization		Meta. realization	
	Modal verb	Adverb	Projecting clause	'shi...de' 'you...'
Probability	*keneng* (can) *hui* (can) *gai* (should)	*Yiding kending biding zhun* (must)	*wo xiangxin* (I believe) *wo xiang* (I think) *wo renwei* (I reckon)	*shi kending de* (is must Sub.) *you keneng* (have possibility)
Usuality		*yizhi* (always) *jingchang* (usually) *youshi* (sometimes)		*shi changyou de* (is often Sub.)
Inclination	*yao* (will) *xiang* (wish) *yuanyi* (will)	*yiding/pian/ fei* (must)		*shi ziyuan de* (is willing　Sub.)
Obligation	*bixu* (must) *gai* (should) *keyi* (may)		*wo yaoqiu* (I require) *wo rang* (I let) *wo yunxu* (I permit)	*shi bixu de* (is necessary Sub.) *you biyao* (have necessity)

2.2   Framework for Interpersonal GM Categorization

This study develops a framework for categorizing interpersonal GM in Chinese by focusing on the realization forms of different types of interpersonal meaning. In particular, the metaphor of mood is categorized by specifying the mood choices involved in the metaphorical expression of speech functions. The metaphor of modality, on the other hand, is categorized by differentiating the grammatical methods which realize four types of modality metaphorically. An overall picture of the framework is presented in Table 3.

Table 3   Framework for interpersonal GM categorization in Chinese

Interpersonal GM	Categories
Metaphor of mood	1. Expressing command with interrogative mood
	2. Expressing command with declarative mood
	3. Expressing statement with interrogative mood
	4. Expressing question with declarative mood
Metaphor of modality	1. Metaphorical realizations of probability
	2. Metaphorical realization of usuality
	3. Metaphorical realizations of obligation
	4. Metaphorical realizations of inclination

In order to facilitate the identification of individual GM instances, the GM categories in Table 3 are subdivided in terms of the grammatical methods involved in relevant metaphorical expressions.

2.2.1 Metaphor of mood

Category 1: Expressing Command with Interrogative Mood

According to Li and Thompson (1981), there are three types of interrogative clauses in Chinese, i.e., question-word, A-not-A or Mood particle interrogatives. The meaning of command can be metaphorically expressed by each type of interrogative in Chinese, as demonstrated by Examples (1) to (4):

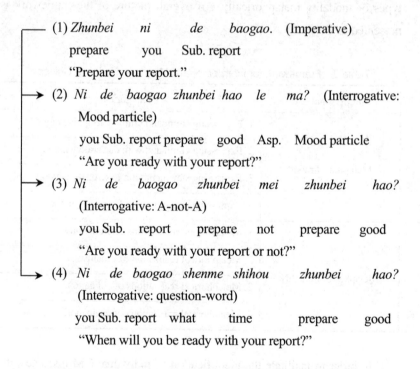

(1) *Zhunbei   ni   de   baogao.*   (Imperative)
    prepare   you   Sub. report
    "Prepare your report."

(2) *Ni   de   baogao   zhunbei   hao   le   ma?*   (Interrogative: Mood particle)
    you Sub. report prepare   good   Asp.   Mood particle
    "Are you ready with your report?"

(3) *Ni   de   baogao   zhunbei   mei   zhunbei   hao?*
    (Interrogative: A-not-A)
    you Sub.   report   prepare   not   prepare   good
    "Are you ready with your report or not?"

(4) *Ni   de   baogao   shenme   shihou   zhunbei   hao?*
    (Interrogative: question-word)
    you Sub. report   what   time   prepare   good
    "When will you be ready with your report?"

Some specific patterns of expression are also deployed in Chinese to realize certain speech functions, which are referred to as speech-functional formulae by Halliday (1994). The most frequently used speech-functional formulae for the expressions of command are as follows:

A. *Hai bu*...(yet not)

The formula of *hai bu* ... (yet not) is the most salient one in the interrogative expressions with command meaning and could be translated into the English expression of 'why not ...', as in Example (5).

(5) *Xiexie   na   ge   jingcha.* (Cong.: Imperative)
    thank   that   Clas.   policeman
    "Say thank you to the policeman."

    Hai bu xiexie na ge jingcha ? (Meta.:Interrogative)
    yet not thank that Clas. policeman
    "Why not say thank you to the policeman?"

B. *Nan dao*... (difficult say)

The formula *nan dao* is used in negative expressions indicated by *bu* (not) and frequently followed by the Mood particle *ma*. See Example (6):

(6) *Na   xie   yinliao.* (Congruent: Imperative)
    take   some   drink
    "Take a drink."

    Nan   dao   ni   bu   ke   ma? (Metaphorical: Interrogative)
    difficult   say   you   not   thirsty   Mood particle
    "Why don't you feel thirsty?"

C. ...*hao/xing/keyi ma* (good + Mood particle)

With the Mood particle *ma*, the formula ...*hao/xing/keyi* introduces interrogative clauses with the meaning of request. The Chinese clause with this formula could be expressed in English as "Would you mind doing something." as shown in Example (7):

(7) *Dao   wo   jia   lai.* (Congruent: Imperative)

reach   I   home   come

"Come to my home."

Dao wo jia   lai hao   ma? (Metaphorical: interrogative)

reach   I   home come   good Mood particle

"Would you mind coming to my home?"

Category 2: Expressing Command with Declarative Mood

Compared with interrogative clauses, the utterances in a declarative form do not imply the meaning of command so obviously. In many cases, the speech function of command is realized by a declarative clause with reference to a particular context. The declarative clauses involved in the expression of command can be further divided into two types according to whether the structure of *shi...de* is deployed or not, as shown in Examples (8) and (9).

A. *Normal form*

(8) *Shoushi   ni   de   fangjian.* (Congruent: Imperative)

clean up you Sub.   room

"Clean up your room."

Ni de fangjian tai luan. (Metaphorical: Declarative)

you Sub. room   very   in a mess

"Your room is in a mess."

B. *shi...de* structure

(9) *Bu   zhun   zai zhe   li   xiyan.* (Congruent: Imperative)
    not   permit   in   here inside smoke
    "Do not smoke here."

Zhe li   shi   jinzhi xiyan de. (Metaphorical: Declarative)
here   inside   is   prohibit   smoke   Sub.
"Smoking is prohibited here."

Category 3: Expressing Statement with Interrogative Mood

Rhetorical interrogatives are used to express the meaning of statement in Chinese. This type of interrogative is distinguished from the normal interrogative in that they are ordinarily concerned with some speech-functional formulae in Chinese. The most frequently used formulae are as follows:

A. *bu shi...ma?* (not is … Mood particle)
(10) *Gen   ni   shuo   guo   le.* (Congruent: Declarative)
     to   you talk   already   Asp.
     "I've already talked to you."

Bu   shi gen ni   shuo   guo   le ma? (Meta: Interrogative)
not   is   to you   talk   already Asp.   Mood particle
"Haven't I talked to you?"

B. *nan dao* ... (difficult say)

The formula ('*nan dao...*') has been discussed in the analysis of commands realized by interrogative mood. In some contexts, it also functions to realize the speech function of statement.

(11) *Bu yiding   qu   tushuguan.* (Congruent: Declarative)
　　 not must   go   library
　　 "We do not necessarily go to the library."

　　 Nan dao   yiding qu tushuguan? (Meta: Interrogative)
　　 difficult say must go   library
　　 "Is that necessary to go to the library?"

C. *you shenme* … (have what)

This type of formula ordinarily appears in a relational clause consisting of Carrier and Attribute. It realizes the speech function of statement by negating the Attribute in the clause. In Example (12), the meaning of *budui* (wrong) is negated.

(12) *Ta   de kanfa   shi   dui   de.* (Congruent: Declarative)
　　 he   Sub. opinion is correct   Sub.
　　 "His opinion is correct."

　　 Ta de kanfa you shenme budui? (Meta: Interrogative)
　　 he   Sub. opinion have   what   wrong
　　 "What's wrong with his opinion?"

D. *nali* … (where)

(13) *Zhe   ge   fangchengshi mei   cuo.* (Cong: Declarative)
　　 this Clas. equation   not   wrong
　　 "This equation is not wrong."

　　 Zhe ge fangchengi nali cuo le? (Meta: Interrogative)
　　 this Meas. equation where wrong Asp.
　　 "Where does the equation go wrong?"

Category 4: Expressing Question with Declarative Mood

The declarative clauses involved in the metaphorical expression of questions is characterized by the structure of '*Wo xiang zhidao/liaojie* …'(I want to know/enquire…). The declaratives concerned have the intention of obtaining information from the person addressed, which is shown in Example (14).

(14) *Ni shenme shijian neng wancheng lunwen*? (Inte.)
      you   what   time   can   finish   thesis
      "When can you finish your thesis?"

Wo   xiang   zhidao   ni wancheng   de shijian. (Decl.)
I   want   know   you   finish   Sub. time
"I want to know the ending time of your thesis writing."

It is worth pointing out that any metaphorical realization of speech function is construed in a certain context. It is possible that the same clause expresses various types of speech function in different linguistic environments. For the convenience of discussion, this study exemplifies the metaphorical forms of speech function without stating the context of these expressions. In the practical analysis of interpersonal GM in Chinese, the context in which metaphorical expressions occur must be taken into consideration. A smaller corpus is thus extracted from the large one for the purpose of manual analysis. This point is explained in more detail in Section 3. According to the discussion above, the detailed categorization of metaphor of mood in Chinese is summarized in Table 4.

Table 4 Categories and subcategories of metaphor of mood in Chinese

Categories of Metaphor of mood	Subcategories	
1. Expressing command with interrogative mood	(i) Normal form	Question-word A-not-A structure Mood particle
	(ii) Special formula	'*hai bu…*' (yet not); '*nan dao…*' (difficult say); '*…hao ma*'(good + Mood particle)
2. Expressing command with declarative mood	(i) Normal form	
	(ii) Special formula	'*shi …de*' (is … Sub.)
3. Expressing statement with interrogative mood	(i) Normal form	Rhetorical interrogative
	(ii) Special formula	'*bu shi…ma?*' (not is … Mood particle); '*nan dao …*' (difficult say); '*you shenme*' (have what); '*nali …*' (where)
4. Expressing question with declarative mood	Special formula	'*Wo xiang zhidao/liaojie …*' (I want to know/enquire…)

2.2.2 Metaphor of Modality

Metaphor of modality in Chinese is subdivided by considering the grammatical methods involved in the metaphorical realization of each type of modality. As revealed in Section 2.1, the grammatical methods concerned are projecting clause, *shi … de* structure, and *you…* structure.

Category 1: Metaphorical Realizations of Probability

Probability can be metaphorically expressed by projecting clause, *shi…de* structure, and *you…* structure.

(i) Expressing probability with projecting clause

When probability is construed as a projecting clause in Chinese, the metaphorical realization generally involves a mental process with a first person participant. The verbs *xiang* (think), *renwei* (reckon), *guji* (estimate) are used most frequently to construct the mental process involved. The probability meaning in Chinese is congruently realized by modal verbs and adverbs, which are functionally referred to as Finite and Adjunct in SFL. The grammatical movements from Finite and Adjunct to mental clause are illustrated by Examples (15) and (16).

(15) *Ta   keneng   qu   jisuanji   zhongxin.*
　he   might   go to   computer   center
　"He might go to the computer center."
　　　Subject Finite   Predicator   Complement

　　Subject Pred.//Subj. Pred.   Complement
　　Wo   xiang ta   qu   jisuanji   zhongxin.
　　I   think   he   go to   computer   center
　　"I think he goes to the computer center."

(16) *Ta   yiding   zai   8   dian   qian   huilai*
　He   definitely   in   8   o'clock   before   come back
　"He definitely comes back before 8 o'clock."
　Subject   Adjunct   Adjunct   Predicator

　Subject Pred.   // Subject Adjunct   Pred.
　Wo xiangxing ta   8   dian qian   huilai
　I   believe   he   8   o'clock before   come back
　"I believe he comes back before 8 o'clock."

(ii) Expressing probability with *shi...de* structure

The structure of *shi...de* in Chinese is generally used to emphasize the information inserted between *shi* and *de*. When the information to be inserted involves comments addressed by a speaker, the structure expresses a modal meaning. Although the structure is generally translated as 'It is ...' in English, it is deployed with a broader semantic scope in Chinese. Any type of modality can be metaphorically realized in the form of '*shi...de*', while the 'It is ...' structure in English is not involved in the expression of inclination. As far as the probability is concerned, almost every modal verb and adverb involved can be inserted into the *shi...de* structure to form a metaphorical realization. The realizations involving adverb and modal verb are shown respectively in Examples (17) and (18).

(17) *Xiangmu   keneng   zai   san   tian   nei   wancheng.*
Project   can   in   three   day   inside   complete
"The project can be completed in three days."
Subject   Finite   Adjunct   Predicator

Adjunct   Predicator   Complement   // Pred. Complement
Zai santian nei wancheng   xiangmu   shi   keneng   de.
In   three   day inside   complete   project   is   can   Sub.
"It is possible to complete the project in three days."

(18) *A   dui   yiding   huosheng.*
A   team   certainly   win
"Team A will certainly win."
Subject   Adjunct   Predicator

Subject   Predicator //   Pred. Complement
A   dui   huosheng   shi   yiding   de.
A   team   win   is   certainly   Sub.

"It is certain that team A will win."

(iii) Expressing probability with *you…* structure

There is also the possibility to express probability through *you…* structure in Chinese. To be more specific, the meaning of probability is construed as an isolated clause. See Example (19):

(19) *Ta*   *keneng*   *hui*   *jia*   *le.*
       he   probably   go back   home   Asp.
       "He probably went back home."
       Subject   Finite   Predicator   Complement

       Pred.   Complement//Subject   Predicator   Complement
       You   *keneng*   *ta*   *hui*   *jia*   *le.*
       have   possibility   he   go back   home   Asp.
       "There is the possibility that he went back home."

Category 2: Metaphorical Realizations of Usuality

The structure of *shi…de* is the only method for the metaphorical realization of usuality in Chinese. Adverbs, on the other hand, are the sole resource for the congruent construal of usuality in the language. Therefore, the metaphorical expression of usuality with *shi…de* involves the grammatical movement from Adjunct to isolating process, which is represented by Example (20).

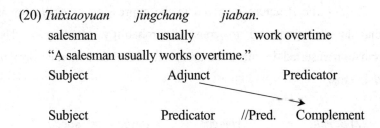

(20) *Tuixiaoyuan*   *jingchang*   *jiaban.*
       salesman   usually   work overtime
       "A salesman usually works overtime."
       Subject   Adjunct   Predicator

       Subject   Predicator   //Pred.   Complement

Tuixiaoyuan	*jiaban*		*shi*	*jingchang*	*de.*
salesman	work overtime		is	usual	Sub.

"It is usual for salesman to work overtime."

Category 3: Metaphorical Realizations of Obligation

With respect to the meaning of obligation, three kinds of metaphorical realization are involved: projecting clause, *shi...de* structure and *you ...* structure. In addition, the obligation in Chinese is construed congruently through modal verbs. The metaphorical realizations of obligation are therefore concerned with the grammatical movement from Finite to projecting clause, *shi...de* and *you...* structures.

(i) Expressing obligation with projecting clause

The projecting clause involved in the expression of obligation consists of a mental process with a first-person participant.   For example:

(21) *Xuesheng* *bixu* *zai* *23* *hao* *jiao* *zuoye.*
students must in 23 day submit assignment
"Students must submit their assignments in 23."
Subject Finite Adjunct Pred.   Complement

Subject Pred.// Subject   Adjunct Pred.   Complement
Wo *yaoqiu* *xuesheng* *zai* *23* *hao* *jiao* *zuoye.*
I require students in 23 day submit assignment
"I require my students to submit their assignments in 23."

(ii) Expressing obligation with *shi...de* structure

The *shi...de* structure involved in the expression of obligation is similar to the one used to construe probability meanings.   The information inserted in the structure is also encoded in the form of modal verbs.

(22) *Banche*   *yinggai*   *anshi*   *daoda.*

shuttle bus	should		on time	arrive

"The shuttle bus should arrive on time."

Subject		Finite		Adjunct	Predicator

Subject	Adjunct	Pred.//	Pred.	Complement
Banche	*anshi*	*daoda*	*shi*	*yinggai*	*de.*
shuttle bus	on time	arrive	is	should	Sub.

"It is sure that the shuttle bus arrives on time."

(iii) Expressing obligation with *you*...structure

Like those expressing probability, the *you*...structure in the metaphorical realization of obligation is an isolated process. This is illustrated by Example (23).

(23) *Women*   *bixu*   *zhichi*   *zhengfu*

We   must   support   government

"We must support our government."

Subject	Finite	Predicator	Complement

Pred.	Complement//Pred.		Complement
You	*biyao*	*zhichi*	*zhengfu*
have	necessity	support	government.

"There is a necessity to support our government."

Category 4: Metaphorical Realizations of Inclination

The only approach to realizing inclination metaphorically in Chinese is *shi*...*de* structure. As the meaning of inclination is congruently realized by modal verbs and adverbs, this category of modality metaphor involves the grammatical movement from Finite or Adjunct to *shi*...*de* structure. See Examples (24) and (25).

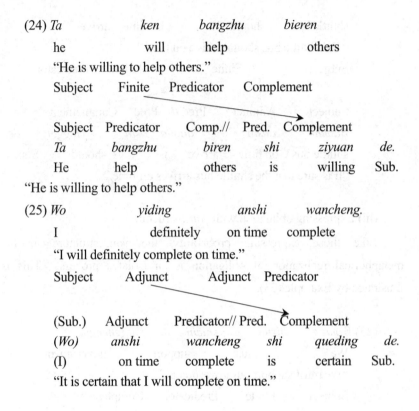

(24) *Ta*　　　　*ken*　　　*bangzhu*　　　*bieren*
　　　he　　　　　will　　　help　　　　　others
　　　"He is willing to help others."
　　　Subject　　Finite　　Predicator　　Complement

　　　Subject　Predicator　Comp.//　Pred.　Complement
　　　Ta　　　*bangzhu*　　*biren*　　*shi*　　*ziyuan*　　*de.*
　　　He　　　help　　　others　　is　　willing　　Sub.
　　　"He is willing to help others."

(25) *Wo*　　　　*yiding*　　　*anshi*　　　*wancheng.*
　　　I　　　　definitely　　on time　　complete
　　　"I will definitely complete on time."
　　　Subject　　Adjunct　　　Adjunct　　Predicator

　　　(Sub.)　　Adjunct　　Predicator//　Pred.　Complement
　　　(Wo)　　*anshi*　　　*wancheng*　　*shi*　　*queding*　　*de.*
　　　(I)　　　on time　　complete　　is　　certain　　Sub.
　　　"It is certain that I will complete on time."

Depending on the description of metaphorical realizations of various types of modality, the categories of metaphor of modality and their subcategories in Chinese are displayed in Table 5.

Table 5　Categories and subcategories of metaphor of modality in Chinese

Categories of Metaphor of modality	Subcategories
1. Metaphorical realizations of probability	(i) projecting clause; (ii) *shi...de* structure; iii) *you* ... structure;
2. Metaphorical realizations of usuality	*shi...de* structure
3. Metaphorical realizations of obligation	(i) projecting clause; (ii) *shi...de* structure; (iii) you ... structure
4. Metaphorical realizations of inclination	*shi...de* structure

3. Corpus Selection and Corpus Analysis

This section describes the corpus on which the analysis of interpersonal GM deployment in Chinese is based, clarifying the size of the corpus and the process of corpus selection and analysis. The corpus used for the present research is a very large corpus of spontaneous spoken Chinese, which is composed by recordings of television programs broadcasted in mainland China.

3.1 Methodological Issues

Two methodological issues must be considered before the selection of corpus: 1) the frequency of GM instances in spoken Chinese and 2) the feasibility of identifying GM instances with specific words or structures in the language. Prior to this study, there is no research on interpersonal GM in Chinese. The lack of information about the real frequency of GM instances in Chinese gives rise to the difficulty of corpus selection. In order to determine the size of spoken Chinese corpus to be used, a pilot study should be conducted to test the occurrence of GM instances in spoke Chinese.

A spoken Chinese corpus of 60,000 characters is collected for this purpose. Although the corpus is numerically small by current standards of corpus linguistics, it is adequate for the pilot study of interpersonal GM. The size of the corpus is not all-important. It follows design principles that make its material represents major varieties of naturalistic spoken Chinese. The corpus is assembled by recording spontaneous formal and informal conversations in the Chinese department of a Singapore university. It is collected between January 2010 and January 2011 as part of a research project on the grammatical characteristics of spoken Chinese. The speakers involved in the corpus are male and female native speakers of Mandarin Chinese aged between 20 and 50 year-old. The corpus contains text types of daily conversation, class session, study group and staff meeting, each of which is represented by two discourses.

This small corpus is analyzed with the framework developed for interpersonal GM identification and categorization in Section 2. It is found that interpersonal GM instances tend to occur much less frequently than expected. Most categories of interpersonal GM occur fewer than 5 times per discourse, and some types of GM are observed only once (or not at all) in a discourse. In addition, the distribution of GM instances in the corpus is not uniform across discourses. The occurrence of GM instances may be accidentally high in a particular discourse, leading to the incorrect conclusions about the frequency of GM deployment. For example, a discourse of class session in the corpus happens to have 27 metaphorical expressions because the teacher uses interrogative clauses as examples of his teaching. Because of the low frequency and unbalanced distribution of GM instances, this study requires a very large corpus to examine the use of interpersonal GM in spoken Chinese. It is worth noting that this pilot study merely provides an indication of the scope of interpersonal GM in spoken Chinese. Sections 4 and 5 reveal the distribution of GM in more detailed ways, ranging from the topic of discussion and the relation between speaker and addressee.

The feasibility of identifying GM instances with specific words and structures is also investigated in the pilot study. Section 2 discusses three critical lexico-grammatical phenomena for the identification of interpersonal GM in Chinese, namely Mood particle, '*shi...de*' and '*you...*' structures. The pilot study shows that they have distinctive impacts on the GM instance recognition in the corpus. Mood particles increase the difficulty of identifying GM instances, while '*shi...de*' and '*you...*' structures make the identification easier.

Previous research on Mood particles in Chinese reveals that these particles are often associated with metaphorical realizations of speech functions (Li and Thompson, 1981; Zhu, 1996). Some of these particles like *ne* and *a/ya* are capable of expressing different types of mood without changing the main structure of the clause. This characteristic of Mood particles determines that they cannot be used as the keywords for an automatic search of GM instances in a corpus. In other words, the metaphorical expressions engendered by the use of Mood particles have to be manually identified. This is practically impossible for the analysis of a very large corpus required by the present research. In order to solve this problem, this study assembles a relatively small corpus from the large one to conduct a manual analysis. This point will be explained in Section 3.3 with more details.

Section 2 shows that grammatical structures of '*shi...de*' and '*you...*' are involved in the expression of each type of modality in Chinese. The modality meanings construed by '*shi...de*' and '*you...*' structures are expressed explicitly with specific words. This feature determines that GM instances with these structures are appropriate for an automatic search in a large corpus. In this sense, the special structures of '*shi...de*' and '*you...*' actually increase the feasibility of identifying GM instances in Chinese.

3.2   Selection of Spoken Chinese Corpus

The focus of this study is to reveal the overall profile of interpersonal GM use in spoken Chinese and the distribution of GM across registers. For this purpose, a corpus formed by different registers of spoken discourses is required for the detailed analysis. The corpus must be large enough to contain sufficient GM instances due to the fact that interpersonal GM are not observed very frequently in spoken Chinese. In addition, it should compose of authentic examples of contemporary spoken Chinese and naturalistic conversations.

Authentic spoken language samples are always difficult to obtain although they are valuable for the linguistic studies. In the past five decades, great efforts have been made to build spoken language corpora. The most important and notable corpora developed since the 1960s include Oral Vocabulary of the Australian Worker Corpus (Schonell et al., 1956), London-Lund Corpus (Svartvik, 1990), COBUILD Bank of English (Moon, 1997) and British National Corpus (Crowdy, 1993; Rundell 1995). However, these spoken corpora are assembled for the study of English or other western languages. There have been few spoken Chinese corpora because of the complexity of the language and the delayed development of relevant research. Since the 1990s, some corpora have been developed in mainland China, Taiwan and the UK to collect spoken data for the study of Chinese Language.

Mandarin Conversational Dialogue Corpus (MCDC) and Mandarin Topic-oriented Conversation Corpus (MTCC) are the representatives of spoken Chinese corpora developed in Taiwan. They are developed by Taiwan's Academia Sincia respectively in 1997 and 2001. Each corpus contains conversations produced by three groups of randomly selected speakers in their twenties, thirties and forties. The conversations were transcribed so that it is possible to work out syntactic structures and discourse devices used by speakers in different ages. The size of the two corpora is relatively small (120,000 characters for MCDC and 200,000 characters for MTCC).

The Lancaster Los Angeles Spoken Chinese Corpus (LLSCC) is a corpus of spoken Mandarin Chinese developed in the UK. The corpus is composed of 1,002,151 words of dialogues and monologues, both spontaneous and scripted, in 73,976 sentences and 49,670 utterance units (paragraphs). The corpus has seven sub-corpora, i.e., conversations, telephone calls, play & movie transcripts, TV talk show transcripts, debate transcripts, oral narratives and edited oral narratives.

The corpora for spoken Chinese complied in mainland China are normally large in size. The most ambitious spoken Chinese corpus under construction is Modern Spoken Chinese Corpus (MSCC), which contains about one billion Chinese characters. Broadcast Media Spoken Chinese Corpus (BMSCC) is a 100 million-character corpus developed by Media University. It is the largest spoken Chinese corpus readily available until now.

This concise review of major spoken Chinese corpora demonstrates that the resource of spoken Chinese corpus is very limited compared to that of English. Given the low occurrence of interpersonal GM in spoken Chinese, the analysis in this study needs a corpus large in size. Those small corpora, such as MCDC and MTCC, are obviously not suitable for the present research. The wide range of text types in LLSCC is very appropriate for the exploration of GM distribution across registers, although the corpus is still relatively small. The major limitation to LLSCC is that it has not been released to the public because of copyright restrictions. There are some other spoken Chinese corpora not mentioned above. However, these corpora are ordinarily small in size and not open to external users. Taking all these factors into consideration, BMSCC is the only corpus eligible for the analysis in this study.

BMSCC is a corpus of spoken Mandarin Chinese consisting of monologues and dialogues recorded from selected television programs broadcasted in mainland China from 2008 to 2010. The corpus comprises about 100 million Chinese characters in 15871 program episodes. The discourses in the corpus can be divided into smaller corpora according to their media form, source channels, communicative mode, discussion topic and even program host. The content of the corpus covers both read speech and spontaneous dialogues and multipart discussions. The discussion topics involved in the corpus includes news, arts, economy and society. In summary, the sub-corpora of BMSCC cover the major varieties of modern spoken Chinese. Such a design of corpus building allows insights to be developed concerning distinctions between different registers of spoken Chinese with regards to the use of interpersonal GM.

It is relatively easy to build a large corpus by recording television and radio output. However, the corpus developed in this way has its own limitation in that part of the corpus is not representative of typical conversation. For instance, some speakers in a program may prepare what they are going to say before the program is broadcasted. This research is very careful in the selection of sub-corpora in BMSCC to minimize the effect of this limitation. The spoken discourses used for the analysis in this study are drawn from spontaneous programs broadcasted in television. Moreover, only spontaneous dialogues in the corpus are selected for the analysis of GM, while read speech and multipart discussions are not included. After these selections, a corpus including 4182 spoken Chinese discourses is utilized for the detailed analysis.

As discussed in Section 3.1, certain types of metaphorical expressions are not appropriate for automatic corpus search. This chapter thus needs a corpus which is smaller and more manageable for a manual analysis which takes the context of relevant expressions into consideration. There are two methods to realize this aim: 1) using the small corpus developed for pilot study and 2) selecting discourses from the large corpus. This research adopts the second method in order to integrate the results of analyzing small and large corpora. According to the register theory of Halliday (1978), there are two considerations that should be borne in mind for the assembly of small corpus from the large one: the topic of dialogue and the relationship between speaker and addressee. This research first uses the relationship between speaker and addressee as a parameter to sample speeches from BMSCC. It is found that in some episodes speakers are equal and in other units they are unequal in social relations. Both discourses with equal and unequal social relations are selected from the large corpus. In addition, the small corpus covers the full range of discussion topics found in BMSCC, i.e., news, arts, economy and society. The detailed composition of the small corpus is shown in Table 6.

Table 6　Composition of the small corpus

Relationship	Topic			
	News	Arts	Economy	Society
Equal relation	5	5	5	5
Unequal relation	5	5	5	5

Table 6 shows that the small corpus consists of 40 discourses, 20 involving equal relationship between participants and 20 unequal. On the other hand, 10 discourses are collected from each area of discussion. To sum up, the exploration of interpersonal GM deployment in spoken Chinese is based on the analysis of a large corpus (hereinafter Corpus A) with 4182 discourses and a small one (hereafter Corpus B) containing 40 transcripts of speech.

3.3　Corpus Analysis

The analysis of corpus is carried out in two steps: 1) identification of GM instances and 2) the quantification of GM instances. The identification of GM instances is mainly implemented with the search engine on the website of BMSCC. Manual annotation of Corpus B is sometimes required to compensate the deficiency of Corpus A for the analysis of certain types of GM. The quantification of GM instances is realized by adding up the amount of each types of GM instance in the corpora. In order to conduct an automatic search of GM instances, this research needs a search engine with the following three functions:

1) to search for particular categories of GM instances;
2) to show distributions of GM instances across different text types;
3) to visualize the source text in which GM instance are located.

BMSCC has the functions of automatic keyword searching and keyword search statistic on its website. The user of the corpus may search the corpus for single Chinese character, word or phrase. The corpus allows users to search a pair of keywords at the same time. It provides different search options, enabling the user to select the area in which he wants to search for the required information. For example, a user can search the use of particular words or phrases in different television programs or time periods. In addition, the corpus permits its users to read the source text in which the words or phrases are included. Moreover, a user has the option to select the linguistic unit in which his search results are displayed, i.e., in clause, paragraph or text.   Finally, the results of search can be downloaded into a new file for further analysis. The search engine of BMSCC thus fulfills the requirements of the present study.

The identification of interpersonal GM instances in the corpus begins with the choosing of words and structures to be used for automatic search. Following this, BMSCC is automatically processed with the search engine on its websites. The task of quantifying interpersonal GM instances depends on the identification of metaphorical expressions in the data. The GM instances found in the corpus are first counted according to their subcategories in individual sub-corpora.   The GM instances in different sub-corpora are then added up in terms of category to measure the numbers of each category of interpersonal GM in the corpus. In the light of the quantifying work, this study defines the distribution of each elemental GM category in spoken Chinese.

4. Overall Distribution of Interpersonal GM Categories

This section examines how the two types of interpersonal GM, namely, metaphor of mood and metaphor of modality are distributed in spoken Chinese. The metaphorical expressions of speech functions and modality are further divided into subcategories as shown in Tables 4 and 5 (see

Section 2.2 for further details). This section explores the distribution of each subcategory of GM in Tables 4 and 5 through a quantitative analysis of GM instances in the corpora selected.

4.1 Metaphor of Mood

Section 2 shows that the metaphor of mood in Chinese has four subcategories in terms of the mood choices involved in the metaphorical expression of speech functions: 1) expressing command with interrogative mood, 2) expressing command with declarative mood, 3) expressing statement with interrogative mood, and 4) expressing question with declarative mood. In addition, metaphor of mood in Chinese may be classified according to the two major forms of realization: 1) normal form of mood expression and 2) speech-functional formulae. The combination of the two ways of categorization thus results in a realization system of metaphor of mood in Chinese as shown in Figure 3.

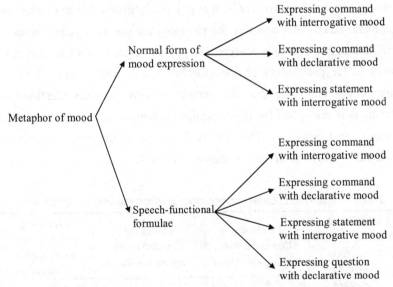

Figure 3   Realization system of metaphor of mood in Chinese

The analysis of the distribution of metaphor of mood in spoken

Chinese is conducted with reference to this realization system. The GM instances in the selected corpora are first identified according to their forms of realization, namely normal form and speech-functional formulae. The metaphorical expressions involved thus fall in two groups: 1) normal form group and 2) speech-functional formulae group. These two groups of GM instances are then differentiated and quantified with respect to mood choices in expressing speech functions. As shown in Figure 3, the normal form group includes three types of speech function expressions. The speech-functional formulae are involved in all the four types of speech function expressions discussed in Section 2.

Metaphor of mood in Group 2 is appropriate for the automatic search of Corpus A because speech-functional formulae are words or structures easy to define. The metaphorical expressions in Group 1, on the other hand, must be recognized by manually analyzing a small corpus because they are usually realized with Mood particles involved in the expression of different types of mood. In other words, it is practically impossible to conduct an automatic search of Corpus A for metaphorical expressions in Group 1. This section thus manually analyzes Corpus B composed of 40 discourses to estimate the distribution of metaphor of mood with normal form of expression. Following this, the number of GM instances identified in Corpus B is multiplied by 10 to acquire the approximate quantity of GM instances in Corpus A. The estimated number of the three subtypes of metaphor of mood in Group 1 is shown in Table 7.

Table 7   Estimated number of metaphor of mood realized in normal form

Metaphor of Mood realized in normal form (Group 1)	Expressing Command with Interrogative Mood	Expressing Command with Declarative Mood	Expressing Statement with Interrogative Mood
Estimated number	290 (29 x 10)	530 (53 x 10)	1470 (147 x 10)
Estimated Percentage	12.7%	23.1%	64.2%

Table 7 shows that the metaphorical expressions of statement occur much more frequently than those construed for the purpose of expressing command. Moreover, the speech function of command is expressed more commonly with declarative mood. The results in Table 7 should be considered preliminary because they are estimated on the basis of an analysis of a corpus small in size. However, they are useful for describing the major trends of how metaphor of mood realized in normal form are deployed in spoken Chinese.

The identification of metaphor of mood realized in speech-functional formulae is more straightforward because relevant expressions are concerned with words and structures easy to search in the corpus. Table 8 illustrates the breakdown of GM instance numbers in Corpus A across different subtypes of metaphor of mood in Group 2.

Table 8　Number of metaphor of mood realized in speech-functional formulae

Metaphor of mood realized in speech-functiona l formulae (Group 2)	Expressing Command with Interrogative Mood	Expressing Command with Declarative Mood	Expressing Statement with Interrogative Mood	Expressing Question with declarative Mood
Number	544	671	2928	352
Percentage (%)	12.1	14.9	65.1	7.9

Table 8 shows that distribution of GM instances realized in speech-functional formulae is very similar to that of metaphor of mood in normal form. The metaphorical expressions of Statement are by far the most common GM instances observed in the corpus. Declarative mood is used more frequently for expressing command than interrogative mood. In order to show the overall profile of metaphor of mood in spoken Chinese, the results in Tables 7 and 8 are combined in Figure 4.

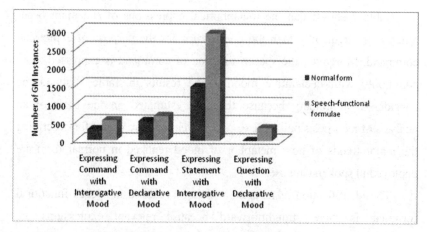

Figure 4   The distribution of metaphor of mood in spoken Chinese

As shown in Figure 4, there are three major characteristics in the distribution of metaphor of mood in Chinese:

1) The metaphor of mood in Chinese is mainly expressed by speech functional formulae including '*haibu...*' (yet not), '*bushi...ma?*' (not is ... Mood particle), '*Wo xiang zhidao/liaojie ...*'(I want to know/enquire...), etc.   To be more specific, GM instances realized in speech-functional formulae are almost three times as many as those realized in normal form.

2) Interrogative mood is especially prevalent in the metaphorical realization of speech functions, accounting for half of the instances of metaphor of mood in Chinese.   More specifically, interrogative mood is used in relation to the expression of statement in the majority instances of metaphor of mood.

3) The metaphorical expression of command is also common in Chinese although its frequency is not as high as that of statement.

It seems that the last two characteristics of metaphor of mood in Chinese are associated with the politeness strategies described by Brown and Levinson (1987). A speaker uses an interrogative to express a statement because he or she intends to minimize face-threatening acts (FTAs). Similarly, the command metaphorically expressed by an interrogative or a declarative has the effect of maintaining face of speaker or hearer involved. This point is not discussed in detail here as it is not the main focus of this research.

4.2   Metaphor of Modality

As revealed in Section 2, the metaphorical realizations of modality in Chinese can be classified from two perspectives: 1) the types of modality, and 2) the grammatical methods involved in metaphorical realization. To be more specific, there are four types of modality in Chinese, i.e., probability, usuality, obligation and inclination. The grammatical methods involved in the metaphorical realization of modality meaning are projecting clause and special structures of *shi* ... *de* and *you*... . Modality type and grammatical method are combined in this section to establish a realization system of metaphor of modality in spoken Chinese, as shown in Figure 5.

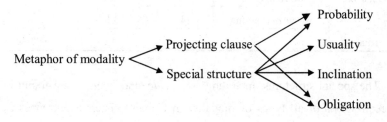

Figure 5   Realization system of metaphor of modality in Chinese

This section first explores the distribution of metaphor of modality realized by projecting clauses. Figure 5 shows that only probability and obligation meanings are involved in this form of realization. All the projecting clauses listed out in Table 2 are searched one by one in Corpus A. Their frequencies in the corpus are displayed in Table 9.

Table 9 shows that projecting clauses realizing probability meaning are used much more frequently than those with the obligation meaning in Corpus A. To be more specific, metaphorical expression of probability is almost 50 times more frequent than that of obligation in the corpus. This distribution of GM instances demonstrates that the primary purpose of using projecting clause in spoken Chinese is to construe the meaning of probability.

Table 9　Number of metaphor of modality realized by projecting clauses

Modality	Projecting clause	Number	Percentage(%)	Total
Probability	*wo xiangxin* (I believe)	1278	13.8	9263
	wo guji (I estimate)	608	6.6	
	wo xiang (I think)	4937	53.3	
	wo renwei (I reckon)	2440	26.3	
Obligation	*wo yaoqiu* (I require)	47	21.8	216
	wo rang (I let)	158	73.1	
	wo yunxu (I permit)	11	5.1	
Total				9479

The special structures, including *'shi ... de'* and *'you...'*, are found in the realizations of all types of modality in Chinese. Their occurrences in Corpus A are displayed in Table 10.

Table 10   Number of metaphor of modality realized in special structures

Modality	Special structure	Number of GM instances	Total	Percentage (%)
Probability	*shi kending de* (is must Sub.)	42	416	39.5
	you keneng (have possibility)	374		
Obligation	*shi bixu de* (is necessary Sub.)	70	571	54.2
	you biyao (have necessity)	501		
Usuality	*shi changyou de* (is often Sub.)	39	39	3.7
Inclination	*shi ziyuan de* (is willing Sub.)	28	28	2.6
Total			1054	100

Table 10 shows that metaphorical expressions realized by special structures are distributed in different ways across four types of modality. In general, the expressions with probability and obligation meanings are much more common in the corpus. Those expressing usuality and inclination meanings are obviously rare, reaching just over 7 percent of relevant GM instances. Unlike the unequal distribution of GM instances with the meaning of probability and obligation in Table 9, the deployment of these two types of GM in Table 10 is more balanced.

The comparison of Tables 9 and 10 reveals that GM instances realized by projecting clauses are used nine times more frequently than those expressed in the form of special structure. This distribution of grammatical methods realizing modality meaning in Corpus A shows that projecting clause is the dominant method used for the expression of metaphor of modality in Chinese. In order to demonstrate the general patterns of how metaphor of modality is distributed in Chinese, the findings in Tables 9 and 10 are integrated in Figure 6.

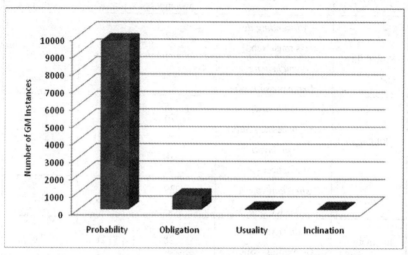

Figure 6   General distribution of metaphor of modality in spoken Chinese

Figure 6 shows that two general patterns of GM deployment in Chinese emerge from the corpus analysis: 1) the distribution of interpersonal GM instances is very uneven across the four types of metaphor of modality; and 2) the metaphorical expressions of probability are used much more commonly in spoken Chinese than those of any other types of modality.

This section also attempts to describe the distribution of metaphor of modality observed with reference to the value of modality.   According to Halliday and Matthiessen (2004: 620), one of the major variables of modality is "the value that attached to the modal judgement: high, median or low". The projecting clauses and special structures involved in the realization of metaphor of modality are differentiated in terms of their value of modality, as shown in Table 11.   In addition, the numbers of each type of expression observed in Corpus A are included in Table 11 to show the distribution of GM in terms of modality value.

Table 11   Distribution of GM in terms of modality value

Level	Type				
	Probability	Usuality	Obligation	inclination	Total
High	Certain: *wo xiangxin* (1278) *shi ...de/you* (416)	Always: *shi...de* (39)	Required: *wo yunxu* (11) *shi...de/you* (571)	Determined: *shi...de* (28)	2343 (22.3%)
Median	Probable: *wo renwei* (2440)	Usually	Supposed: *wo yaoqiu* (48)	Keen:	2488 (23.6%)
Low	Possible: *wo guji* (608) *wo xiang* (4937)	Sometimes	Allowed: *wo rang* (158)	Willing:	5703 (54.1%)

Table 11 shows that the metaphorical expressions with a low value of modality are highly preferred in Chinese conversations.   More than half of the GM instances in the domain of modality are used to express the meanings of 'possible' and 'allowed'.   Given that the proportion of the GM instances with the meaning of 'allowed' is small, the primary purpose of using metaphor of modality by Chinese speakers is to show that they are not certain about their conclusions. On the contrary, the metaphorical expressions with high and median values of modality are employed less commonly by Chinese speakers.

5. Distribution of Interpersonal GM across Registers

This section compares how the two types of interpersonal GM, i.e., metaphor of mood and metaphor of modality are distributed across different registers.   In order to describe the situation in which language is used,

Halliday (1978) develops register theory and recognizes three dimensions of situation:

    1) Field of discourse: what language is being used to talk about
    2) Tenor of discourse: the role relationships between the participants
    3) Mode of discourse: the role language is playing in the interaction

According to Eggins (1994), the variable of Field includes the topic and the interactants of discourse. The topic of discourse can be specialized or everyday, while the interactants may have specialized or common knowledge of the field. The variable of Tenor varies according to the change of status, affective involvement and contact between the participants. The variable of Mode is mainly concerned with the difference between written and spoken languages. For example, a conversation is spontaneous while a composition is planned. Given that Mode of discourses in the corpus selected has been clearly defined as spontaneous conversation, the analysis of GM deployment across registers focuses on the effects of Field and Tenor. The contextual factors involved in the description of Field and Tenor are summarized in Table 12.

Table 12   Contextual factors in Field and Tenor of discourse

Field	Topic	Specialized
		Everyday
	Interactant	Specialized knowledge
		Common knowledge
Tenor	Status	Equal
		Unequal
	Affective involvement	High (family/friends)
		Low (business clients)
	Contact	Frequent
		Occasional

The corpus used in the present research is composed of conversations broadcasted on television programs. The affective involvement in these programs is normally low, while the contact between speakers is occasional. The status between participants in relevant programs is thus the major consideration of Tenor analysis. This study thus selects two groups of program from Corpus A in which the status between participants is respectively equal and unequal. With respect to Field of television conversations, the factors of topic and interactant are in fact interrelated. Experts with specialized knowledge are usually invited to participate in television programs with specialized topic. It is very rare to see ordinary people in a television program talking about a professional issue. This study concentrates the analysis of Field on the topic of discussion because BMSCC allows the automatic search of discourses according to their topics. Taken all these considerations together, the present research examines the use of interpersonal GM in different registers from two perspectives:

1) The connection between the deployment of interpersonal GM and the topic of discussion;

2) The correlation between the deployment of interpersonal GM and the status between speaker and hearer.

One critical methodology issue in the comparison of GM distribution across different registers is that relevant registers are not equally represented in the corpus selected. For example, the sub-corpus for register of society consists of 1030 texts, while the sub-corpus of arts includes only 318 discourses. This section thus changes all raw frequency counts to a rate of occurrence per text to compensate the unbalance between sub-corpora of different registers. For instance, the metaphorical expressions of Probability occur 201 times in register of arts and the total number of texts in the register is 318. Thus, the rate of occurrence for this type of interpersonal GM in arts register is:

201/318 = 0.63 times per text

The corpora selected for the analysis in this study falls into four registers in terms of topic: 1) news, 2) arts, 3) economy and 4) society. This study first inspects the frequency of two types of interpersonal GM across these registers. The rate of occurrence for the four subtypes of metaphor of mood in different registers is illustrated in Table 13.

Table 13   Distribution of metaphor of mood across topics

Topics	Metaphor of mood			
	Expressing Command with Interrogative Mood	Expressing Command with Declarative Mood	Expressing Statement with Interrogative Mood	Expressing Question with declarative Mood
News	0.17	0.28	1.03	0.08
Arts	0.19	0.26	1.05	0.07
Economy	0.21	0.29	1.01	0.08
Society	0.17	0.30	1.04	0.06

Table 13 shows that the conversations with different topics are similar in using different types of metaphor of mood. In other words, the deployment of metaphor of mood in Chinese is not greatly affected by the change of conversation topic.

As discussed above, the distribution of GM instances is very uneven across different types of modality in Chinese. It is not necessary to discuss the occurrence of metaphorical expressions with the meanings of usuality and inclination since they are observed less than 40 times in the corpus.

This study only calculates the rate of occurrence for GM instances with the meanings of probability and obligation, as illustrated in Table 14.

Table 14　Distribution of metaphor of modality across topics

Topics	Metaphor of Modality			
	Probability (9679 instances)	Obligation (787 instances)	Usuality (39 instances)	Inclination (28 instances)
News	3.11	0.18	Not calculated	Not calculated
Arts	0.63	0.19	Not calculated	Not calculated
Economy	1.74	0.15	Not calculated	Not calculated
Society	4.07	0.19	Not calculated	Not calculated

Table 14 shows that GM instances with obligation meaning are evenly distributed across registers with different topics. But the occurrence rate of metaphorical expressions with probability meaning differs dramatically in different registers. The discourses in the fields of news and society have a much higher frequency of GM deployment than those in the other two areas. It means Chinese speakers use a much larger set of GM instances to express probability when they discuss news and society. Among the four types of discourse in the corpus, news and society belong to everyday topics requiring less professional knowledge. Arts and economy are relatively more specialized topics that only a few people are qualified to discuss in depth. Those who are invited to participate in a television program covering these two topics are frequently top specialists in relevant fields. In this case, the speakers involved are very confident about their own opinions. This may be the reason why the occurrence of GM instances expressing probability meaning is low in arts and economy registers.

The examination of how GM deployment is affected by the change of social status between speaker and hearer is more complicated because the metaphorical expressions must be searched program by program. This research selects 17 programs from Corpus A in which the status between participants can be clearly defined as equal or unequal, including 2132 spoken discourses. Considering that the number of discourses involved is smaller, only the most frequently observed GM categories are covered in this examination. The results of examination are displayed in Table 15.

Table 15 shows that the most striking contrast between programs involving participants with equal and unequal status is their differential reliance on interrogative mood. The conversation participants unequal in status prefer to use more interrogatives to express the meanings of statement and command than those equal in status. In order to explore the reason for this preference on interrogative mood, this study conducts a thorough analysis of 50 spoken discourses in which the status between participants is unequal. The analysis demonstrates that interrogative mood is ordinarily used by speakers lower in social status, such as program host. In other words, the reliance on interrogative mood in programs with unequal participants is largely engendered by the need of speakers low in status to show their respect to hearers with higher status. More generally, the deployment of metaphor of mood in Chinese is related to the status relationship between speaker and hearer. Table 15 also demonstrates that the use of two major types of metaphor of modality, i.e., probability and obligation, is not greatly affected by the status between relevant speakers and hearers.

Table 15 Distribution of GM instances in relation to status

| Status | GM | | | | |
| | Metaphor of Mood | | | Metaphor of Modality | |
	Expressing Command with Interrogative Mood	Expressing Command with Declarative Mood	Expressing Statement with Interrogative Mood	Probability	Obligation
Equal (10 programs 1287 discourses)	0.10	0.24	0.83	2.01	0.15
Unequal (7 programs 845 discourses)	0.23	0.27	1.57	2.37	0.18

6. Conclusions

The discussion in this study has been focused on the use of interpersonal GM in spoken Chinese. A large corpus of natural spoken Chinese is analyzed to explore how interpersonal GM instances are distributed in the language and how the frequency of different types of interpersonal GM is affected by the change of dialogue topic and social relationship between speaker and addressee. Prior to the actual corpus analysis, this study develops a framework for identifying and categorizing interpersonal GM in Chinese by distinguishing congruent and metaphorical realizations of semantic meanings in interpersonal domain and differentiating grammatical methods involved in metaphorical expressions.

The framework is the first attempt to describe interpersonal GM systematically, providing a basis for further research in this area. Moreover, the framework reveals that certain lexical and grammatical phenomena, including Mood particles and structures of *shi* ... *de* and *you* ..., are critical for the recognition of interpersonal GM instances in Chinese.

In this study, the distribution of metaphor of mood and metaphor of modality are examined separately to simplify discussion. The overall picture of interpersonal GM distribution in spoken Chinese emerging from the corpus analysis is as follows:

1) Metaphor of modality is used much more frequently than metaphor of mood in spoken Chinese;

2) The majority cases of metaphor of mood in Chinese are realized in the form of speech-functional formulae;

3) Interrogative is the most commonly used mood in the metaphorical expression of speech functions in spoken Chinese;

4) Metaphor of modality is predominantly realized in the form of projecting clause in spoken Chinese;

5) Metaphor of modality has a very uneven distribution in spoken Chinese, with a particular high occurrence in the expression of probability;

6) Metaphorical expressions with a lower value of modality are used more frequently in spoken Chinese.

It is important to recognize from these characteristics that interpersonal GM in spoken Chinese has a greater reliance on certain types of metaphorical expressions. In general, metaphor of modality is the major part of interpersonal GM in spoken Chinese. To be more specific, GM instances realized by speech-functional formulae, projecting clauses and interrogatives are used more frequently in the language. The metaphorical expressions with the meaning of probability and lower value of modality are highly preferred by Chinese speakers. The reason for these patterns of interpersonal GM deployment in Chinese is an interesting direction for further research although it is not explored in this study.

In order to reveal the relationship between social factors and the meaning creation in spoken Chinese, this study also investigates the use of interpersonal GM in different registers. The investigation focuses on the correlation between the deployment of GM instances and the register variables of Field and Tenor. It is found that the use of interpersonal GM in spoken Chinese is affected by the conversation topic and the social status between speaker and hearer. In particular, the use of metaphor of modality is sensitive to the change of conversation topics which require different degrees of professional knowledge. The deployment of metaphor of mood reflects the variation of social status between speaker and hearer. There are other contextual factors which may affect the use of interpersonal GM in Chinese. Restricted by the corpus selected, they are not discussed in this study.

References

Crowdy, S. 1993. Spoken Corpus Design. Literary and Linguistic Computing 8(2), pp. 259-265.

Chao, Y. 1968. A Grammar of Spoken Chinese. Berkeley & Los Angels: University of California Press.

DeFrancis, J. 1984. The Chinese Language: Fact and Fantasy. Honolulu: University of Hawaii Press.

Eggins, S. 1994. An Introduction to Systemic Functional Linguistics. London: Pinter.

Halliday, M.A.K. 1978. Language as Social Semiotic: The Social Interpretation of Language and Meaning. London: Edward Arnold.

Halliday, M.A.K. 1985. *Spoken and Written Language.* Geelong Victoria: Deaking University Press.

Halliday, M.A.K. 1994. An Introduction to Functional Grammar. London: Edward Arnold.

Halliday, M.A.K., 1998. Things and Relations: Regrammaticising Experience as Technical Knowledge. In J.R. Martin and R. Veel (eds.). Reading Science: Critical and Functional Perspectives on Discourses of Science. London: Routledge. pp. 185-236.

Halliday, M.A.K. Matthiessen, C.M.I.M., 1999. Construing Experience through Meaning: A Language-based Approach to Cognition. London: Cassell.

Halliday, M.A.K. Matthiessen, C.M.I.M., 2004. An Introduction to Functional Grammar. London: Edward Arnold.

Li, C., Thompson, S. A. 1981. Mandarin Chinese: A Functional Reference Grammar. Berkeley: University of California Press.

Lü, S. X., 1982. Zhongguo Wenfa Yaolüe. (An Outline of Chinese Grammars). Shanghai: Commercial Press.

Moon, R., 1997. Vocabulary Connections: Multi-word Items in English. In Schmitt, N. and McCarthy, M.J. (eds.) Second Language Vocabulary: Description, Acquisition and Pedagogy. Cambridge: Cambridge University Press, pp. 40-63.

Palmer, F.R., 2001. *Mood and Modality.* Cambridge: Cambridge University Press.

Ravelli, L., 1985. Metaphor, Mode and Complexity: An Exploration of Co-varying Patterns. BA Dissertation: University of Sydney.

Romero, E. & Soria, B., 2005. The Notion of Grammatical Metaphor in Halliday. In J.L. Martínez-Dueñas Espejo, C. Pérez Basanta, N. Mclaren L. Quereda Rodríguez-Navarro (eds.), *Towards an Understanding of the English Language: Past, Present and Future. Studies in Honour of Fernando Serrano,* Granada: Universidad de Granada, pp. 143-158.

Rundell, M., 1995. The BNC: A Spoken Corpus. Modern English Teacher 4(2): 13-15.

Schonell, F., Meddleton, I., Shaw, B., Routh, M., Popham, D., Gill, G., Mackrell, G. Stephens, C., 1956. A Study of the Oral Vocabulary of Adults. Brisbane: University of London Press.

Svartvik, J., 1990. The London-Lund Corpus of Spoken English: Description and Research. Lund: Lund University Press.

Tsang, C.L., 1981. *A Semantic Study of Modal Auxiliary Verbs in Chinese*. PhD Thesis: Stanford University.

Wang, L., 1956. Zhongguo Xiandai Yufa (Modern Chinese Grammar). Shanghai: Commercial Press.

Zhu, Y., 1996. Modality and Modulation in Chinese. In M. Berry (ed.). Meaning and Form: Systemic Functional Interpretations. Norwood, N.J.: Ablex Pub. Corp.

A Corpus-based Study of Interpersonal Grammatical

Metaphor in Spoken Chinese

Abstract: As a phenomenon arising from the interaction of semantics and lexicogrammar, Grammatical Metaphor (GM) occurs in the expression of both ideational and interpersonal meanings. Ideational GM is mainly deployed in written texts, while interpersonal GM is frequently observed in spoken discourses. Previous studies on the phenomenon focus their discussion on ideational GM and the use of GM in English. This study is the first attempt to explore the use of interpersonal GM in spoken Chinese. The study develops a framework for the identification and categorization of interpersonal GM in the language. On the basis of the framework, a large corpus of spontaneous conversation is analyzed to reveal how different types of interpersonal GM are distributed. The analysis shows that spoken Chinese has a preference for certain types of metaphorical expression. This study also investigates the relationship between interpersonal GM in spoken Chinese and its immediate context of situation, demonstrating how the deployment of interpersonal GM is affected by the topic of conversation and the social status between speaker and hearer.

Key words: Grammatical Metaphor; spoken Chinese; corpus of spontaneous conversation

此文发表于 *Language Sciences*，2013 年第 38 卷

从教师听觉评价和语音分析软件看
跟读法训练对改善日语韵律错误的效果

尹松

提　要：国内大学日语专业很少开设语音课程，在零起点入门阶段往往用 2-4 周时间完成以单音为主的发音学习，因课时所限无法进行高低强弱、节拍、停顿、语调等韵律方面的训练。而韵律被认为是影响日语语音语调是否自然流畅的一个重要因素。本研究利用课外时间进行了为期 3 个月的跟读法训练，以期解决学生的韵律问题。通过教师听觉评价和语音分析软件这两种主观客观相结合的方法，证明在音拍、声调、句末文末语调、句子整体语调等方面，训练后错误率减少，实验表明跟读法对改善学生的韵律问题有一定的作用。本研究成果可为现有的音声教育提供借鉴，亦为学生在自主学习中自行改善韵律问题提供了一种新的可能性。

关键词：韵律；跟读法；基频曲线；听觉评价

1. 问题的提起

长期以来，国内日语教学界非常重视培养学生掌握标准地道的语音语调。遗憾的是，受教学进度课程设置等客观条件所限，音声教育往往被忽略，很少有学校单独设立语音课，长期有效地进行语音指导。

日语专业是零起点教学，语音指导即指发音阶段的教学。大部分学校发音阶段教学只有 2-4 周，教学重点亦停留在单词层面的发音，无法进行高低强弱、节拍、停顿、句子整体的语调等韵律方面的训练。而比起单个单词，韵律是决定外语语音语调是否自然流畅的重要因素（佐藤 1995）。笔者在日语专业三年级教学中经常会遇到学生语音语调不标准不自然的情况，比如把长音发成短音，音调高低起伏剧烈等基础性错误。在课堂教学时间允许的情况下，笔者会指出学生的问题并加以矫正。但是这种矫正受课堂教学时间、教学目的以及授课教师主观意识影响，有很大的随意性及局限性，结果往往是相同的问题反复出现，说明学生在语音语调方面已经出现了石化现象。那么，有没有方法在现有的教学环境下通过学生课外的自主学习改善语音语调中的问题呢？跟读法为问题的解决提供了一种新的可能性。

2. 文献回顾

跟读法是尽量准确地把听到的音声即时或延时进行口头复述的一种语言行为（玉井，2005）。一直用于口译人员的培养，近年来在第二语言教学中受到关注。跟读法分为两种，一种是韵律跟读法（prosody shadowing），注重培养准确流畅的韵律，另一种为内容跟读法（contents shadowing），通过帮助听者延长音声信息在大脑中的保存时间，完成音声、字形、意义的解码，提高内容理解的准确率。前者可以用于矫正发音，训练正确的语音语调，后者被视为可以提高听解能力。

跟读法在国外的英语教学中已经积累了一些理论与实证方面的成果，如鸟饲（2003）曾指出，跟读训练法可以改善音调、拍节以及重音等韵律方面的问题；提高语速，使句子、文章整体听起来较为自然，接近母语话者；为听解打下基础。玉井（1997）以日本大学英语专业3-4 年级学生为对象，连续 5 天进行跟读法训练，并选取 TOEFL 试题测试跟读法的效果。结果表明跟读法在短期内可以提高听解能力。随后玉井又进行了一系列实验，认为跟读法不仅可以提高听解能力，还可以提高复述能力改进语速。

日语教学中有关跟读法的研究才刚刚起步，主要为韵律跟读法的效果研究。以在日留学生为对象的研究有荻原（2005）和清水·齐木（2011）两篇。荻原（2005）以 8 名中国留学生为对象，在日语课堂中引入跟读法进行了为期 3 个月的语音矫正。结果表明，与训练前相比，学生的促音、长音以及拨音等错误大幅度减少，浊音半浊音、清音浊音以及母音无声化等错误减少了 40%。清水·齐木（2011）以 4 名初级和中级学习者为对象，每周一次共进行了 12 次跟读法训练，从正确率和流畅性两方面考察跟读法训练的效果。结果显示，虽然在训练期间内会出现波动，但从长期观点看不论是正确率还是流畅性，整体上还是稳步上升的。松见等（2013）以国内日语专业 2 年级学生为对象，在日语课上进行了 32 次跟读法训练，结果表明跟读法可以提高学生朗读日语时的流畅性。

荻原、清水·齐木以及松见等的研究都是根据错误率的减少来判断跟读法训练的效果，属于教师听觉上的主观评价，虽然主观性不可避免，但这是基于教师的教学经验及对语言敏感程度的值得信赖的一种评价方法，遗憾的是这种方法只能回答语音改善的结果，不能回答改善的过程。随着计算机技术的成熟，专业性极强的语音数据分析软件逐渐进入外语教学领域，其可以把语音数据可视化，通过基频曲线直观反映语音的变化过程，可以弥补听觉评价的主观性与不可视性。

鉴于此，本研究使用教师听觉评价和语音分析软件中的基频曲线两种方法考察韵律跟读法训练与改善日语专业学生韵律错误之间的关系。

3. 研究目的

本研究探讨跟读法对改善韵律错误的作用以及学生对跟读法的看法。研究课题如下。（1）跟读法是否可以改善学生的韵律问题？（2）学生怎样看待跟读法及其作用？

4. 研究方法

课题（1）以 12 名日语专业 2 年级学生为实验对象，其中男生 2 名，女生 10 名。实验利用下午课外时间，每次 30 分钟左右，每周 2 次，共进行了 16 次。参加实验的学生均为自愿参加。使用『日本留学試験対策スコアアップ問題集』（アルク，2003）中的 16 篇听解文章作为实验材料。文章均为口语体文章，其中会话 10 篇，演讲 6 篇。每篇文章时间约为 1 分 30 秒。直接使用书中附带的 CD 音声资料，作为日语母语话者的标准音声，没有进行语速上的改动。

实验步骤参照门田（2007）[①]，在语音教室进行。（1）不看录音原稿听一遍录音。（2）看录音文字确认单词读音、语法意思[②]。(3)读录音原稿，把自己的录音录在 MP3 中。（4）不看录音原稿，跟随耳机中的音声进行跟读法训练，要求尽量跟上录音节奏模仿跟读 4 次。（5）读录音原稿，把自己的录音录在 MP3 中。步骤（3）和步骤（5）作为前测和后测的数据。之所以每次收集前测和后测的数据，是为了让学生即时意识到自己的语音语调和标准音声之间的差距，有意识地对照标准音声朗读。同时也是为了排除影响实验效果的其他因素，如课堂教学中教师的发音矫正等。由于学生请假等原因在 16 次训练中选择 12 名同学全部参加的 10 次作为分析数据。

课题（1）采用教师听觉评价和基频曲线两种方法分析。根据教师的教学经验以及已有研究的结果，我们把评价标准定为学生较难准确掌握的音拍、声调、句末文末语调和句子整体语调四个方面。教师听觉评价方法由笔者和担任实验对象会话课教学的日本外教两人完成，对二人有分歧的判断通过协商决定正误，二人的判断一致率为 95%。具体判断标准如表 1。

---

① 详见门田（2007）pp. 227-230。
② 韵律跟读法最主要目的是促进音声知觉的自动化处理（门田，2007），但考虑到如果学生不理解内容会影响到实验结果，故在此步骤中对学生提出的单词、句型、语法等语言知识点进行讲解，并在确认学生理解内容后再开始下一步骤。

表 1 教师听觉评价标准

1. 音拍：长音、促音、拨音发音是否到位。
2. 声调：是否有明显的声调错误。
3. 句尾语调：句末文末是否上扬，疑问句是否降调。
4. 句子整体语调：是否平白无抑扬顿挫。

基频曲线使用 PRAAT Version 4.3（Boersma，P & Weenink，D，2008）语音实验分析软件。课题（2）采用开放式问卷方法，内容包括学生对跟读法训练的看法以及训练的效果。

5. 实验结果

5.1 跟读法的训练效果

5.1.1 教师的听觉评价

表 2 为教师听觉评价结果，跟读法训练前后的误用变化。

表 2 跟读法训练前后的误用变化

时段	音拍	声调	句末文末语调	句子整体语调
训练前	468	481	372	497
训练后	332	343	254	367
减少率	29.0%	28.7%	31.7%	26.2%

从表2中可以看出通过跟读法训练，4个方面的错误率均有所下降，下降率在 30%左右。结果说明跟读法训练对改善学生的语音语调问题有一定的作用，但效果并未如预想的那样大。

5.1.2 基频曲线分析

为了解韵律问题的改善过程，我们采用语音实验分析软件 PRAAT Version 4.3（Boersma，P & Weenink, D，2008）对教师听觉评价中的改善事例进行分析，测定基频曲线作为分析对象。

图 1 是音拍的基频曲线，从左至右依次为日语母语话者、学生 A 训练前后的数据。在例句"この授業は人間とファッションというテーマだが"中选取"授業"这个单词考察学生的长音发音。从基频曲线中可以看出日语母语话者的长音"ぎょう"比短音"じゅ"发音时间长充分，而学生训练前后变化不大。

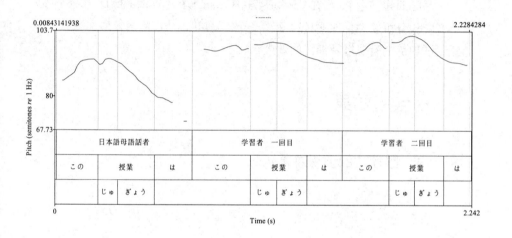

图 1 "この授業"的基频曲线

为了更清楚地看出区别，我们对于"授業"这个单词中长音的持续时间进行了分析。表 3 是"授業"的持续时间。

表 3 "授業"的持续时间

被式	"この授業は"整句持续时间	音节"じゅ"的持续时间	音节"ぎょう"的持续时间
母语话者	0.736 s	0.111 s	0.195 s
A 训练前	0.804 s	0.141 s	0.162 s
A 训练后	0.691 s	0.135 s	0.158 s

如表 3 所示，日语母语话者的长音"じゅぎょう"中的"ぎょう"持续时间接近普通音节的两倍。相比之下，学生 A 训练前的长音并没有发到位，没有足够的时长，训练后长音的相对时长反而变得更加短促。从基频曲线和发音持续时间看训练后学生的长音问题并未得到改善，但"この授業は"这个句子在教师的听觉评价中却为音拍改善的例子。重听该句前后两次语音资料，我们发现训练后，"この授業は"这个句子的整体速度上升了。正是由于句子整体速度的上升，使句子整体听起来语调较为自然，教师听录音时才把这个例子当成音拍改善例。这个例子给我们的启示是，在接受了跟读法训练以后，虽然音拍问题没有得到较大的改善，依然有值得研究和探讨的余地。但句子整体语速会得到相应的提升，今后学生通过有意识地强化练习，可以接近日语母语话者的语速，从而可以较为准确自然地朗读。

下面是对声调的分析。图 2-图 4 所示为例句"あてはまらない例もたくさんあるんだ"的日语母语话者与学生 B 训练前后的录音基频曲线的对比。

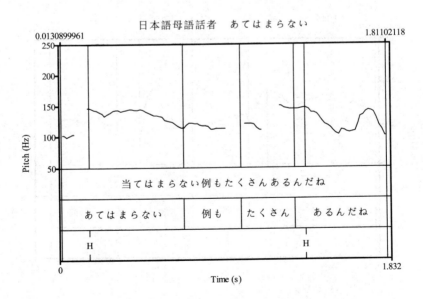

图 2 日语母语话者的"あてはまらない"基频曲线

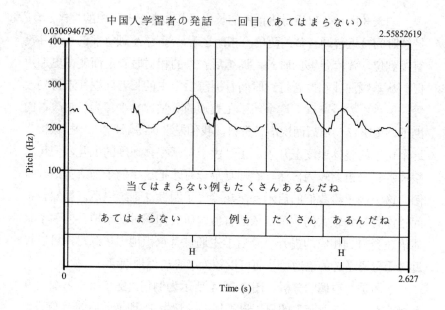

图3 学生 B 训练前基频曲线

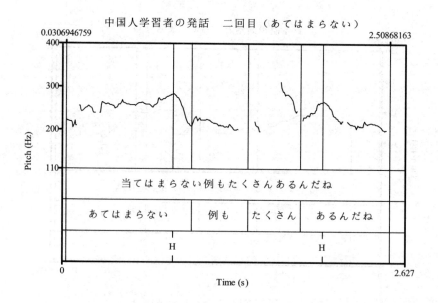

图4 学生 B 训练后基频曲线

　　观察图 3 可以发现，学生 B 在接受跟读法训练之前的第一次录音中，"あてはまらない"的声调读成了头高型，正确读音为中高型。而且听录音可以发现"は"的部分读作了"wa"①。而在接受了跟读法训练后的第二次录音中，如图 4 所示"あてはまらない"的部分改变成了中高型声调。虽然和母语话者相比，基频曲线的形状仍有区别，但教师听觉评价认为此部分的声调已经有了明显的改善。句尾"あるんだね"的部分，正确应为头高型声调，学生 B 两次录音中却均读成了中高型声调，也就是说训练后声调并未有明显的改善。

　　下面讨论语调，分成句子整体的语调和句尾的语调。图 5 是日语母语话者"山田さんの結婚式でやることを考えた？"的基频曲线。图 6 和图 7 是学生 C 训练前后的对比。

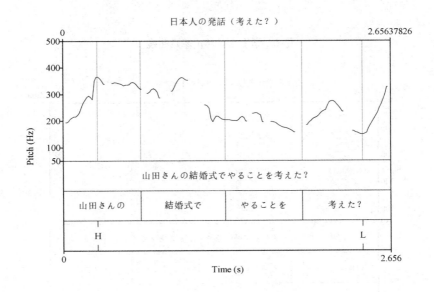

图 5　日语母语话者的基频曲线

---

　　① 由于在跟读法训练前，已经对跟读内容的理解进行了确认，排除了未知的语言知识对跟读的影响，故此处可以理解为学生的语音误读，而非读成助词的"wa"。

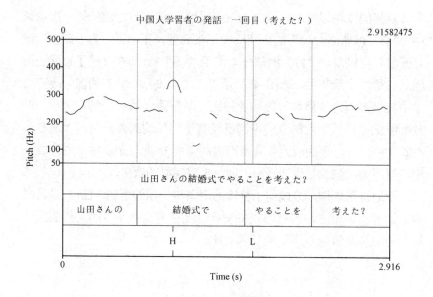

图 6 学生 C 训练前基频曲线

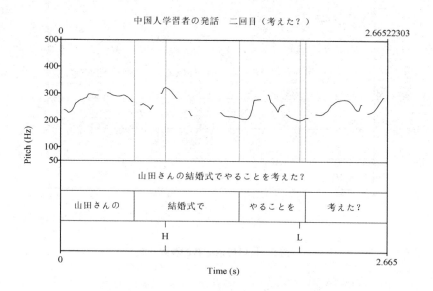

图 7 学生 C 训练后基频曲线

日语标准语调呈"へ"字形曲线（金田一，1967），这种语调易听易懂（藤崎，1989）。观察日语母语话者的 F0 走势，"山田さんの""結婚式で""やること"从高到低呈下降趋势，描出"へ"字形曲线，而学生 C 的结果中并没有呈现相似的曲线。第一次录音中，"結婚式で"处的 F0 明显高于"山田さんの"处的 F0。在接受了"跟读法"训练之后，虽依然没有呈现清晰的"へ"字形曲线，但比起训练前已经有所改观。

下面看句尾语调。因为该句是没有疑问助词"か"的疑问句，故日语母语话者的句尾处"考えた？"的 F0 明显呈现升调的走势。学生 C 在训练前的第一次录音中，句尾处 F0 几乎无上升的趋势。但在训练后第二次的录音中，句尾处 F0 略显上升的趋势。虽然和日语母语话者相比，升幅不够明显，但教师听录音时可以感到较之训练前的进步。

综合以上教师听觉评价以及语音分析软件的统计结果，我们认为跟读法训练可以改善学生的韵律问题，但短期训练并不能改进所有问题，而且改进的幅度亦有起伏，尚不能完全达到日语母语话者的水平。

5.2　学生问卷结果

跟读训练结束后进行了问卷调查。有关跟读法训练本身，学生认为训练内容不难（简单 5 人，一般 7 人），应该增加难度，比如加快速度，或使用能力考试 1 级内容增加新单词，不使用能全部听懂的内容。对于话题的选择，学生认为语音语调明显且表现日本人日常生活的会话或者讲演比较有意思。关于跟读法训练次数，多数学生认为 4-6 次比较好，少数学生认为次数并不重要，自己认为完全可以准确跟读后就可停止。

有关跟读法训练的效果，实验对象认为跟读法对改善语音语调的错误有效，还可以帮助他们意识到自己发音方面的问题，提高语速和注意力。结果如下：通过跟读法训练，（1）我了解到了正确的日语语音语调（12 人），（2）我掌握了正确的日语语音语调（9 人），（3）我意识到自己的日语发音错误（11 人），（4）我有意识地注意自己的日语发音（12 人），（5）我朗读日语时的语速变快了（7 人），（6）加强了我听日语时的注意力（11 人），（7）跟读法训练可以帮助我学新单词和日语表达方法（9 人）。

6. 考察

实验结果表明跟读法训练对改善学生的语音语调问题有一定的作用，这与已有研究结果一致（荻原，2005；唐泽，2009；松见，2013）。实验同时也证明了跟读法训练的理论基础。即学生通过跟读训练，完成了音声知觉的自动化，通过把听到音声信息瞬时或稍微延时地复述出来，使语音环中的音声信息不会消失在语言处理之前，从而延长工作记忆时间，有时间认知并处理语音语调、音声解码方面的问题。

实验结果同时表明音拍、声调、语调的改善幅度并不是很大，这与以下原因有关。汉语和日语虽然同为高低声调，但表现形式截然不同。相比汉语单音内的四声高低起伏，日语单音与单音之间高低不同，而且第一拍音和第二拍音声调一定高低不同。受汉语母语发音影响，学生读日语时起伏剧烈，这也是矫正语音语调的难度所在。改善幅度的大小与学生是否适应了跟读法训练、学生的日语语言能力以及跟读法训练的使用材料等因素有关。跟读法要求听到音声信息后瞬时解码音声、字形、意义，并复述出来，是一项需要较高认知能力的训练，与重复内容这一方法不同，并不是简单的鹦鹉学舌。尽管实验开始前对学生进行了跟读法的讲解，通过十余次的训练学生是否基本掌握了跟读法的要领仍有待商榷。这次实验使用的跟读材料为日本留学考试中的听力考试录音，语音语调清晰明了，内容也都是贴近学校生活和日常生活的会话或讲演，但学生在问卷中仍希望跟读语音语调明显的内容，这说明学生日常接受的音声信息量过少，对音声信息不敏感，"耳感"有待加强。上述原因也可以解释至今为止有关跟读法训练效果的研究多为教学实践研究，即研究结果反馈教学，再通过长期的教学实践检验训练效果这一现象。

与已有研究不同，本实验发现通过跟读法训练，虽然有些语音语调没有得到改善，但训练后学生整体语速增快，使得句子整体听起来较为自然。这个新发现说明如果坚持跟读法训练，学生最终可能使用接近日语母语话者的语速自然发音。

研究结果是否可以回馈教学，亦与学生的意识有关。本次问卷调查中，大部分学生"意识到自己发音错误""有意识地注意自己的发音"。这个结果令人欣慰，也和二语习得理论中"注意（noticing）"在语言形式的加工和获得上所发挥的重要性相吻合，即"注意"是将语言输入转化为习得知识的充分条件。对本研究而言，实验对象对跟读法音声材料中的语音语调注意得越多，获得的该方面的知识就会越多，会有意识地在朗读中模仿标准音声，具体表现在语音语调错误率的减少上。

7. 结语

本研究结果证实了二语习得理论和跟读法训练的理论基础，为今后开展跟读法训练的研究积累了第一手资料，同时也为跟读法训练提供了可能性与可操作性。本研究所用语音分析软件，可免费网上下载，操作简单。今后，教师可以提供给学生日语母语话者和学生的基频曲线图，使音声数据可视化，让学生一目了然地意识到自己和标准音声的差距何在，并通过课后的自主学习改善日语韵律问题。

音声教育的重要性毋庸置疑，但在外语教学界使用"文字"教材"用眼睛"学习仍是主流。希望本研究结果可以抛砖引玉引发思考，重视"音声"教材"用耳朵"学习，不仅仅在发音阶段而应长期有效地坚持音声教育，最终促进日语语言习得。

参考文献

荻原廣，2005，「日本語の発音指導におけるシャドーイングの有効性」『京都経済短期大学論集』第 13 巻第 1 号，55-71。

金田一春彦，1967，「コトバの旋律」『日本語音声の研究』，東京堂出版社，78-110。

唐澤麻理，2009，「シャドーイングが日本語学習者にもたらす影響—短期練習による発音面及び学習者意識の観点から」『お茶 の 水女子大学人文科学研究』第 6 巻，209-220。

鳥飼玖美子ほか，2003，『はじめてのシャドーイング』，学習研究社。

玉井健.1997， 「シャドーイングの効果と聴解プロセス における位置づけ」『時事英語学研究』，36，105-116。

玉井健，2005，『リスニング指導法としてのシャドーイングの効果に関する研究』，風間書房。

佐藤友則，1995，「単音と韻律が日本語音声の評価に与える影響力の比較」『世界の日本語教育』5，139-154。

清水慶子・斉木ゆかり，2011，「シャドーイングを用いた中級学習者の正確さと流暢さ強化タスクの検証」『日本語教育方法研究会誌』Vol,18,No.1。

藤崎博也，1989，「日本語の音調の分析とモデル化」『講座日本語と日本語教育日本語の音声・音韻（上)』明治書院，266-297。

門田修平，2007,『シャドーイングと音読の科学』コスモスピア。

松見法男・韓暁・于一帆、ほか，2013，中国国内の中級日本語学習者におけるシャドーイングの有効性—シャドーイング訓練と音読訓練を導入した実験授業を通して『学校教育実践学研究』19，113-122。

Effects of Shadowing on Improving Prosody in Japanese Learning through Teacher's Listening Assessment and Phonetic Analysis Software

Abstract: Phonetic courses are not commonly provided for Japanese majors in Chinese universities. Pronunciation practice mainly concerning individual phonemes usually takes 2-4 weeks at the beginning of Japanese learning. The prosody training involving pitch, mora, pause and intonation is absent due to limited courses. However, prosody is regarded as one of the important factors marking naturalness and fluency of Japanese pronunciation and intonation. The present study, based on an experiment conducted in off-class time and focusing on "shadowing" practice for three months, proves that students after the practice make less mistakes in mora, tone, intonation at the end of a sentence or text, and overall intonation by combining subjective teacher's listening assessment and objective phonetic analysis software. It is thus concluded that "shadowing" practice has exerted a strong influence on the phonetics and intonation improvement of the students and provides new possibility for students to improve their prosody performance in their self-study.

Key words: prosody; shadowing practice; pitch; teacher's Listening Assessment

此文发表于《外语教学理论与实践》2015 年第 4 期

从特征赋值看吴语内部语言距离
与互通度的关系①

张吉生

摘　要：国内外对方言间互通度与语言距离研究的传统方法都是以音段为基本单位分析、计算语言距离。本文以音系特征为基本单位，通过分析同源词音段特征赋值的异同来计算语言距离，揭示了吴语内部互通度低与声母韵母的历时和共时音变结果的关系。研究发现，吴语内部的历时音变主要发生在韵母，因此，影响其互通度主要是韵母的语言距离；其语言距离由音段的音系特征决定，主要特征赋值差异感知明显，对互通度的影响大于次要特征；以音系特征为基本单位测出的语言距离与互通度有高度相关性，距离越大，互通度越小，反之亦然。

关键词：特征赋值；语言距离；吴语；互通度

1. 引言

吴方言是内部互通度较低的汉语方言之一。普遍认为：南北吴语差别很大，南部吴语相互间的互通性很低。张吉生等（2014）对吴语区五个代表性方言点（吴江，黄岩，永康，衢州，温州）的互通度进行了测

---

① 本文为上海市教委重点课题"吴方言内部互通性音系学研究"（项目编号：11ZS47）成果之一。

量①，根据数据统计结果，其相对的互通度均值排序如下：

表 1　互通度均值排序②

方　言　对	互通度（均值%）	方　言　对
温州–衢州	12.5	衢州–永康
温州–永康	15	衢州–吴江
温州–黄岩	20	永康–黄岩
温州–吴江	23.5	衢州–黄岩
永康–吴江	25	黄岩–吴江

　　张吉生等（2014）的研究表明温州话是吴语中最难懂的，因此任何方言与温州话互通，其互通度很低。这一结果与人们的感觉和许多相关研究（Kilpatrick，2014）一致。影响方言内部互通度的因素很多，有语言内部因素和语言外部因素。语言外部因素主要涉及语言交际双方的社会背景、文化程度、生活经历、心理和身体状况、年龄等。语言内部因素包括语音、音系、词汇、语法等语言结构。就音的结构而言，还可能与各方言和普通话的语言距离远近有关③。国外的许多关于同族语言互通度的研究（Gooskens & Heeringa，2004）等发现语言（语音）距离对于语言间互通度的干扰起关键作用。王璐（2014）根据测试五个吴方言互通度的 30 个三字组词和 20 个句子的转写语音材料，计算分析了 10 对吴方言的语言编辑距离（包括辅音距离、元音距离和声调距离），发现音段（包括辅音和元音）的编辑距离对吴语内部互通度的影响很大，与互通度有

---

　　① 张吉生等（2014）设计了 30 个三字组词汇和 20 个句子，分别在五个吴方言点各选取了 15 位受试人进行了互通度的听力测试，具体测试方法和相关数据参考《吴语内部互通度实验研究报告》。

　　② 张吉生等（2014）对吴语内部互通度的研究证实他们设计的 30 个三字组词与 20 个句子有极高的相关性，即各自得出的互通度基本一致。此处提供的是基于 30 个词汇测出的互通度，由于篇幅有限，本研究只分析 30 个词的语言距离。影响互通度测试结果可能涉及其他非语言因素，如受试人的心理状态、测试态度等，因此表（1）提供的互通度绝对值不一定准确，但相对值是可信的。

　　③ 荷兰著名音系学家 Haike Jacobs（2014 个人书信）认为，因为不同方言区的人都能听懂普通话，某个方言的可懂度大小很可能与其语言结构和普通话的语言结构的远近有关，虽然这一推断尚未得到实证分析的验证，但从理论上讲有一定道理。

紧密相关性。

迄今为止，国内外分析影响同族语言间或方言间互通度的语言距离都以音段为基本单位进行计算分析（Chiswick & Miller，2004；Heeringa，2004；Gooskens & Heeringa，2004；Gooskens，2013；王璐、张吉生，2014；王璐，2014 等）。但实际上，不同音段之间的距离差别很大，如[e],[ɛ]和[ɔ]三个不同的音段相互间的差异大小不同，音段[e]与[ɛ]只区别于一个[紧张性]特征，其感知差别也不大；而[e]与[ɔ]区别于[紧张性]、[后位性]和[圆唇性]三个特征。其感知的差异也很大。因此，传统方法以音段为基本单位来计算语言距离的准确性不够高。本研究将根据音段的音系特征赋值，运用莱文斯坦（Levenshtein，1966：707-710）的编辑距离计算方法来计算五个吴方言之间同源词的语言距离，揭示方言间同源词音段变化大小与互通度之间的关系。

2. 音段的特征赋值

如果说方言形成就是"一种语言随着时间的推移而逐渐分化成不同的语言或方言"（徐通锵，1991：39），那么吴语在它形成以来的某个时期其内部应该没有多少差别。研究认为（高本汉，1915—1926），汉语在中古时期（约1000年前）差别不大，所有汉语方言（除闽语）都出自《切韵》。然而，在历史长河中，由于语言系统的内部演变和语言的外部接触，语言的结构产生变异。本文主要关注音系结构，音系结构的主要单位是音节。古汉语作为单音节语言，早期吴语每个相同字的音节结构（即声母和韵母）应该基本一样。在一千多年的历时演变中，不同地域的吴语音节结构发生变化。根据赵元任（1928）和钱乃荣（1992）等学者对吴语的田野调查，吴语内部的音节结构变化主要发生在韵母，有的鼻韵母变阳声韵，有的撮口韵变合口韵，有的双元音变单元音等。声母的变化相对较少。有的声母辅音变化很小，感知区别不大，如黄岩话的"臭"[tɕʰiu]与衢州话的"臭"[ʧʰɯ]；有的变化较大，如黄岩话的"外"[ŋa]与温州话的"外"[va]。因此，从音系特征赋值异同的多少可以准确地看出音变程度的大小。

根据发声学（Bickford，2006；Ladefoged & Maddieson，1996）和音系特征赋值原理（Chomsky & Halle，1968）以及本研究所涉及的五个吴方言的实际语料，我们选择[位置]①、[舌边]、[延续]、[鼻音]、[浊音]、[塞擦]、[前部]、[响音]、[舌面]②九个音系特征视角来分类区别吴语的声母辅音音段，其特征赋值如表 2 所示。

表 2　声母辅音特征赋值

辅音 特征	p pʰ	b	t tʰ	d	k kʰ	g	f	v	s	z	⊲	/	↩	h	ɦ	ts tsʰ	dz	tʃ tʃʰ	dʒ	tɕ tɕʰ	dʑ	m	n	ŋ	l
[位置]	L	L	C	C	D	D	L	L	C	C	C	C	C	G	G	C	C	C	C	C	C	L	C	D	C
[舌边]	-	-	-	-	-	-	-	-	-	-	-	-	-	-	-	-	-	-	-	-	-	-	-	-	+
[延续]	-	-	-	-	-	-	+	+	+	+	+	+	+	+	+	-	-	-	-	-	-	-	-	-	-
[鼻音]	-	-	-	-	-	-	-	-	-	-	-	-	-	-	-	-	-	-	-	-	-	+	+	+	-
[浊音]	-	+	-	+	-	+	-	+	-	+	-	-	-	-	+	-	+	-	+	-	+	▨	▨	▨	▨
[塞擦]	-	-	-	-	-	-	-	-	-	-	-	-	-	-	-	+	+	+	+	+	+	▨	▨	▨	▨
[前部]	+	+	+	+	-	-	+	+	+	+	-	-	-	-	-	+	+	-	-	-	-	+	+	-	+
[响音]	-	-	-	-	-	-	-	-	-	-	-	-	-	-	-	-	-	-	-	-	-	+	+	+	+
[舌面]	▨	▨	▨	▨	▨	▨	-	-	-	-	+	+	-	-	-	-	-	-	-	+	+	▨	▨	▨	▨

表 2 共涉及 34 个辅音，其中，只有六对阻塞音的送气与不送气没有加以区别。就本研究所涉及的五个吴方言的语料所示，"帮"母和"并"母保持不变，因此我们无需用[送气]这一特征来度量音变的距离。但清浊需要区别，因为有些摩擦音的清浊有变，如"臭豆腐"的永康话和吴江话的不同语音表达如下：

---

① 此处的[位置]包括[唇部]（LAB）、[舌前]（COR）、[舌根]（DORS）、[喉部]（GLO），四个发音部位。

② 特征[舌边]、[延续]、[鼻音]、[浊音]、[前部]、[响音]六个音系特征分别指[lateral]，[continuant]，[nasal]，[voice]，[anterior]和[sonorant]，在音系学中被广泛运用（Chomsky & Halle，1968；Kenstowicz，1994 等）；[舌面]指[laminal]与[舌尖]（[apical]）对立，Ladefoged 和 Massieson（1996：164）专门用来区别一些[嗞音性]摩擦音和塞擦音，如普通话中的[s]和[ʂ]是[+舌尖]摩擦音，[ɕ]是[+舌面]摩擦音。

（1）　　　　　　　　　　　　　臭　　　　　　豆　　　　　　腐

永康话　　　　　　　　tɕieu³³　　　　　dəu²²　　　　fu³⁵

吴江话　　　　　　　　tsʰɵ³¹　　　　　dɵ²⁵　　　　vu³¹

表 2 中我们没有给响音赋值[浊音]特征，一方面大量跨语言语料证明，有些语言的[浊音]特征对于响音是默认的，不赋值[浊音]特征（van der Torre，2003），如吴语声母阻塞音的清浊与声调阴阳调域匹配，但响音却可以与阴调和阳调共现（张吉生，2006：121-128）。另一方面，响音不赋值[浊音]特征表示声母辅音[t]，[tʰ]或[d]变成鼻音[n]，它们的音变距离相等。

此外，我们用与[舌尖]（[apical]）对立的[舌面]（[laminal]）特征来区别后齿龈音（如[ʃ]和[ʧ]）与齿龈硬腭音（如[ɕ]和[tɕ]）。因此，[舌面]特征只用来赋值与舌面有关的摩擦音和塞擦音，在普通话中也只有摩擦音和塞擦音才与舌尖元音和舌面元音搭配的制约。本来汉语音系中没有后齿龈音（[ʃ]或[ʧ]），由于（历时或共时）音变，有的方言用[ʃ]和[ʧ]分别代替了[s]、[ɕ]或[ts]、[tɕ]，如衢州话的"臭豆腐"说[ʧʰiu⁴³dei⁴⁴fu⁵²]，"红烧肉"说[ɦõ²²ʃɔ³⁴ŋyəʔ³¹]。赖德福吉和麦迪逊（Ladefoged & Maddieson，1996：164）认为，摩擦音[s]和[ʃ]赋值[舌面]还是[舌尖]特征因不同语言或不同语音环境而定。[舌面]和[舌尖]的主要区别是舌头位置，汉语普通话的[s]和[ʂ]是舌尖音（Ladefoged & Maddieson，1996：164），而[ʃ]的舌头位置处于[s]与[ʂ]之间，因此，本文认为一些吴方言中的[ʃ]或[ʧ]也是舌尖音[①]。另，我们用[塞擦]（[±affricate]）来区别塞音和塞擦音，因此其它音段不赋值[塞擦]特征。

我们对比声母就是对比一个辅音音段，因为汉语没有辅音群，但韵母的情况就复杂多了。汉语韵母的最大结构是 GVX，即一个介音（glide），一个韵核元音和一个韵尾成分（X），X 可以是一个元音或鼻音或喉塞音。汉语音节就是声母和韵母两个成分，在传统音韵学中，韵母是一个整体，不再细分。所谓同源词就是源词的每个音节都是相同的声母和韵母。因此，从互通度看吴语音变产生的语言距离，韵母是个整体。根据本研究

---

① [舌尖]和[舌面]是对立的，[-舌面]就是[+舌尖]。

所涉及的语料，五个吴方言全部韵母的所有音段主要涉及[前]、[后]、[高]、[低]、[圆唇]、[紧张]、[舌尖]、[鼻音]、[声门]九个音系特征。韵母音段的特征赋值如表3所示。

表3　韵母音段特征赋值

音段\特征	i	∩	ɿ	y	ʮ	ɥ	u	ʊ	e	ˍ	ˌ	ɜ	∵	E	æ	‖	o	ˍ	ʌ	ɐ	ɐ	A	≙	ɒ	N
[前]	+	+	+	+	+	+	+	-	-	+	+	-	-	+	+	+	-	-	-	-	+	-	-	-	
[后]	-	-	-	-	-	-	+	+	-	-	-	+	+	-	-	-	+	+	+	-	-	+	+		
[高]	+	+	+	+	+	+	+	-	-	+	+	-	-	+	+	+									
[低]	-	-	-	-	-	-	-	-	-	-	-	-	-	+	+	-	-	+	+	+	+	+	+		
[圆唇]	-	-	+	+	+	+	+	-	-	-	-	-	-	-	-	-	+								
[紧张]	+	-	-	+	-	+	-																		
[舌尖]	-	-	+	-	+	-																			
[位置]																									P
[鼻音]																									+
[塞音]																							+		

表3韵母音段中有两个是辅音，一个声门塞音，一个鼻音。鼻音用N表示，意为任何发音部位的鼻音，因此特征用[P]表示"位置"。实际语料中多是舌根鼻音[ŋ]，其[位置]赋值是[DORS]，也可能是舌前鼻音[n]，[位置]赋值是[COR]。吴方言有入声韵，只以声门塞音[ʔ]结尾，因此用一个[塞音]特征表示即可（不像粤语或闽语有三个不同发音部位的塞音结尾，需赋值不同[位置]特征）。如果元音鼻化[a]，[A]等就赋值[鼻音]特征。

吴语韵母的另一特点是表层语音实现时前高元音多，一共七个，基本是圆唇与非圆唇成对，如例（2）所示：

（2）　　　　　　　圆唇　　非圆唇

　　[+紧张]　　　y　　　　i

　　[-紧张]　　　Y　　　　ɪ

　　[+舌尖]　　　ʮ/ʯ　　　ɿ

例（2）中有两个圆唇舌尖元音[ɥ]和[ʮ]①，两者区别不大，只是舌位前后有细微的差异，往往与[s]和[ʃ]互补，如黄岩话的"水"[sɥ]和衢州话的"水"[ʃʮ]，因此，在本研究中[ɥ]和[ʮ]不予以赋值区别性特征。此外，还有一些区别不大的表层元音变体，如[e]和[E]只有舌位高低的稍微区别，没有一个方言会有[e]和[E]的对立分布，且感知区别也不大，故在此研究中也不予以赋值区别性特征。

上述表 2 和表 3 是本研究所涉五个吴方言声母和韵母表层语音表达的特征赋值。如果吴语内部同源词的早期底层音系结构相同，通过不同的历时和共时的音变，其表层的语音实现差异会很大。通过对比分析同源词声母和韵母表层音段特征赋值的差异就能计算出方言间的语言距离。

3. 基于特征的语言距离计算

国外有许多关于同族语（如日耳曼语）之间或方言之间互通度与语言距离关系的研究（Chiswick & Miller，2004；Heeringa，2004；Gooskens & Heeringa，2004；Gooskens，2013 等），这些研究证明了互通度与语言（语音和音系）距离有很大的相关性。以前的这些研究都是基于音段为计算单位来测算语言（方言）间的语言距离。王璐（2014:135）根据 30 个三字组词汇的语音转写语料，用相同方法测出的 10 对方言语言距离（从小到大）的排序为：黄岩-吴江＜黄岩-衢州＜黄岩-永康＜黄岩-温州＜温州-永康＜吴江-衢州＜温州-吴江＜衢州-永康＜吴江-永康＜温州-衢州②。这一语言距离与我们测出的互通度等级（见表 1）总体基本吻合，但仍有出入，如黄岩-温州，温州-永康和吴江-永康，它们的语言距离与互通度的关系。本研究认为，以音段为基本单位计算语言距离不够准确，如"八仙桌"一词，衢州话、温州话、永康话的语音表达如下：

---

① 国外语音学家们通常用来标示前高圆唇的半元音（Ladefoged & Maddieson，1996：322）。

② 此处提供的只是王璐（2014）用 30 个三字组词汇测出的语言距离排序。她通过综合 20 个句子和 30 个词汇共同测出的语言距离排序为（从小到大）：黄岩-吴江＜黄岩-衢州＜黄岩-永康＜黄岩-温州＜温州-永康＜吴江-衢州＜温州-吴江＜衢州-永康＜温州-衢州＜吴江-永康。（王璐，2014：157）

（3）　　　　　　方言点　　　　八　　　　　　仙　　　　　　桌
　　　　　　　　衢州话　　　　pʮ/⁴⁴　　　　ɕie⁴³　　　　ʧo/⁵⁵
　　　　　　　　温州话　　　　pʊ³³　　　　ɕi⁵⁵　　　　ʨiu³¹
　　　　　　　　永康话　　　　pʊ²⁴　　　　ɕiE³³　　　　tsuo³¹

根据莱文斯坦（1966：707-710）的编辑距离计算方法①，以音段为基本单位，"八仙桌"一词，衢州话、温州话、永康话相互间的语言编辑距离如表4所示（此处不计算声调）：

表4　基于音段的语言编辑距离统计

方言对	衢州-温州			方言对	衢州-永康			方言对	温州-永康		
方言	八	仙	桌	方言	八	仙	桌	方言	八	仙	桌
衢州	p /	‿ie	ʧo/	衢州	p /	‿ie	ʧo/	温州	pʊ	‿i	ʨiu
温州	pʊ	‿i	ʨiu	永康	pʊ	‿iE	tsuo	永康	pʊ	‿iE	tsuo
编辑	2	1	3	编辑	2	1	3	编辑	1	1	3
距离	6			距离	6			距离	5		

根据表4，温州-衢州和衢州-永康的编辑距离都是6次，温州-永康的编辑距离是5次，因此就"八仙桌"一词而言，它们的语言距离（从大到小）排序是：温州-衢州，衢州-永康＞温州-永康。但实际上，同样是一个编辑距离的音段差异，可能其变化的程度差别很大。如[y]，[ʮ]，[A]三个元音都不一样，以传统的方法，这三个元音之间的编辑距离都为1。但[y]与[ʮ]只有一个[紧张性]特征不同，差别不大，相比较[A]与[y]区别于[高]、[低]、[前]和[圆唇]4个特征，其差别要大得多，这种不同特征差别引起的感知也大相径庭。因此，计算五个吴方言同源词的语言编辑距离要观察构成每个音段的音系特征，并测算所有特征的不同赋值。根据音段的特征赋值（如表2和表3所示），以特征为计算单位，"八仙桌"一词，衢州话、温州话、永康话相互间的语言距离的计算结果

---

① 该方法比较两种语言（方言）同源词的每个音节的音段，音段不同计1次替换操作；音段多少不同，计1次添加或删除操作，权重一样（详细计算方法见王璐（2014:108-116））。

表示如下①：

根据表 5 的特征距离计算，就"八仙桌"一词而言，衢州话、温州话、永康话三个方言对之间的语言距离（从大到小）排序为：温州-永康＞温州-衢州＞衢州-永康。显然，以特征为计算单位的语言距离与以音段为计算单位的语言距离其结果可能不同。以特征为计算单位考量了音段变化大小的距离，这个语言距离的大小与互通度的大小（如表 1 所示）有更直接的关系。

表5　基于特征的语言距离统计

方言对	衢州-温州			衢州-永康			温州-永康			方言对
词汇	八	仙	桌	八	仙	桌	八	仙	桌	词汇
前词读音	p /	˨ie	ʧo/	p /	˨ie	ʧo/	pʊ	˨i	tɕiu	前词读音
后词读音	pʊ	˨i	tɕiu	pʊ	˨iE	tsuo	pʊ	˨iE	tsuo	后词读音
声母特征 [位置]									1	[前] 韵母特征
[延续]		1			1				1	[后]
[鼻音]	1	1	1				1	1		[高]
[浊音]					1		1			[低]
[前部]					1				1	[圆唇]
[舌边]						1			1	[紧张]
[舌面]			1							[舌尖]
[响音]										[鼻音]
[塞擦]	1	1	2			2	1			增音
语言距离	0　4	0　2	1　3	0　4	0　1	1　2	0　2	0　3	2　4	语言距离
	1		9	1		7	2		9	
		10			8			11		

注：表中每个音节下面分两行，左行格记左边的声母特征，右行格记右边的韵母特征。

另一方面，以特征为计算单位比以音段为计算单位要复杂得多。一般而言，一个特征赋值不同就计 1 分，但复杂的是增加一个音段应计几分？本研究对增音分为三种，根据增音的复杂度和感知的区分度分别计 1 分、2 分或 3 分。如音节末增加一个声门塞音，计 1 分，因为韵尾塞音只

---

① 基于特征的计算是对比每个音段的特征赋值，一个特征的赋值不同，计 1 分；"增音"这行表示两个方言同一音节的音段数不同，但有的音段增音计 1 分，有的计 2 分，有的计 3 分，具体方法下面详细说明。

赋值一个[塞音]特征（如[po]与[po/]）；音节末增加一个鼻音，计 2 分，因为韵母鼻音赋值两个特征（如[pA]与[pAŋ]）；如一个元音鼻化，计 1 分，因为与口腔元音比它只多赋值一个[鼻音]特征，与鼻韵母比它只少赋值一个鼻音[位置]特征，（如[pA]与[pA]）；[pA)]与[pAŋ]）。如果增音的是介音，要看此介音与声母和韵核元音的关系，如[pe]与[pie]或[go]与[guo]，后者增加一个介音[i]或[u]，都计 1 分，因为[i]与[e]或[u]与[o]都只差一个特征赋值；如[ɕi]与[ɕie]计 2 分，因为后者增加一个介音计 1 分，韵核元音[e]与[i]的特征赋值差别计 1 分；如[ʈʂu]与[tɕiu]的韵母距离也计 1 分（声母也计 1 分的特征赋值差），尽管[i]与[u]差 3 个特征，但此时的[i]与[tɕ]是必然匹配。但[tɕi]与[tɕia]的差别计 3 分。本研究以这样一种精细的计算方法对测试互通度的 30 个三字组词汇 10 个方言对的音段特征距离进行计算，具体语料如下①：

（4）拍马屁　　八仙桌　　黄梅天　　照相馆　　糯米饭　　发横财
　　赚外快　　小学生　　元宵节　　上半夜　　老花眼　　喷农药
　　臭豆腐　　东南风　　五斗橱　　红烧肉　　毛线衫　　读书人
　　外甥女　　蒸馒头　　裁缝店　　送彩礼　　表兄弟　　面皮厚
　　耳朵痒　　看电视　　水蜜桃　　油菜花　　胡萝卜　　新水桶

本研究基于表 2 和表 3 的特征赋值，以音系特征为基本单位，运用莱文斯坦（1966：707-710）的编辑距离计算方法，对上述 30 个三字组词五种方言语音的转写语料进行 10 个方言对之间的语言距离测算。即通过约 100 张类似表 5 的特征距离分析计算②，得出下列数据：

---

① 本研究的分析语料就是上述 30 个三字组词汇五个不同吴方言的录音转写材料。代表这五个吴方言（温州、衢州、永康、黄岩、吴江）的录音转写语料中，可能个别音节的读音与标准或传统文献的记音有所不同，因为实际的语音实现，有些发音会因人而稍有差异。本研究的全部语音转写材料经复旦大学陈忠敏教授审核和修正，借此，作者对陈忠敏教授的帮助表示衷心感谢。

② 表 8 只计算了 3 个方言对一个词的语言距离，10 个方言对一个词的计算需要这样 3—4 张表，30 个词需要做约 100 张这样的计算。

表6 基于特征的语言距离均值

方言对	声母距离	韵母距离	语言距离
黄岩-衢州	1.20	4.30	5.50
黄岩-吴江	1.70	3.80	5.50
吴江-衢州	1.43	4.97	6.40
黄岩-永康	1.23	5.80	7.03
温州-吴江	2.27	6.06	8.33
吴江-永康	2.30	6.70	9.00
衢州-永康	1.67	7.33	9.00
黄岩-温州	1.93	7.37	9.30
温州-永康	1.87	7.46	9.33
温州-衢州	2.07	7.66	9.73

表6反映了基于30个三字组词汇10个方言对之间的音段特征距离平均值（平均每个三字组词的特征赋值差异），根据声母加韵母的语言距离平均值，10个方言对的语言距离（从小到大的排序）是：黄岩-衢州，黄岩-吴江＜吴江-衢州＜黄岩-永康＜温州-吴江＜吴江-永康，衢州-永康＜黄岩-温州，温州-永康＜温州-衢州。

4. 分析与结论

根据音系学特征赋值理论（Chomsky & Halle，1968：301-329），辅音特征分为主要特征（primary class）和次要特征（secondary class）。主要特征指用来区别音段的自然分类和位置分类，如辅音的响音和阻塞音（[±响音]）区别，鼻音和非鼻音（[±鼻音]）区别以及主要发音部位节点特征（[唇部]、[舌前]、[舌根]①）。赖德福吉和麦迪逊（1996：282-306）根据 Jones（1956）的基本元音，提出[高]、[低]、[前]、[后]、[圆唇]为主要元音特征（major vowel features），其他特征（如[鼻化]、[紧张]等）为附加特征（additional vowel features）。一般来说，一个由主要特征赋值不同改变的音段比一个由次要特征赋值不同改变的音段差异更大，如[i]与[e]、[F]与[o]、[t]与[k]的变化比[i]与[I]、[ε]与[e]、[ʧ]与[tɕ]要大得多。基于特征为计算单位的语言距离（如表 6 所示）不仅更合理地反映了与表 1 所示的互通度的高度相关性，更主要的是通过不同类型特征赋值异同的分析，使我们清楚地认识和了解了引起互通度低的真正原因。

汉语音节的音段组合很简单，最多四种结构：CV，CGV，CVG 和CGVX，吴方言 70%多是前两种。如果一个三音节词基于特征的语言距离在 9.00 以上，意味着每个音节的主要元音基本不同，这无疑给互通制造了巨大困难。一种语言由于语言系统的内部演变和语言的外部接触慢慢地发生变异，这种变异无疑首先是音变，其次才是语法、词汇的变异。因此，决定吴语内部互通度的首要因素是音的结构，其次才可能是词汇和语法。

从表 6 数据看，吴语内部的音变主要是韵母，声母变化不大，即影响吴语内部互通度的音变主要来自元音，而非辅音。一些对欧洲同族语言的互通度与语言距离的研究（如 Gooskens，2007：445-467；2013：195-213；Ashby & Maidment，2005 等）表明，影响互通度的关键因素是辅音，他们的研究发现，往往同族语中同源词保持了相同的元音。也许辅音的变异影响更大，它将分化出不同的语言，而元音的变异往往发生在一种语言的不同方言，或一种方言的不同变体（varieties）。如英国英语

---

① 早期乔姆斯基和哈勒（Chomsky & Halle，1968：307）曾用[前部]（anterior）、[舌前]（coronal）、[高]、[低]和[后]五个特征作为主要特征（primary class）来区别不同发音部位的辅音。以后在特征几何（feature geometry，见 Clements（1985:225-252））理论里，辅音的不同发音部位通过[唇部]、[舌前]、[舌根]的位置节点特征来区别，这些位置节点下面的特征（如[anterior]和[distributed]）属于次要特征（McCarthy 1988:84-108；Roca 1994:91-96）。

和澳大利亚英语的许多常用词汇的不同读音都是元音的变异（Harrington,
Cox & Evans 1997：155-184）。也许正是由于辅音变异具有更大影响因素，
所以温州-吴江的互通度（从大到小）排序第七，而其语言距离（从小到
大）排序第五，但温州-吴江的声母特征距离是第二大。所以，以音系特
征为视角，不仅要计算各方言音变特征赋值不同的数量，还需分析不同
类型特征赋值不同引起的差异。就本研究涉及五个吴方言声母辅音音段
有九个音系特征，有些特征赋值的不同，感知差别不大，有些特征的不
同产生巨大的感知差异。我们统计了全部声母特征赋值在 10 个方言对中
的差异，数据如表 7 所示。

从表 7 可以看出，声母辅音特征赋值差异最大的是[前部]和[舌面]，
其实[前部]和[舌面]特征的不同赋值引起的差异往往是表层的变体，如
[s]与[ʃ]，[ts]与[ʧ]，[ʧ]与[ʨ]，[ʃ]与[ɕ]等，往往不是底层的两个音
位，其感知区别也不大。而[位置]的不同往往是不同的音位，如[p]，[t]，
[k]，[f]，[s]，[h]，[m]，[n]，[ŋ]等。另，[鼻音]特征的不同就是鼻
音与非鼻音的区别，感知差异很大。温州-吴江在[位置]和[鼻音]这两个
感知明显的特征差异都远远高于 10 对方言的平均值。因此，不同特征的
差异距离产生不同的感知，导致不同的互通度。总体来说，吴语的声母
辅音变化不大，相互间的差异较小。

我们已知影响吴语内部互通度的音变主要是韵母，而影响韵母音变
的特征也有九个，不同的特征差异产生不同的感知和互通度。10 个方言
对的韵母不同特征差异统计如表 8 所示。①

表 8 说明韵母音段赋值不同最多的是[紧张]特征，居九个特征之最，
并且远远高出其他特征，也就是说元音的[紧张]特征很容易改变。但单
独[紧张]特征赋值的不同感知区别不大，对互通度的影响也较小，如[i]
与[ɪ]，[y]与[ʏ]，[e]与[ɛ]，[ʌ]与[ɐ]，[u]与[ʊ]等。

---

① 在表 5 基于特征的语言距离统计中，韵尾有无声门塞音，计入"增音"一栏，但此处作为一个
特征，单独计算。

表7　声母特征距离统计

方言对	[位置]	[延续]	[鼻音]	[浊音]	[前部]	[舌边]	[舌面]	[响音]	[擦音]	增音
黄岩-吴江	9	5	3	2	13	1	13	2	0	3
黄岩-衢州	6	2	4	3	9	1	3	3	0	0
吴江-衢州	2	4	1	4	18	0	10	1	0	3
黄岩-永康	8	3	4	4	5	2	7	4	0	0
吴江-永康	8	8	5	6	16	1	16	6	0	3
温州-吴江	12	6	6	3	18	0	11	6	1	6
温州-永康	9	2	5	4	13	1	9	6	0	9
温州-衢州	12	6	5	3	14	0	7	5	1	9
黄岩-温州	13	3	7	2	11	1	7	6	0	9
衢州-永康	6	6	6	5	6	1	8	7	0	0
均　　值	8.5	4.5	4.6	3.6	12.3	0.8	9.1	4.6	0.2	4.2

表8　韵母特征距离统计

方言对	[前]	[后]	[高]	[低]	[圆唇]	[紧张]	[舌尖]	[鼻音]	[塞音]	增音
黄岩-吴江	4	8	12	6	11	20	1	4	0	26
黄岩-衢州	15	8	6	14	15	24	1	6	2	25
吴江-衢州	12	6	9	10	13	31	0	6	3	33
黄岩-永康	24	12	11	15	15	24	4	5	11	31
吴江-永康	12	11	15	13	13	20	3	7	10	50
温州-吴江	16	18	19	18	19	25	0	9	10	26
温州-永康	26	15	16	23	13	31	4	10	10	36
温州-衢州	26	18	11	11	26	25	0	11	11	45
黄岩-温州	21	22	21	18	25	24	1	12	11	36
衢州-永康	27	18	10	17	17	40	4	7	11	49
均　　值	18.3	13.6	13.4	14.5	18.4	26.4	1.8	7.7	6.9	35.7

根据表6的全部特征赋值，衢州-永康的语言距离排序（从小到大）第七，但其互通度排序（从高到低）第五，两者稍有差异，其主要原因就是衢州-永康的[紧张]特征赋值差别最高（40），远远超过了10个方言对的平均值（26.4），使其整个特征距离拉大。另一方面，温州-吴江[紧张]特征的赋值差异低于均值，但感知区别比较明显的[高]、[低]、[圆唇]这些

主要特征赋值差异都高于均值，这也是导致温州-吴江的语言距离排序与互通度排序有一些差异的重要因素。因此，只有观察音段具体的特征差异，才能更准确地测出语言距离，了解影响互通度的真正原因。

综上分析，本文以特征赋值为视角，以音系特征为基本单位，运用莱文斯坦（1966：707-710）的编辑距离计算方法，对测试五个吴语相互间互通度30个三字组词汇的语言距离进行了分析计算。

本文不仅测算出了10个吴方言对的语言距离排序，更重要的是通过对音系特征赋值异同的观察，揭示了音变的趋势和特点，阐释了产生语言距离的真正原因。就声母辅音而言，与其他特征相比，[前部]和[舌面]特征赋值差别最大，发音部位的变化也不小；相对而言，清浊的变化不大，对互通度影响最大的还是发音部位的变化。对韵母来说，结构简化的不对等是较大的差异，如 GV 中 G 的丢失：（G）VX 中 X 的丢失（包括[/]，[ŋ]，[n]，[i]或[u]），即有的鼻韵变成阳声韵，有的双元音变成单元音，有的入声消失，这给同源词的音节结构带来很大变化，较大程度上影响了互通性。韵母核心元音差异最大的是[紧张]特征，但这一特征对互通度的影响不大。元音的主要特征（[前]，[后]，[高]，[低]，[圆唇]）赋值的不同差异与方言对的互通度大小排序基本一致，这充分说明了同源词核心元音主要特征的历时音变对方言间的互通性影响很大。

通过系统分析，我们可以得出这样的结论：（1）音的语言距离由音段的音系特征决定，不同类型的特征有不同的感知效果，导致不同的互通度；主要特征赋值差异对互通度的影响要大于次要特征。（2）吴语内部的历时音变主要发生在韵母，因此，影响其互通度主要是韵母的语言距离。（3）音变是影响吴语内部互通度最重要因素，这种基于特征的语言距离越大，互通度越小，反之亦然；两者有高度相关性。

基于本文以计算音系特征赋值差异为方法，研究分析吴语内部语言距离与互通度的关系所得出较为科学、合理、准确的结果，我们认为，这一方法同样可以用来科学解读影响汉语其他方言内部间的互通度，以及汉语不同方言间互通度的音系理据。

参考文献

Ashby, M. & J. Maidment. 2005. *Introducing Phonetic Science*. Cambridge: Cambridge University Press.

Bickford, Anita. 2006. *Articulatory Phonetics: Tools For Analyzing The World' s Languages* (4th ed.). Summer Institute of Linguistics.

Chiswick, B. and P. Miller. 2004. Linguistic distance: A quantitative measure of the distance between English and Other Languages. IZA Discussion Paper No. 1246.

Chomsky & Halle. 1968. *Sound Pattern of English*. Cambridge, Mass.: MIT Press.

Clements, G.N. 1985. The geometry of phonological features. *Phonology Yearbook*. Oxford: Oxford University Press, 2: pp. 225-252.

Gooskens, C. 2007. The contribution of linguistic factors to the intelligibility of closely related languages. *Journal of Multilingual and Multicultural Development*, 28(6), pp. 445-467.

Gooskens, C. 2013. Experimental methods for measuring intelligibility of closely related language varieties. In R. Bayley, R. Cameron, and C. Lucas (eds.), *Handbook of Sociolinguistics*, Oxford: Oxford University Press, pp. 195-213.

Gooskens, C. and W. Heeringa. 2004. Perceptive evaluation of Levenshtein dialect distance measurements using Norwegian dialect data. *Language Variation and Change*, 16(3): pp. 189-207.

Harrington, J., Cox, F., & Evans, Z. 1997. An acoustic study of broad, general and cultivated Australian English vowels, *Australian Journal of Linguistics*, 17:pp. 155-184.

Heeringa, W. 2004. Measuring Dialect Pronunciation Differences Using Levenshtein Distance. Ph.D. dissertation. Groningen: University of Groningen.

Heeringa, W., K. Johnson & C. Gooskens. 2005. Measuring Norwegian dialect distances using acoustic features. In *UC Berkeley Phonology Lab Annual Report 2005*, University of California, Berkeley, pp. 312-336.

Jones, Daniel. 1956. *An Outline of English Phonetics*. (8th edition.) Heffer, Cambridge.

Kenstowicz, Michael J. 1994. *Phonology in Generative Grammar*. Cambridge: Blackwell.

Kessler, B. 1995. Computational dialectology in Irish Gaelic. In *Proceedings of the 7th Conference of the European Chapter of the Association for Computational Linguistics*. Dublin: Association for Computational Linguistics, pp. 60-67.

Kilpatrick, Ryan. http://shanghaiist.com/2014/05/20/chinas_ten_most_difficult_dialects.php. 2014.

Ladefoged, Peter and Ian Maddieson 1996 *Sounds of the World's Languages*. Oxford: Blackwell Publishers Ltd.

Levenshtein, V. I. 1965. Binary codes capable of correcting deletions, insertions and reversals (in Russian), *Dokl. Akad, Nauk SSSR* 163, No. 4, pp. 845-848; English Translation in *Soviet Physics Doklady*, 1966, 10:8. pp. 707-710.

McCarthy, J. 1988. Feature geometry and dependency: a review. *Phonetica*, 43: pp. 84-108.

Roca, Iggy. 1994. *Generative Phonology*. London: Routledge.

Serva, M. & F. Petroni. 2008. Indo-European Languages Tree by Levenshtein Distance. *Europhysics Letters* 81, pp. 1-5.

Van der Torre, E.J. 2003. Dutch Sonorants. Doctorial Dissertation. Utrecht: LOT.

Van Hout, R. & H. Münstermann.1981. Linguistische afstand, dialekt en attitude [Linguistic distance, dialect and attitude]. *Gramma*, 5, pp. 101-123.

高本汉（B.Karlgren），《中国音韵学研究》（*Etudes sur la Phonologie Chinoise*, Stockholm, Gotembourg, 1915-1926, 赵元任、李方桂、罗常培，译），北京：商务印书馆，1940 年。

钱乃荣，《当代吴语研究》，上海：上海教育出版社，1992 年。

徐通锵，《历史语言学》，北京：商务印书馆，1991 年。

王璐，《编辑距离与吴语间的互通度》，博士学位论文，华东师范大学，2014 年。

王璐、张吉生，吴语互通度与编辑距离之间的关系，《语言研究》2014 年第 2 期，第 65-69 页。

张吉生，从吴方言看声母-声调的相互关系，《当代语言学》2006 年第 2 期，第 121-128 页。

张吉生、王璐、朱音尔，吴语内部互通度实验研究报告，《吴语研究》，游汝杰主编，上海：上海教育出版社，2014 年。

赵元任，《现代吴语的研究》，北京：商务印书馆，1928[2011]年。

A Study of Correlation between Linguistic Distance and Mutual Intelligibility Among Wu Dialects in Light of Feature Specification

Abstract: Traditionally, studies on correlation between linguistic distance and mutual intelligibility are based on calculation of segmental differences. This article focuses on the differences of feature specification of segments to examine the linguistic distance and the mutual intelligibility between the five Wu dialects. From the perspective of feature specification, the present study has found that the differences in major features cause more salient perception and bigger influence on intelligibility than those in minor features and that there is high correlation between linguistic distance and mutual intelligibility: the bigger the linguistic distance, the lower the mutual intelligibility.

Key words: feature specification, linguistic distance, Wu dialects, mutual intelligibility

此文发表于《中国语文》2015 年第 6 期

六国基础教育英语课程比较研究①

邹为诚

摘　要：在全球化的时代，一国的外语教育政策会受到其他国家政策和实践的影响，因此国际的课程比较具有重要的价值。本研究采用文化人种志的方法研究了法国、俄罗斯、巴西、日本、韩国和中国六国的基础英语教育课程体系。研究表明，六国的政策所规定的目标要求和学习者实际上所承担的学习负荷是完全不同的。造成这种差异的原因是六国的"英语泡沫"程度不同和教师的职业自主性差异。研究还表明，世界各国的英语课程虽然有很多相似性，但其背后有着丰富的文化和历史传统差异，国际的课程比较必须深入研究这些因素，才能真正理解他国的课程特点，理性地学习他人的经验。

关键词：基础教育；英语课程；比较研究

1. 研究背景

　　自从二十一世纪起，我国的基础英语教育以颁布《课程标准》(中华人民共和国教育部 2003,2011)为标志发生了重要变化，我国高中毕业生的英语水平逐年提高，但学生学业负荷过重是最突出的问题之一。这是一种普遍性问题还是我国特有的现象？为探究这个问题，我们依

———————
　　① 本研究为龚亚夫、邹为诚主持的国家社科基金"十二五"规划教育学重点课题"中小学英语课程与教材难度国际比较研究"（AHA 120008-1）的成果。

据文化类型比较了欧洲文化区的法国和俄罗斯，东亚文化区的日本、韩国、中国，以及南美文化区的巴西。

我们的研究问题是：①六国的基础英语课程体系各有何特点？②六国的基础课程体系所产生的学习压力各有多大？③六国的课程体系为何是这样的？上述国家的基础英语课程体系对我国并不十分陌生，学界已有很多关注和讨论。现有的大部分研究都采用文本分析的方法解读其外语教育政策，这种研究的局限性是不能展示"实施的课程"，而"实施的课程"背后有丰富的社会文化意义，对理解相关国家的外语教育政策和课程实践有着重要的意义。

本研究采用"社会文化调查"的手段，开展了文本分析和知情者访谈的调查。文本分析对象是各国的英语课程标准、考试大纲、政策性文件、课程表和考试试卷。访谈对象有驻我国和我国驻外外交文化官员、在华留学生、学者以及目标地区的初高中英语教师和学者。

2.　研究结果

2.1　课程负荷

本研究首先分析了各国高中英语课程的负荷，课程负荷是三个要素综合作用的结果：课程目标、学习量和课程资源（课时）。为了统一负荷值，研究者采用 CEFR 的能力等级对六个国家的课程目标进行估计和比较。教材的学习量以教材内总词汇数来计算。课程资源指课程标准规定的课时数。在中国，课程标准规定的课时数与学校实际所用的课时数会有很大差异，例如我国很多学校都实施"阴阳课表"，即学生上课的实际课时与学校公布的课时不一样（邹为诚，2013），这种数据未被纳入统计范围。其他国家也有类似情况，如韩国、俄罗斯的学生也花费大量的时间去校外补习。六国的课时在高中阶段略有差异，但大体都在 40-50 分钟之间，为方便起见，本研究一律按照该国课程标准的课时数计算，如遇选修性质的课程，按最高课时计算。单位课时内学习量指如果教师要教完全书，在单位课时内要处理的学习量，计算方法是教材总字数／课程标准规定的课时。

表1 六国高中英语课程负荷比较

国家	课程目标	学习量	课程资源（课时）	单位课时内学习量	负荷比较结果
法国	B2	36353	360	101	高负荷课程
俄罗斯	B2	30211	400	76	
中国	B1	32749	600	55	中等负荷课程
日本	B1①	23397	760	31	
巴西	A2	16278	240	68	低负荷课程
韩国	A2	26160	392	67	

由表1可见，六个国家的课程负荷可划分为三类，法国和俄罗斯为高负荷课程，中国和日本为中等负荷课程，韩国和巴西为低负荷课程。韩国和巴西的单位课时内学习量较大，但这是数据的假象。韩国教材中有三层练习，分别面向所有的学生、低水平学生和高水平学生，这大幅度提高了统计时的教材字数。巴西单位课时内学习量高是因为其课时数很少。

2.2 课程体系

课程体系描写了六个国家基础英语课程的主要特点。

2.2.1 中国基础英语课程特点

我国的英语课程标准倡导把语言知识与语言运用教学相结合，提出了以语言技能为基础的教学方案，重视学生在情感态度、学习策略、语言技能、语言知识和文化意识这五个方面的发展。在教学过程中，教师对教材的依赖程度非常高，教师职业自主性比较弱，高度重视课标指定的词汇表和语法清单。教师强调学生对学习材料的熟记，运用

---

① 根据日本文部科学省最近公布的最新英语教育的改革计划，日本高中毕业生在2020年时需达到B2的目标（日本文部科学省 2013）。

背诵所获得的语块和语法知识开展技能训练。

中国基础教育面临的一个现实问题是考试。中国的教育属于竞争性文化，高一级的教育机会需要通过竞争性考试获得，由于目前的语言测试兼具有智力测试和个人倾向特质检测的性质（崔允漷 2013），因此，课堂教学很难在测试中表现出来，由此造成的后果是应试教育泛滥。

中国基础英语课程的师资能力不均衡，在英语语言与教学能力方面存在着巨大差异。中国基础英语教师缺乏外语方面的职业入门门槛（如英语水平等级）和发展的等级（如英语教师的职业阶梯）要求，擅长利用考试的压力推动学生的学习。此外，中国社会巨大，地区和城乡差异特别明显，东西部地区和城乡学校之间在英语学习条件方面存在巨大差异。

2.22 法国基础英语课程特点

英语是法国基础教育中学习人数最多的一门外语，学生一般都从小学开始学习第一外语，到初中高年级时，第一外语要求达到 CEFR 的 B1 水平，同时学生开始学习第二外语，要求达到 A2 的水平。学生在高中阶段开始重视第二甚至是第三外语，学习两门外语以上的学生占学生总数的 77%以上（Goullier，2012）。

法国社会对英语学习持有复杂的心态（Phillipson，2007），精英阶层、社会大众和学生三角之间存在严重分歧。法国精英推崇多元外语政策，其初衷是抵抗英语霸权，但是法国的大众却推崇英语学习，而学生却普遍缺乏外语学习的动力（Goullier，2012）。

法国的外语教学把口语表达能力放在教学的第一位，推崇"行动教学"理念，提倡外语学习以活动为主，反对把外语教学变成知识竞技场（Castelloti，2012）。法国是世界上最难获得教师职业证书的国家之一，教师因而也是比较优秀的社会精英，他们根据 CEFR 的能力指标自主选择教材。但是任何教育改革都是批评传统的过程，法国也不例外。对于以听说交际活动为基础的课堂教学，"很多法国教师也不完全接受"（受访者），很多外语教师在学术上仍然不能很好地理解现代语言教学观，掌握与之相适应的教学手段。传统的教学观，如重视语法和语言知识的学习，仍占有很大市场，这也是法国当前英语教学改革的阻力之一（Castelloti，2012）。

2.2.3　日本基础英语课程特点

日本英语课程的理念非常独特。传统上，它视英语能力为"与西方强权分霸世界"的工具（Kubota，1998），因此，日本的英语教育长期以来一直是"精英主义"盛行。但是近年来，英语教育正在出现平民化、大众化的趋势，如广泛地在小学开设英语课。"分霸世界"的观念正在逐渐转向"文化学习"和"人本主义教育"观（Butler & Iino，2005）。

日本的课堂教学受"生本化"（即教师视学生的能力确定教学目标，以学生的需求和情感态度为中心）思想的影响非常大，不主张"强行干预"学生的学习过程，承认学生在能力、性情、智力和兴趣等方面的差异（Tobinetal & Davidson，1989）。日本英语课堂重视语法和翻译、阅读和写作，轻视听说训练，因而学生的听说能力薄弱。日本的教师迁就学生的语音，造成日本学生普遍的"英语语音本地化的倾向"（受访者）。

日本与中国一样有着浓厚的考试文化情结。日本的高考分为全国性的大学考试和高校的独立考试。前者叫作 STEP，与 CEFR 水平挂钩，STEP 的二级相当于 CEFR 的 B1（Masako & Yuichi，2012）。学生通过STEP 之后，很多名牌大学还将要求学生再参加一次各高校单独组织的考试。由于学生追逐名校成风，因此这些高校所出的五花八门的考试对日本高中英语教学产生了严重的负面影响（Butler & Iino，2005）。日本高中英语采用分流的政策来解决人际差异的问题，高中英语分为选修课和必修课。必修课只有 5 个学分，要求很低。但选修课达 21 学分（日本文部科学省，2008），与中国的高中英语教育目标要求相当。

日本的英语课程整体上看还没有完全抛弃"精英教育"的传统，日本的私立高中（Super Science High school）和特色高中（Liberal Arts High school）有非常优秀的学生，"他们的英语水平非常高，完全可以达到 B2 的水平"（受访者）。但是在公立的普通高中，政府虽然投入巨资、聘请外教、提供教师的在职训练，"公立学校的英语教育（仍）

举步维艰"（受访者）。

2.2.4 俄罗斯基础英语课程特点

俄罗斯的基础教育体系目前正处在教育体制转型期，因此，苏联时期的教育遗产仍在发挥着重要的作用。俄罗斯的课堂教学在苏联时期以经典文学研读、语法分析和文本翻译为主。由于与西方长期对立，其英语教学脱离西方语言教学思潮，被称为"闭门造车"，或"坐在铁窗后学习莎士比亚和狄更斯"（Ter-Minasova，2005）。21 世纪以来，"俄罗斯基础教育转型顺利，教师开始实施以交际能力为核心的教学原则。课堂教学强调交际活动，小班教学；教材除了本土教材以外，世界的主要英语教材出版商都在俄罗斯推广他们的产品。学校实行一纲多本的政策，教师或学校可以自主决定教材"（受访者）。外语教育政策与欧洲 CEFR 框架挂钩，采用 CEFR 的能力等级作为联邦或州的英语课程的基础，采用 B2 为教学目标，与法国水平相当。从 2009 年起，还开始学习中国设置统一的高考，称为 Unified State Exam，简称 USE。据 2013 年考题，高考覆盖 CEFR 的三个等级：A2 水平题目占 40%，B1 水平题目占 25%，B2 水平题目占 35%（俄罗斯联邦教育评估研究院 2012）。在教材的设计方面，传统的追求高难度和培养交际能力的做法在教材中共存，俄罗斯教材虽然语言素材的学术性比较强，但其设计的活动却非常现代化，注重在任务的引领下学习语言。

目前，俄罗斯社会正出现一股重视英语学习的热潮，"大量的正规学校转型为'外语特色学校'。在这些学校里，英语是最重要的课程之一，在课时、活动、教材要求和师资方面都远远高出国家对普通学校的办学要求"（受访者）。俄罗斯的英语学习热潮有三个特点：1）英语学习的起始年龄越来越低。越来越多的学校从学前、甚至从幼儿园开始英语教育；2）英语学习的社会化程度越来越高；3）越来越多的年轻学生利用假期赴欧美等英语国家参加社会实践，以提高英语的语言与文化的综合能力（McCaughey，2005）。

随着改革的推进，一些困扰我国的问题也开始在俄罗斯出现。原本教师自主的课堂、充满交际活动的课程"正在向应试教育转变"（受访者）。目前由于统一高考实施的时间不长，它的负面影响尚未成为全局性问题。

2.2.5　巴西基础英语课程特点

巴西是世界上教育公平问题最突出的国家之一，这个问题甚至引起了国际组织的关注（经合组织，2011）。巴西实行半日学制，学生只上半天课，结果是"经济条件好的家庭可以在公立学校放学后把孩子送入私立语言学校（约40%）"（受访者）。巴西有非常悠久的私立英语教育传统，学生在这些学校可以接受优质的外语教学。这些学生通过公立和私立两种系统的教育，获得教育上的优势，"利用这种优势最后通过竞争性的大学考试（ENEM）"（受访者），"进入价廉物美的公立名牌大学"（受访者）。而对于"贫困家庭的孩子，他们在基础教育阶段完全依赖公立的半日制学校读书"（受访者），而"公立学校的教师只有约一半人具有教师资格证"（受访者），教师基本用葡萄牙语讲课，教学手段是语法解释和翻译，教学内容主要是应试性质的。这些穷学生没有条件去私立学校读书，"他们在竞争性的高考中很难获得好成绩，最后只能进入收费较高、但是口碑不高的私立大学"（受访者）。"应届高中生中约 85%的人可获得高等教育的机会"（受访者）。

2.2.6　韩国基础英语课程特点

英语在韩国社会中具有极高的地位，韩国社会普遍认同英语在社会生活中的价值，已被认为是国际通行证、谋生工具和社会地位的象征。由于这些带有夸大性质的认识，"英语教育已经成为韩国教育的重负和争论的焦点"（受访者）。但不可否认的一点是，"韩国近年来年轻人的英语水平上升很快，尤其是 20 世纪 60 年代以后出生的人"（受访者）。

韩国的学习文化"注重应试和书面语，不注重人际交流和语言运用"（受访者）。"学生在课堂中以书面语学习为主，热衷钻研应试问题，擅长应付考试，韩国学生在 TOEFL 和 TOEIC 等国际性考试中，常有令人惊异的高分出现"（受访者）。

韩国有公立学校和私立学校两种英语教育。公立学校的教师主要来自韩国的师范院校，"教学方式比较传统"，应试教育是主流，"师范生的语言交际能力比较弱",连英语教育硕士都"不能自由地在课堂上用英语与教授讨论问题"(受访者)。因此,"师范教育培养的教师能力不高"(受访者)。社会"私立外语学校的教师大都是来自英美国家的韩裔,他们在语言能力和教学水平上远远高于公立学校",但"他们对公立学校的英语教育方式和教学改革影响甚小"(受访者)。这也是韩国补习班盛行的原因之一。学生的学业从小学到高中不堪重负,这种情况甚至引起了国际社会的批评(Shin,2007;Koo,2014)。

韩国的基础英语教育政策与我国一样,都处于非常难以调和的一对矛盾之中。一方面决策者希望提高全民族英语水平,但另一方面又要降低学生学业负荷。韩国的教育政策高调强调英语教育的作用,并且对学生提出了不切实际的期望,例如小学生要能够融会贯通地掌握520个词,高中生要达到能学习学术内容的水平(韩国科学技术教育部,2008);另一方面,又把具体的学习量降到很低水平,如整个基础阶段累计词只有 1920 个,勉强接近英语阅读的门槛词汇量要求(2000)(Nation,2014),只有中国学生一半左右的学习量。由此可见,韩国外语教育的"象征性政策"与"实质性政策"(邹为诚,2011)差别很大,象征性政策起到一种呼吁的作用,但真正落实到具体的课程要求时,政策不得不向现实低头。

3. 讨论

3.1 课程理念、社会环境和英语学习

六国的基础英语课程虽然在政策文本上对各自的理念有不同的表述,但共同点是"学习英语是为了获得社会经济利益"。在这个共同点上,六国之间也存在着一些细微差别。法国和日本更加倾向于文化和多元发展,中国和俄罗斯倾向于融入国际社会和加入世界经济的潮流,韩国和巴西则是为了国家的经济发展,在强国林立的国际社会中求得生存之道。

六国的英语学习社会环境有一个共同点，英语与民众生活之间的关系主要局限在与教育有关的领域，譬如升学和学校的学术活动。普通民众仅仅是在涉及出国事务、旅游观光、接待游客等狭窄的领域中接触到有限的英语。与中国香港地区、新加坡或者双语国家如加拿大对第二语言的依赖程度相比，这六国的民众在日常生活中对英语的需求是非常微弱的。

对比六国的教育理念、社会环境和文化历史，可以发现六国在英语学习方面都存在比较严重的泡沫，我们姑且称其为"英语泡沫"。泡沫的表征就是六国教育对英语学习目标存在着缺乏理性的一面，英语学习的要求不是产生于理智的思考和判断，而更多的是在社会逼迫之下妥协的结果。法国的泡沫根源是文化精英与普通民众的分歧，文化精英希望抵抗英语霸权，而普通民众则更多地考虑子女在未来世界经济中参与全球化竞争的能力。于是，法国最后只好规定每个学生要学习 2 门甚至 3 门外语，从而实现双方的妥协。至于学生的个人发展是否需要这么多门外语，学生是否愿意或者是否有能力学习这么多门外语，似乎无人关心。

巴西所面临的矛盾与法国类似，巴西政府为了发展南美统一市场，号召民众学习西班牙语，但是民众和学术界并不看好这个南美统一市场，更倾向于参与全球化竞争，因而更愿意学习英语。作为妥协，公立学校必须学习英语和另一门外语（实际上是西班牙语）。但是由于巴西半日制的体系，非常有限的课时被社会的分裂浪费掉了。学生不得不利用社会化的商业资源学习英语，这不仅催生了英语泡沫，还使得教育公平问题变得更加严峻。

在俄罗斯、日本、韩国和中国，英语泡沫更为严重。四个国家的共同点是高考，高考的本质就是追求高一级的教育机会和在未来获取更好的经济利益。当经济利益成为课程背后的推动力时，教育一定会产生"泡沫"并且导致学习变质。例如，日本教育界在十年前坚守学术，认为小学不必开设英语课，并且在英语教学中坚守"生本教育"的理念。但是在工商界的压力下，在看到中国和韩国的小学英语教育发展后，日本被迫放开小学英语教育，同时将英语高中毕业的要求从目前的 B1 提高到 B2，向欧洲高水平国家看齐。

纵观六国的英语教育政策，矛盾的焦点是工商界（包括学生家长）的利益与教育界之间的分歧。无论学校和社会是否有条件，从小学开始教英语已经成为一个不可逆转的国际性趋势。因此，语言教育界当下要讨论的问题已经不是小学要不要教英语的问题，而是要如何教的问题。不仅如此，社会甚至还要求提高高中的出口水平等级。在这种情况下，教师的作用就变得非常重要，因此，各国面临的另一个重要问题是什么样的教师才能应付社会发展的挑战。

3.2　英语教师的职业特性

六国的英语教师的职业特点有很大差别。六国对英语教师都有英语能力和教育能力方面的要求，都有教师职业证书体系，但只有法国、日本和俄罗斯比较严格地实施了这个体系。我国对英语教师的英语水平和教学能力没有明确要求。韩国的情况类似，公立师范院校对英语教师的培养并不严格，师范教育与教学实践脱节。巴西的教师资格也不健全，近一半教师没有教师资格证。

六国的英语教师在教师的职业自主性方面差异更大。在法国、俄罗斯和日本，教师的职业自主性比较强，其中尤以法国为最高。教师的职业自主性高低对教学的影响很大。职业自主性高的教师可以灵活地根据学生情况来决定教学内容，可以在课堂上灵活地评价学生，利用形成性评价的方法促进学生学习，可以用等级评价的方式代替一刀切的考试。如果课程标准用能力等级的方式来规定教学内容和评价方式，这就更加需要教师的职业自主性做保障，否则社会就需要投入巨大的成本来设计教学和评价体系。在六国的教育体系中，没有哪一个国家具有能够满足这种需要的经济和社会条件。因此，一个理性的做法就是社会给予教师足够的信任，让教师有足够的自主权来选择教学内容、教学方法和评价方式。

六国在职业自主性方面都有最低限度的保障，在教学内容的选择方面，都实行"一纲多本"的教材政策，教师都可以在选择教学内容方面有一定的自主权。但是在教学评价方面，法国的教师自主性最强，他们对学生的能力评价能够为社会所信任和接受。韩国、日本、中国的教师自主性最弱，社会信任度很低，因而要用各种目的考试来选拔学生。俄罗斯社会处在转型之中，社会的变化使得俄罗斯的教师正在逐渐地丧失教师的自主性，传统的形成性评价和等级制评价正在逐渐地失去其作用，一刀切的"全国统考"（USE）正使得俄罗斯传统教学中的优点逐渐消失。日本的情况有些特别，日本是一个高度发达的精英社会，但是，日本社会中还有一种"名校"情结在起作用。对学生和社会来说，受什么教育不重要，重要的是"在什么地方受教育"，形式的重要性大于实质性内容。因此，英语教师给学生的评价不起作用，社会最后只承认学生去了哪所学校，而不是学生到底具有什么样的语言能力。

3.3　学习负荷

对比六国的基础英语教育，我们发现了一个值得深思的问题，批评英语学习造成学习负荷过重的问题主要集中在中国和韩国。为何法国和俄罗斯理论上学习负荷最高，他们的学术界和社会却没有提出这样的批评？日本的学生也有种种考试，为何他们现在已经没有了这样的批评？答案可能存在于两个方面，一是课程标准要具有足够的灵活性，能够兼顾各种学习能力和特性的学生；二是教师的职业自主性强，社会给予教师充分的信任，让他们能够在教学中灵活地选择教学内容、教学方法和评价方式，尊重学生发展的规律，最大限度地在认知发展、情感需求和社会能力三者之间求得平衡，而不是完全被高风险、大面积、标准化的考试所左右。在更深层次上的学习负荷过重的问题不仅是课程的问题，还是一个社会问题，需要全社会反思，从我们的教育体系、社会文化和历史传统中寻找原因。

4.　结论

本文比较了六个国家的基础英语课程体系，研究表明，我国的英语课程体系虽然在理论上学习负荷不是最大，但却是社会争议最大的国家之一。研究还表明，六个国家的英语课程体系各有各的特点，这些特点是各自的社会文化和历史传统所形成的结果，其独特之处难以被其他国家所效仿。这些结论告诉我们，当我们向别国学习时，一定要深刻理解这些国家为何会有如此的教育政策和实践方法，这才是国际比较教育中最有意义的问题，这样我们才能真正以"他山之石"攻我国之"玉"。

参考文献

Butler, Y. & M. Iino. 2005. Current Japanese reforms in English language education: The 2003 Action Plan. *Language Policy,* 4/1: pp. 25-45.

Byram, B. & L. Parmenter. (eds.). 2012. *Common European Framework of Reference: The Globalization of Language Education.* Bristol: Multilingual Matters.

Castelloti, V. 2012. Academic perspectives from France. In B. Byram & L. Parmenter (eds.). *Common European Framework of Reference: The Globalization of Language Education.* 45-52. Bristol: Multilingual Matters.

Cummins, J. & C. Davision (eds.). 2007. *International Handbook of English Language Teaching.* New York: Springer.

Goullier, F. 2012. Policy perspectives from France. In B. Byram & L. Parmenter (eds.). *Common European Framework of Reference: The Globalization of Language Education.* 37-44. Bristol: Multilingual Matters.

Koo, S. 2014. An assult upon our children. *The New York Times.* August 1, 2014.

Kubota, R. 1998. Ideologies of English in Japan. *World Englishes*, 17/3, pp. 295-306.

Masako, S. & T. Yuichi. 2012. Perspectives from Japan. In B. Byram &

L. Parmenter (eds.). *Common European Framework of Reference: The Globalization of Language Education*. 198-212. Bristol: Multilingual Matters.

McCaughey, K. 2005. The Kasha syndrome: English language teaching in Russia. *World Englishes*, 24/4, pp. 455-459.

Nation, I. 2004. The goals of vocabulary learning and vocabulary size. In I. Nation (ed.). *Teaching and Learning Vocabulary*. 11-30. Beijing: Foreign Language Teaching and Research Press.

Phillipson, R. 2007. English no longer a foreign language in Europe? In J. Cummins & C. Davision (eds.). pp. 123-136.

Shin, H. 2007. English language teaching in Korea: Toward globalization or glocaolization? In J. Cummins & C. Davision (eds.). pp. 75-86.

Ter-Minasova, S. 2005. Traditions and innovations: English language teaching in Russia. *World Englishes* , 24/4, pp. 21-44.

Tobin, J. , D. Wu & D. Davidson. 1989. *Preschool in Three Cultures: Japan, China, and the United States.* New Haven: Yale University Press.

崔允漷，2013，迎接新的教育评价范式，载崔允漷、周文胜、周文叶（编），《基于标准的课程纲要和教案》，上海：华东师范大学出版社。

俄罗斯联邦教育评估研究院，2012，《俄罗斯 2013 国家统一外语考试试卷标准》，莫斯科：俄罗斯联邦教育评估研究院。

韩国科学技术教育部，2008，《英语教育课程标准》，首尔：韩国科学技术教育部。

经合组织（OECD），2011，《教育概览2011》，北京：教育科学出版社。

日本文部科学省，2008，《中小学英语学习指导要领》，东京：日本文部科学省。

日本文部科学省，2013《日本英语教育改革实施计划书》，东京：日本文部科学省。

中华人民共和国教育部，2003，《高中英语课程标准（实验）》，北京：人民教育出版社。

中华人民共和国教育部，2011，《义务教育英语课程标准》，北京：北京师范大学出版社。

邹为诚，2011，论外语教育政策研究的性质、任务和方法——代《中国外语》外语教育政策研究专栏主持人话语，《中国外语》第 4 期，26-30。

邹为诚，2013，教育部八省市高中英语课程标准（实验）实施情况调查报告，北京：中华人民共和国教育部。

An International Comparative Study of Six Nation's English Education at the Foundation Stage

Abstract: In the increasingly globalized world, English language policy makers often borrow from other nations in order to improve one's policy and practice in English language curriculum. As a result, internationally comparative studies of English language curriculum have a particular significance in understanding and learning from other nation's practice. This research project compared six nations' enacted English language curriculums (France, Russia, China, Japan, South Korea and Brazil) for the foundation stage through an ethnographic approach in addition to policy document analysis. The study reveals the goals set by the six nations' policies do not correspond to the workload borne by the students in these nations. The variation is attributed to the different degrees of English Learning Bubbles in each of the social, cultural and historical environments and English language teacher's autonomy. The researcher finally argues that in spite of the similarities of English language curriculums of the six nations, behind them are deep social, cultural and historical factors which finally determine the substance of the English language curriculum for the foundation stages in one nation. Therefore, rational borrowing from other nations must be based on the proper understanding of these factors behind a nation's experience.

Key words: comparative education; English education; curriculum studies

此文发表于《外语教学与研究》2015 年第 3 期